AN APPROACH TO THE OLD TESTAMENT

AN APPROACH
TO THE
OLD TESTAMENT

BY

HORACE CLEAVER
B.D.

LONDON : THE EPWORTH PRESS

THE EPWORTH PRESS
(FRANK H. CUMBERS)
25-35 City Road, London, E.C.1

MELBOURNE   CAPE TOWN
NEW YORK   TORONTO

SET IN MONOTYPE BASKERVILLE AND PRINTED IN
GREAT BRITAIN BY THE CAMELOT PRESS LTD.,
LONDON AND SOUTHAMPTON

PREFACE

THE purpose of this text-book is to help Methodist Local Preachers on Trial as they pursue their prescribed studies in the Old Testament. It is hoped, however, that it will also prove useful to the preachers, Bible Class leaders and Sunday School teachers of other communions.

The author, the Rev. Horace Cleaver, B.D., has given much time to the study of the Old Testament, and has been for some years one of the examiners in that subject in connexion with the examinations for Methodist Local Preachers on Trial. Though a busy circuit minister, he willingly responded to the request of the Studies Board that he should write this official text-book.

In an introductory chapter, Mr Cleaver shows the importance of the Old Testament to the Christian and the preacher, reminds the student of certain facts which he must bear in mind as he reads the Hebrew Scriptures, and gives him a preliminary 'bird's-eye view' of Israel's history.

As will be seen from the Syllabus of Study (pp. vii–viii) the course of instruction deals with carefully selected sections of the Old Testament. Help is given to the student as he passes from one period of Hebrew history to another, and more detailed guidance is given as he reads the Bible itself, paragraph by paragraph.

Those chapters which often cause trouble to the novice, Gen. 1-4, are postponed to *Study Eleven*, where they are included among 'The Writings'. The formation of the Old Testament is not discussed until the concluding section of *Study Twelve*. The book concludes with two useful Maps, a Table of Dates, and an Index of Subjects.

GREVILLE P. LEWIS
Connexional Secretary

Local Preachers' Department
1 Central Buildings
Westminster, S.W.1

v

TO THE STUDENT

1. In all your study of the Old Testament, you should use a *Revised Version* with marginal references. You should also keep a good dictionary at your elbow.

2. The title of this text-book, *An Approach to the Old Testament*, is meant to suggest that its purpose is to *introduce* you to the thrilling message of the Hebrew Scriptures. In the Syllabus of Study (*see opp.*) some passages are printed in brackets, and, in the body of the text-book, the paragraphs which comment on these passages are marked with a star (thus ★). These sections of the Old Testament are omitted from your present course of study, *not* because they are unimportant, but because the Old Testament syllabus must be kept within reasonable limits. No questions on these passages will be set in the On Trial examination, but the student must *read* these passages and the comments on them in this text-book, so that he can understand the subsequent passages.

3. For the purpose of cross-references, the paragraphs have been numbered consecutively from 1 to 450. Whenever, in the Studies, you are asked to turn to other Biblical passages (e.g. '*see* Josh. 11¹⁻⁹') or to other paragraphs in the text-book (e.g. '*see para.* 448'), it is most important that you should do so. Do not ignore these directions.

4. From time to time throughout your study, the Maps and the Table of Dates printed in the Appendix should be consulted.

5. The titles of O.T. and N.T. books are printed in italics; e.g. *Genesis, Mark*, etc. The abbreviation '*ANT*' stands for *An Approach to the New Testament* (Greville P. Lewis).

6. Before you begin each of the Studies 2-12, turn to the Syllabus of Study, and carefully read the Biblical passages which are dealt with in that particular Study, including the passages that are bracketed. Then read the appropriate Study in the text-book, again and again referring to the O.T. passages as they are commented upon.

7. Each of these Studies represents *a fortnight's work*, if you intend to complete the course in six months.

8. *Correspondence Students*. Before the end of the fortnight, and using only your Old Testament, write out your answers to the Test Questions which are printed at the end of each Study, and *promptly* post them to your tutor.

SYLLABUS OF STUDY

Study One

Introducing the Old Testament

A. *Why the Old Testament?*

(1) 'Why should we bother about the Old Testament?' We have all heard such a question both from people outside the churches and within; we have probably asked it ourselves on occasion. Often the Old Testament seems very far removed from modern life and likely to be a stumbling block rather than a help to those who are seriously seeking religious truth. It contains many inadequate ideas of God and its characters often show a shocking standard of behaviour. Besides, we are Christians and not Jews, and our religion has its basis in the ministry and work of Jesus Christ. What then do we need beyond the New Testament? Surely it would be better to dispense with a book that can easily be a handicap to faith and that provides our critics with so much ammunition.

(2) This belittling of the Old Testament is by no means a new thing. The Christian Church was scarcely 100 years old when a fierce controversy broke out on this very subject. A wealthy shipowner, Marcion by name, tried to persuade the Church at Rome to abolish the Old Testament from its worship and teaching, and to concentrate entirely upon such books of the New Testament as he considered to contain the pure Gospel of Christ. Only a minority listened to him, and, as a penalty for his rashness, he was excommunicated. This was in the year A.D. 144. Nowadays we take it for granted that the Old Testament will be bound in the same volume as the New. In most church services, extracts from it are read, and to very many Christians parts of it at least are exceedingly precious. In their judgement, either to reject it or to ignore it would be a grave mistake and would lead to an impoverishment of our religion. Just as, in the second century, the Church would not be persuaded by Marcion, so, in the twentieth, we shall be wise not to let the critics of the Old Testament deprive it of its chance to speak to us.

(3) True, the Old Testament does contain many ideas about

God which fall short of our Christian thought of Him as the Father of our Lord Jesus Christ, and it does at times seem to condone and even to commend a standard of conduct that is offensive to consciences made sensitive by Christ. There is a way to deal with these difficulties, as we shall discover in our course of studies. Seen in their proper light they add to the interest and fascination of the Book. The Old Testament is not only full of matchless stories; it is the record of the marvellous way in which God revealed Himself to mankind through the history and experience of the Hebrew race.

Here are four reasons why the Old Testament has been retained by the Christian Church and why we should take trouble to understand its message.

1.   *The Old Testament was the Bible, not only of the early Christians, but of Jesus Himself.*

(4)   The village school at Nazareth was held in the Synagogue with the master of the Synagogue as its warden. In everyday life Jesus would speak Aramaic, the language which had come to be in general use in Palestine; but He must also have been taught the Hebrew in which most of the Jewish scriptures had originally been written. Without Hebrew He would not have been able in later years to have read the lessons in the Synagogue services. There is every reason to believe that He learned many of the outstanding passages by heart. Again and again in His public ministry He made use of quotations. Thus, during the Temptation in the wilderness, He countered each of the three suggestions of the Tempter with a text taken from *Deuteronomy*, and when He returned to Nazareth, and announced in the Synagogue service the kind of ministry He was about to undertake, He found exactly the description He wanted in the writings of Isaiah. There are many other instances in the Gospels. We cannot doubt that His mind and heart were steeped in the ancient scriptures of His race.

(5)   It is only natural that Christians should want to understand the writings which, from a human point of view, provided so rich a nourishment for the spirit of their Master. Certainly it was so in the Early Church. Many of the first members were not Jews; but they gratefully accepted the sacred scriptures of the Jews and claimed them as their own. Very few of them would be able to read them in Hebrew but, happily, they were able to make use of a Greek translation which had been begun by Jewish scholars near Alexandria some 250 years before the birth of

Christ. This version was known as the Septuagint (abbreviated to LXX: *see para.* 448). It was popularly believed that the work had been accomplished by seventy scribes (Septuagint is the Latin word for seventy).

2. *The New Testament can only be understood when we turn to it with an adequate knowledge of the Old.*

(6) Christianity did not enter the world as an entirely new thing. It grew out of the ancient faith of the Hebrew people, Judaism as it is generally called. Although in a very short time Christianity appeared quite separate and distinctive, there is very much in it that we can never understand without a knowledge of the ground from which it sprang. Jesus, in His ministry, took it for granted that His hearers had a sufficient knowledge of their religious heritage, and, since most of them were Jews, this was not an unreasonable assumption. Again and again in His teaching, we find Him making it clear that He had not come to destroy the essence of the old faith, but to build upon it, develop it, fulfil it (*see next para.*). He, therefore, used terms which were quite familiar to Jews of the first century. For us, a great deal in the Gospels is bound to be puzzling unless we put ourselves in the position of those first hearers. Many characteristic words and ideas, such as 'Son of Man', 'Messiah', 'Kingdom of God', only yield their meaning when we try to understand what they meant to Christ's audiences in Palestine. That means we must go back into the Old Testament to discover the history and the meaning of these terms. When we come to the thought of the first Christian leaders, such as Paul, much that they wrote is quite incomprehensible without a competent knowledge of the Old Testament.

3. *Jesus declared that He came not to destroy but to fulfil the Old Testament.*

(7) His mission was to carry it through to its proper conclusion. From one point of view, we may see in the Old Testament the story of man's hunger for God. Always human beings have been seeking for Him, wanting to find a satisfying vision of Him, longing for an experience of Him that would meet their deepest needs. For man has always felt himself weak and puny, and needing to be sustained amidst all the chances and changes of this mortal life. We believe that the answer to man's hunger is in Jesus Christ. Nevertheless, our appreciation of what Jesus means to those who receive Him grows as we realize how desperate

has been man's search. The Old Testament gives us the story of a people who, whatever their faults, and however frequent their rebellions, could not do without God. It is the record of man's brightest hopes and aspirations.

(8)   There is another, and more important, point of view. The Old Testament tells us not only of man's strivings, but of God's self-disclosure. It is the story of what He has been doing amongst men, of how He has taken the initiative and given man a knowledge of His character and His demands, of a purpose that He has been working out in the world. The Jews were convinced that their race had been specially chosen by God in order that He might use them for the accomplishment of His will. In all their history He took an active part. Events, whether great or small, were not simply the result of chance, or of human purpose and activity. God was in them, seeking all the time to achieve through them His own intentions. And what was that purpose? To save men from the sin which had tempted and mastered them; to redeem His world from the infection of selfishness and evil; to create a divine community and to establish His rule of righteousness in their hearts! The story of the Jewish people is the story of the working out of that purpose. From the beginning it was hindered and frustrated by human sin, and God had to overcome an opposition on the part of the very men whom He had created. He had chosen a people for His purpose and they proved stubborn and rebellious. Though their religious leaders did not cease to plead with them to return to God and give Him their full obedience, though they pointed out the signs that He was still at work in their history and urged them to accept His guidance and direction, their success was never more than limited and short-lived. Men went on defying God. To this sinfulness on the part of men there was no answer, until God came Himself in Jesus Christ and brought about its ultimate and final defeat. As Christians we rejoice that the divine purpose is accomplished through Jesus. With reverent hearts and minds we glory in His coming into our world, in His life, His death, His resurrection, His saving power. How much deeper and stronger is our appreciation if we first know something of the story recorded in the Old Testament of God's dealings with His rebellious people.

4.   *The Christian Church claims continuity with the people of the Old Testament.*

(9)   The theme of the Old Testament is that, in order to fulfil

His purpose in the world, God selected Israel to be His chosen people. It was not intended they should boast of their choice as a privilege, but that they should accept it as a solemn responsibility. They were chosen in order to serve, to be His instrument. Alas! The children of Israel proved unworthy of their God-given mission, and failed to rise to the opportunities and demands put before them. How grievously they failed we can see in their blind rejection of Jesus Christ.

(10) The divine purpose was fulfilled in Jesus Christ and in Him we have the assurance of God's ultimate and complete triumph. But, even after the coming of Jesus, God still needed an agency through which He could work. Hence the Church! After the resurrection, the Christian Church took over the mission in which ancient Israel had proved so unsatisfactory. From the beginning, Christians believed that they constituted the new Israel of God. Henceforth, the Chosen People were not confined to members of one specific race: the Church of Christ gathered to itself not only trueborn Jews but men and women of every race under heaven. With an unshakable conviction that their Risen Saviour was gloriously present in their midst, and in the absolute certainty that the Holy Spirit had been poured out upon them, they committed themselves without reserve to the service of God. They were conscious that they had their part to play in His work of setting men free from the chains of sin and of redeeming the whole world. Thus, when we bind the Old Testament with the New and form the sacred book of our Christian faith, we are symbolizing the truth that the mission of ancient Israel led up to and was fulfilled in the mission of the Christian Church. What God had to say to the Jews in those far-off days can still help us in our understanding of Him and His ways and the tasks to which He has called us.

B. *How to Read the Old Testament*

If we are to reach a right understanding of the sacred writings of the Jews, certain points must be kept in mind.

1. *The writings of the Old Testament came from a world that was very different from our own.*

(11) We must try in imagination to picture what it was like.

Perhaps the outstanding difference was that its people were without the vast resources of scientific knowledge which form the basis of our modern civilization and are the source of our modern power. True, they had a certain wisdom in the management of life, born of their observation and thought. They noticed the ways of nature and were able to make use of their discoveries. But they came very far short of that understanding of things which today we call 'scientific'. A second difference was that their social life was much more rough and primitive than ours, and often very cruel. For instance, slavery was an accepted institution. For the most part, people did not stop to ask questions about the value of human life; they simply treated it as a cheap thing. At times we come across a higher conception, as in *Deuteronomy*, where the attitude to their fellows enjoined upon the Israelites comes within sight of the teaching of the New Testament. But the general level of social life in the Old Testament is that of a pre-Christian age. A third difference was the large part played in religion by the ritual of sacrifices. Animals were slain by the thousand in the belief that this practice was what God required. In times of crisis, even human sacrifices were offered, though the nobler Hebrews protested against them. These three examples alone are enough to make us realize that in our studies we are moving in a world vastly different from our own.

2. *In the opinion of most other races, the Hebrews were a difficult people.*

(12) In our time we have witnessed terrible campaigns of persecution launched against the Jews in many European countries. Whilst we have tried to be sympathetic towards them in their sorrows, it may be that we have detected in our own minds an attitude of dislike or distrust. Part of the reason is that they are so very different from ourselves, both in their ways of conduct and of thought, and are therefore hard to understand. The situation at the time of Jesus was very similar. The Jews had spread into every part of the known world and, wherever they went, people were puzzled by them, and often annoyed. For instance, they refused to make a sacrifice to any god or goddess except their own Yahweh. In the Roman Empire, everybody else was prepared to acknowledge the divinity of the Emperor, partly in recognition of the great benefits they had received from him. No doubt to very many it meant no more than a conventional gesture of patriotic loyalty; but the Jews were

prepared to suffer whatever penalties might come their way rather than perform an act which, in their minds, would have seemed an open disloyalty towards their God.

(13) Another factor that made them appear strange in the eyes of their contemporaries was that they maintained that their God, Yahweh, was invisible. He had a temple in Jerusalem —the only place where the Jews were permitted to make their sacrifices to Him—but it was empty of those material representatives of deity which were so familiar to other people. It contained no image of any sort, for images had been expressly forbidden. We can understand how this gave rise to the charge that the Jews were atheists! Moreover, wherever they went, they insisted on building a synagogue in which they could continue their own peculiar form of worship. As far as conduct was concerned, their morals were austere, far more exacting than those of most of their neighbours, and this too did not add to their popularity. In social life, they were determined to preserve the distinctive customs of their race, and set great store upon a multitude of rules and regulations which defined what they could, and could not, eat and drink, and which aimed at keeping them ceremonially 'clean'.

(14) Thus, in one way or another, the Jews gave the impression that not only were they different from the rest of mankind, but that they despised all who had not been privileged by being born into their tradition. How these differences arose, and why, are partly revealed in the Old Testament. In our readings we shall see their sense of racial exclusiveness and superiority becoming a dominant factor in their lives. For the moment, the point is that in the Old Testament we are dealing with a race very different from our own. We cannot hope to understand them without a constant effort of imagination, and we must make that effort if we want to know why they thought and felt and behaved as they did.

3. *The Old Testament, as we have it, is a translation from an old and, in many ways, a strange language.*

(15) In the early centuries of Hebrew history, stories and poems and songs, chiefly about their ancestors, must have been passed from one generation of Jews to the next by word of mouth. Then came writing, first on parchments made of skin, and, much later, on papyrus made of vegetable matter. The first prophet to write down the notes of his message was Amos (about 750 B.C.).

Before his time, however, the earlier schools of prophets probably began to compile connected histories. In these early writings only consonants were used, it being taken for granted that those who read would be able to understand. Later on, long after the time of Jesus, a system of dots and dashes was invented to indicate vowels and these were inserted by scribes into the consonants of the manuscripts they received. In a modern copy of the Hebrew Old Testament, you can see both the consonants and the vowel signs. An important question is: can we be sure that the scribes put in the vowels that were originally intended? In our own language, for instance, if we were given the three consonants B, G, T only, we could not be certain whether the intended word was 'bigot', 'beget', or 'begat'. This is an illustration of just one of the many difficulties faced by Old Testament scholars.

(16) Another is the possibility that in the copying out of manuscripts by hand mistakes may have occurred of one sort or another; a third, the difficulty of translating accurately from the original Hebrew or Aramaic into Greek, Latin, Syriac, or more modern languages. Even when scholars feel sure they know the Hebrew word that was in the original manuscript, they may find great difficulty in translating it so as to convey its exact meaning. Our *Authorised Version* of the Old Testament was published in 1611. In spite of its majestic language, some of its words have changed their meaning since the time of James I. Moreover, in the intervening years, older and more accurate manuscripts have been discovered. In our studies, therefore, we must use the *Revised Version* of 1885; and we may find help in looking at some still later translations, e.g. *Moffatt*, and the *Revised Standard Version* from America.

(17) We owe a tremendous debt to our Biblical scholars. It is unfortunate that we have got into the way of describing them as 'critics', for the word rather suggests an attitude of superiority, whereas the majority of them are very humble men. In the phrase 'Biblical criticism', the word 'criticism' does not mean 'fault-finding'; it refers to the application to the Biblical documents of careful methods of scholarship. The German word *kritik* means 'examination'. Every reputable Biblical 'critic' is seeking to uncover the divine message contained in the Bible and to proclaim it as clearly and as forcibly as he can. Our custom is to divide Biblical criticism into two sections. 'Lower criticism' aims at finding out as nearly as possible the words that were originally written; 'higher criticism' asks who wrote the passage,

what were the circumstances, what purpose was intended, can we rely upon its accuracy, and so forth. After all, these are questions which are bound to arise in the mind of all who read the Bible, though we may not all see eye to eye in the answers we give to them.

4. *The Old Testament is not a single book, but a collection of works of various kinds, and must be treated as such.*

(18) Imagine taking down from the various shelves of a public library thirty-nine books more or less at random—history, philosophy, poetry, politics, sociology, theology, fiction, and so on. A collection of writings hardly less varied has been bound together between the covers of our Old Testament. There are law books, such as *Leviticus* and *Deuteronomy;* histories which stress the ways in which God dealt with His people, *Samuel* and *Kings* for instance; notes of the fervent preaching of the prophets from *Amos* onwards; a great dramatic poem, *Job;* a collection of hymns used in public worship, *Psalms*; and tales with a deep religious meaning, like *Jonah.* When we begin to study any particular book, the first thing we must do is to put it in its proper class. Much misunderstanding of the Old Testament comes from a failure to do this. For instance, it is foolish to read a work of fiction, written to drive home some much needed moral and spiritual lesson, as if it were an account of literal history; or to treat a poem as if it were a collection of scientific facts.

5. *The supreme interest of the Old Testament is in religion and the ways of God with men.*

(19) We might almost say it has no other interest. This interest in religion is the factor that draws all the various books together and gives them a real unity. However different they may seem to be, they are all concerned with the relationship between God and men, with human life set in the fear of the Lord. Two books perhaps seem to stand out as exceptions. At first reading, neither the *Song of Songs* nor *Esther* seems to have any religious message for us, but when we study them more closely, and ask what they meant to their first readers, it is possible to see even here a word from God to man.

(20) We can trace throughout the Old Testament two basic conceptions. The first is that the Hebrew people are under an obligation to worship Yahweh as their God, and Yahweh alone, and that they are bound in duty to live according to His will.

B

Both prophet and priest are concerned to make God real to His people and to leave no doubt in their minds as to what He requires of them. Even the somewhat dull and uninspiring lists of laws and regulations which the Old Testament contains are the outcome of a living faith in Yahweh and lay down the pattern of a life centred in Him.

(21)   The second fundamental idea is that Yahweh was at work in all the affairs of His children. He made Himself known through the events of their history, through the experiences that befell their race. The two most soul-shaking crises the nation had to pass through were the Exodus and the Exile. Both were not only decisive events; they were signs that God was at work amongst them and also revelations of His character. But many smaller and less momentous happenings also brought them insights and visions concerning the divine nature and activity.

(22)   Moreover, God was at work in the lives of *individuals*. The Old Testament is rich in biography. Most of us made our first acquaintance with it through the stories of its outstanding personalities—the Patriarchs, Moses, Samuel, David, Elijah, and others. We are shown these men in their weakness as well as in their strength, their shame as well as in their glory. But they are not significant simply because of their likeness to and kinship with ourselves; the more important thing is that we are permitted to see God's dealings with them and through their stories learn more of what God is like, how He deals with us, and what He expects of us.

6.   *We are to look to the Old Testament for a progressive revelation of divine truth, and watch the way being prepared for the full and final revelation in Jesus Christ.*

(23)   In our mind's eye we must re-arrange the order of the Old Testament books and, as far as is possible, set them in their proper time-sequence. This will enable us to see a very primitive people gradually rising to nobler and loftier conceptions of God and duty. There is a *progressive revelation* at work. Due emphasis needs to be given to each of these two words. The Old Testament is, first and foremost, the record of a divine *revelation*. It is easy to speak of man's search for God and of his slowly developing knowledge. This puts the stress on our human achievement. The deeper truth is that the initiative has come from God's side. He Himself has been intent on revealing Himself to men, on disclosing His nature and His will, and has in fact been more anxious

to give than man has to receive. Therefore the revelation has had to be *progressive*. God has had to wait with patience and restraint until His children were ready to receive His truths, until they were sensitive enough to understand His ways and to interpret what He was saying to them. In the Old Testament we see the light which comes from Him growing stronger and stronger. Gradually men's thoughts of God are spiritualized; slowly their ways of living become more moral in response to their vision of God's requirements.

(24) A word of caution, however, is necessary. We must be careful lest we take the word 'progressive' to mean that the growth in man's knowledge of God can be represented, as on a graph, by a straight line moving gradually, but steadily, upwards. It was a far more complicated business. If we wanted to draw a diagram, we should have to draw a very wavering line, with many ups and downs, but one which did in the end reach the point at which God was able to make His supreme self-revelation in Jesus Christ. The progress was anything but even. Some of the richest conceptions came near the beginning of Israel's history. Moses undoubtedly thought of Yahweh as the Living and Redemptive God, an idea that rose not only far above the minds of his contemporaries, but also far above many of later ages. There were periods of regression as well as progress. During the time of the settlement in Canaan, the level of religion was very much lower than that set by Moses. Centuries after his death, prophets such as Amos seem to be re-discovering and re-emphasizing truths that had been known to the great lawgiver. Once again God had to make known through them the moral quality of His demands, as though the Ten Commandments had never been given or their implications drawn. Moreover, even the prophets were not able to receive the full revelation of the divine character. In some respects their thought was in advance of the religious conceptions of their day: in others they shared its limitations. 'Progressive revelation', therefore, must not be thought of as a steady and inevitable advance of knowledge. What the term means is that, on a broad view, finer ideas of God and life drove out grosser and more primitive ones, until, in the fulness of time, God was able to speak clearly to us in Jesus Christ.

(25) This conception of a progressive revelation will help us to deal with the problems raised by low standards of conduct and unworthy ideas of God in the Old Testament. God was only able to reveal to men as much as they were able to bear. We are

conscious all the time that we are in a period of preparation; the people of God are being made ready to receive His full self-disclosure. Meanwhile His message to us comes through earthen and imperfect vessels, and our business is to discern the treasure and not be put off by the obvious flaws and blemishes of the container. The way is being prepared for God to make His supreme act of revelation and redemption in Jesus. 'God who spoke in many forms and fashions of old to our fathers by the prophets has in these days spoken to us in his Son' (Heb. 1²). The Old Testament means to lead on to Christ, the perfect and all sufficient Word of God. By the light of the revelation that God has given us in Him, we must then turn back and judge what has gone before. Nothing that is contradictory to the mind of Christ can be for us the Word of God, and the Old Testament must be interpreted in the light of the truth that shines from Him. At every point the test question must be, 'What has Jesus to say about this?'

C. *A Bird's-eye View of Israel's History*

(26)   The Hebrews believed that God disclosed His character and His will to men through the events of history, and especially through the events of their own national story. Since we share that belief, before we come to a more detailed study of the Old Testament, it may be useful to take a swift glance over the history of God's Chosen People. Our future work will fill in many details but, at the very beginning, a clear grasp of the broad outline is very necessary. We note four landmarks in the story:

1. *The Exodus*

(27)   A group of Israelite tribes were driven by scarcity of food to the borders of Egypt, where they settled in the Land of Goshen. With a change of dynasty, they passed into slavery, and were compelled by the native Egyptian Pharaohs to provide labour for their building schemes. From this bondage they were rescued by the inspired leadership of Moses, who effected their escape from Egypt and proceeded to guide them back to Palestine where their ancestors had once sojourned. Moses' work was based upon the deep conviction that it was the will of their God, Yahweh, that the liberated slaves should possess this land as a permanent

home. On Mount Sinai, Moses entered into a Covenant on their behalf. They became the People of God. Yahweh would guide them and protect them, and they from their side were to serve Him alone and obey His demands that were expressed in the Law. Amongst other things, this Covenant gave to the various tribes a sense of unity, which varied from time to time in its strength, but which was never completely forgotten. After making their pledges of obedience, the Israelites went on their way, though progress seems to have been slow. Nevertheless, their deliverance from the tyranny of Egypt had been accomplished and, in all their subsequent history, the Exodus was remembered as the mightiest act of God.

2. *The Kingship*

(28) Moses died on the borders of Canaan, having been permitted to see the Promised Land from afar but not to enter it. The tasks of leadership then fell upon the shoulders of Joshua. His conquest of the land turned out to be neither swift nor complete, for the twelve tribes acted independently of each other, or co-operated only in small groups, and had to be content with securing for themselves pockets of land amidst the territory of the native Canaanites. They had to struggle hard to preserve their existence. On the one hand, the inhabitants of the land resented their coming; on the other, various surrounding tribes envied them their success and were determined if possible to wrest their gains from them. The Israelites were also in grave danger of losing their loyalty to Yahweh and adopting the pagan ritual and worship practised in their new home. In these unsettled years, various tribes produced a series of warrior chieftains, known as 'judges', who gained for themselves a local prestige by warding off their tribal enemies. Real unity amongst the tribes was hard to achieve, and came only in face of the serious menace of the Philistines. In the emergency the tribes agreed to appoint a king under whose command they would all be prepared to fight.

(29) The first three kings had varying degrees of success. The first, Saul, failed to achieve a full unity and only temporarily drove back his foes. The third, Solomon, raised the kingdom to a very high degree of power and glory, but in the latter years of his reign he lost territory and his autocratic rule brought about a permanent division of the kingdom after his death. It was David who remained in the hearts and minds of subsequent generations as their ideal king. He broke the power of the Philistines and

fused the separate Hebrew clans into one, giving them Jerusalem as their new capital and the symbol of their unity, and proposing the building there of a temple to Yahweh. Many days of trouble and distress were in store for the Children of Israel, but, whatever their sufferings, they looked forward with hope, believing that a monarch of the same blood and the same character would be sent to deliver them once more.

3.   *The Exile*

(30)   The luxury and extravagance of Solomon brought about a revolution. After his death, ten of the tribes, goaded by economic distress, refused to accept the rule of his son, and the nation split into two parts, Judah in the south, and Israel (or Ephraim) in the north. The next period of Hebrew history is shaped by two major influences—the external threat of the aggressive policies of powerful neighbours, and the attempts of the great prophets at home to recall the people to their loyalty to Yahweh.

(31)   At first, our main interest is with the northern kingdom. Under Omri it rose to great strength and prestige. His son, Ahab, maintained the political influence of Israel, but in religious issues came into serious collision with the prophet Elijah. The little kingdom reached the peak of its power in the reign of Jeroboam II, though, by this time, the renewed menace of Assyria was a very live danger, as Amos in his prophesying realized. Israel lay along the route between the great empires of the east (Assyria and its successors) and their formidable rival, Egypt, and was therefore always exposed to the perils of a buffer state. Frequently it made its position worse by falling into temptation and intriguing between rival powers. Assyria, at this period, had its eye upon Egypt and was not prepared for Israel to be unruly. When, therefore, the little kingdom aroused its wrath, Assyria seized the opportunity and set about reducing it to submission. After a long siege, Samaria, the capital, was captured (721 B.C.) and the majority of its inhabitants were deported. The northern kingdom as such ceased to exist.

(32)   In the south, Judah was smaller and less powerful than its neighbour, and, on the whole, blessed with a series of useful, if somewhat undistinguished rulers. The working out of the divine purpose now lay in its hands. The Assyrian advance threatened Jerusalem as well as Samaria, but an attack under Sennacherib came to nothing. Isaiah, statesman as well as prophet, did his best to keep Judah free of all foreign entanglements, but not

altogether with success. Since the nation's safety was thought to depend upon the protection of Yahweh, religious reforms were introduced by Hezekiah and Josiah, and it was hoped that disaster might be avoided. It was indeed postponed. For over 100 years after the fall of Samaria, the southern kingdom was spared any serious molestation, though it was mostly under Assyrian domination.

(33) In due time, the Assyrian Empire lost its strength and gave place to that of Babylon. The question of world supremacy now had to be settled between Babylon and Egypt. Once more Judah found itself in a position of acute danger. The prophet Jeremiah was even more pronounced in his isolationism than Isaiah, but the politicians of Jerusalem ignored his advice and intrigued with the Egyptians. At last the Babylonians lost their patience, marched against the Holy City, and in 597 B.C. carried off to Babylon the king and many of the leading citizens. The survivors at Jerusalem had not the sense to behave. Their further intrigues brought Nebuchadrezzar back, and, in 586 B.C., after a terrible siege, the city had to surrender. Another deportation was carried out. All the potential leaders amongst the Jews were exiled to Babylon, except a few who fled to Egypt, and only the poor and ineffective inhabitants were left behind. The city and the temple lay in ruins. In all their history, no greater disaster ever befell the Chosen People of Yahweh. It must have looked as if the divine purpose had been brought to a premature end.

4. *The Return*

(34) Events were to prove that the catastrophe of 586 B.C. was not as final as it seemed. Thanks mainly to their prophets, Ezekiel and his disciples, and an anonymous prophet to whom we refer as II Isaiah, the exiles managed to preserve their national identity and to maintain their religious loyalty, even in Babylon with its many temptations. After some fifty years, Cyrus the Persian made himself master of the Babylonian empire, and, as one of his first acts, gave the Jews permission to return to their native land and rebuild their temple (536 B.C.). Only a few availed themselves of this opportunity, though we must assume that, from this time onwards, occasional caravans of pilgrims made their way back. Not until 520 B.C. did a group seriously tackle the job of repairing the ruined temple. They were inspired by the governorship of Zerrubabel and the urgent preaching of Haggai and Zechariah. Nevertheless, for a very long time

depression and anarchy seem to have prevailed at Jerusalem, and any real return of prosperity was postponed until the governorship of Nehemiah (444 B.C.). Together with Ezra the Scribe, he infused a new spirit into the little community and gave it a deepened racial consciousness which it was never to lose.

(35)   The Old Testament has little to tell us of what happened in the next four centuries.* Judah, or Judea as it was now called, evidently had great difficulty in maintaining a sense of national identity. Except for a comparatively short period it was never politically free. In succession it became the dependant of Persia, Greece, Egypt, and Syria. Against the latter, the Maccabees engineered a successful revolt in 165 B.C. With Hyrcanus (135 B.C.) came some eighty years of relative independence, but the opportunity proved more than the nation could take. Its rulers spent their energies in bitter and futile quarrels, and the country was grievously split from top to bottom. Finally, the Romans, who were rapidly rising to world domination, were called in to restore order (63 B.C.), and Judea became a part of the Roman province of Syria. So it was when Christ was born. Nevertheless, in spite of everything they had endured, in spite of everything that had threatened to swallow them up and merge them with other races, the Jewish people had never surrendered their identity or completely lost their sense of being an Elect Nation. Proud and exclusive, they emerged from these centuries of history, still convinced that they, of all the nations of the earth, had been chosen for the fulfilment of Yahweh's purpose.

TEST QUESTIONS

1. Say, in your own words, why you think Christians ought to read and study the Old Testament.
2. How would you deal with the complaint that a great deal of the Old Testament falls below the level of Christian thought?

*See ANT., paras 8-81.

Study Two

The Patriarchs

(36) Every nation likes to believe it has a long past, that its traditions have come down from remote and ancient times. The Hebrews were very proud of their ancestry, for it proved them to be the People of God. It was possible for them to trace their history back as far as Moses and be reasonably confident that they were in touch with men who had actually lived and events that had actually happened. The question was: what lay still further back?

(37) In *Genesis* we read of the adventures of the earliest ancestors of the Hebrew race—the patriarchs Abraham, Isaac, Jacob, and Joseph. These stories are not based quite firmly on the ground of historical fact. In all probability the Patriarchs were real people and many of the incidents ascribed to them actually happened; but we cannot know for certain. For many generations before they were committed to writing, the narratives were passed on by word of mouth. Some scholars think that, whilst we may read these stories as the adventures of individuals in the dawn of Hebrew history, we ought also to see in them the records of the various journeyings of shepherd tribes. They suggest that Abraham, Isaac, Jacob, and Joseph are used to represent groups of nomads in much the same way as we use 'John Bull' as a symbol of the English nation.

(38) From other sources, we know that, many centuries before Christ, people of the same Semitic stock as the Hebrews were driven to migrate from the barren deserts of Arabia. A wave of them, probably about 4000 B.C., moved in search of pasture for their flocks and found a place of settlement near the mouth of the River Euphrates. They became the ancestors of the Assyrians and the Babylonians who were to play such an important part in the later phases of Israelite history.

(39) Round about 2000 B.C. a second movement took place. A settlement was made in the '*Fertile Crescent*', the stretch of productive land running from the Nile Valley to the Tigris and

Euphrates, and including Palestine and Syria.* These peoples are usually known as the Amorites.

(40)   Some 300 years later, probably round about 1700 B.C., a third migration took place. The ancestors of the Hebrew nation set off on their wanderings. If we accept the line of interpretation mentioned in *para.* 37, we can trace their fortunes in the adventures of Abraham and his successors. Their manner of life must have been very simple and primitive. They had no fixed places of abode and built no houses, but carried with them movable tents of goatskin and pitched them wherever they found food for themselves and their flocks. No doubt they had to struggle hard to maintain their existence, and often came into conflict with other groups of wanderers and with the descendants of those who in earlier migrations had settled in the Fertile Crescent. At the head of each tribe was a patriarch whose word was the final law for those under his rule.

(41)   In reading *Genesis*, our primary concern is the religious faith which shines out of the stories of the Patriarchs. The authors who finally committed them to writing were convinced believers in Yahweh. Out of all the families of the earth He had chosen the Hebrew people and appointed them to be His servant to proclaim the knowledge of God to all the world. They believed that from the beginning of their history, even in the dim and misty period before reliable accounts began to be kept, their ancestors had been providentially guided and brought by Yahweh through many sufferings and disasters in order that they could fulfil His purpose. Accordingly Abraham, Isaac, Jacob, and Joseph are represented as conscious instruments in the working out of this divine plan, with a faith as clear and as strong as those who told the stories afterwards. The Old Testament wants us to catch something of that sublime faith in the overruling guidance and protecting power of God.

A.   *Abraham*

(42)   *Gen.* 11²⁷–12⁹.   THE CALL OF ABRAHAM

About 1750 B.C. Abraham moved from Mesopotamia and followed the Fertile Crescent in the direction of Palestine. With

* *See* the map on p. 205.

him went his father-in-law, Terah, and his nephew, Lot. What particular incident provoked this departure we do not know. We are left to conjecture whether he was protesting against the growing luxury and the increasing complexity of the civilization of the day, or resisting certain aspects of the religion of Ur which he felt to be an affront to his conscience. The Biblical writers certainly portray this migration as an act of obedience to the will of God.

For a time, Abraham sojourned at Haran, and some of his relatives seem to have settled there. With his nephew, he himself moved further south into uncharted country. He did not know the name of the land to which he was being called, but he staked everything on the divine promise that through him a new nation was to be founded, a nation which should be 'God's People'. He believed this in spite of the fact that his wife, Sarah, was childless and therefore no direct line of succession was possible. At Shechem, he learned that the land promised to him was Canaan, but he was not yet permitted to settle in it.

(43) *Gen*. 13. ABRAHAM'S SEPARATION FROM LOT

According to 12^{10}, Abraham and Lot made their way as far as Egypt and, after a short stay, moved back towards Canaan. The number, both of their families and their flocks and herds, had greatly increased—so much so that strife arose between their respective herdsmen as they competed for pasturage. The solution was to divide the territory. Anxious for peace, Abraham gave Lot the first choice, though as the senior the right belonged to him, and, if necessary, he had the superior forces with which to have asserted his claim. No doubt he wanted to avoid a conflict which might easily have widened. The land was already occupied by the Canaanites who, if the issue had been pushed to a contest, would have taken sides between the rivals and possibly would have expelled both from the land.

Lot chose the well-watered basin of the Lower Jordan Valley, a country that seemed as fair and as fertile as Egypt itself. Contrary to its appearance, it carried with it the danger of moral contamination through contact with the evil city of Sodom. After that city's destruction, we are left to assume that, in spite of his inclinations, Lot was driven to the mountains, where his descendants became known as Ammonites and Moabites. Abraham himself settled at Mamre, in Hebron, where God renewed His promise to him.

(44) *Gen.* 17¹⁻²². THE COVENANT

The fundamental belief of Hebrew religion was that a Covenant existed between Yahweh and His people. This was not, as the word possibly suggests, in the nature of a commercial bargain. The parties concerned in it did not enter into the Covenant on any basis of equality; the initiative came entirely from God's side. We come nearer to understanding its essential character if we think of the unwritten bond of obligation that exists between a father and his children. He undertakes to look after them; they in return owe him loyalty and obedience.

The Old Testament traces the Covenant relation between Yahweh and Israel back to the time of Abraham. Its terms were simple. Abram, to give him the name by which he was known up to that point in his experience, undertook to do as God told him. It is interesting to notice that, according to *Genesis*, neither Abraham nor any other of the Patriarchs, whatever their personal faults and failings, ever refused a command laid upon them by Yahweh. On the other side of the Covenant agreement, Yahweh undertook the providential care of Abraham and his descendants. He guided their footsteps and provided for their needs.

As an assurance of the faithfulness of this promise, God changed Abram's name from its original form to 'Abraham', and the name of his wife to 'Sarah' (= 'the mother of nations and kings') as a token that she would bear a son whose heirs would receive Canaan as a lasting possession. The practice of circumcision, performed on all Hebrew boys at the age of eight days, was to be the sign that they were true sons of Israel and included under the Covenant.

(45) *Gen.* 18¹⁶–19²⁹. ABRAHAM'S PRAYER FOR SODOM

The exact location of Sodom, with its fellow 'city of the plain', Gomorrah, is not known, but it is generally believed to have been in the region of the Dead Sea. These two cities were notorious for their sexual immorality, until finally God destroyed them by raining down fire and brimstone. Liquid bitumen (petroleum) is found in the district, and an explosion in the soil may very likely have flung quantities of matter skyward, to fall back on the cities as a fiery rain. When Abraham became aware of the doom that was hanging over Sodom, he interceded with Yahweh for the sake of his nephew, Lot, who had chosen to dwell there. Lot was reluctant to leave; possibly he was afraid of the distant mountains and the rougher and more precarious life they had to offer.

His wife's reluctance was even more pronounced. In the retreat from the city, she was commanded not to look behind, either to prevent unnecessary delay in the flight, or to obviate any hankering after what she was leaving, or because God must not be seen at His work of destroying evil. This part of the story may have been told to account for the presence in the neighbourhood of a salt column, which Josephus the Jewish historian says he saw, and which modern travellers tell us is still there.

B. *Isaac*

(46) *Gen.* 21$^{1-21}$. ISAAC AND ISHMAEL

To most people, Isaac is the least vivid of the Patriarchs. His birth created an awkward situation: there was almost certain to be a growing tension between Sarah and Hagar, whose son was thus displaced. The feast in celebration of Isaac's weaning would take place when he was two or three years old. The word 'mocking' (*v.* 9), can be translated better as 'sporting'. It almost seems as if up to this point, the two boys had been regarded as on the same footing, or even that the elder had a priority. The treatment meted out to Hagar and her son was brutal, and the story-teller does not excuse it. Sarah and Abraham certainly do not show up in a very good light. The point of the story, however, is to indicate why the divine race sprang from Isaac and not Ishmael. As a compensation to the banished son, Yahweh ordained that he too should become the ancestor of a great race, the Ishmaelites.

(47) *Gen.* 22$^{1-19}$. THE SACRIFICE OF ISAAC

Human sacrifice was not unusual amongst primitive people, though amongst the Hebrews it does not seem to have been common. There are indications that it was resorted to on occasions of emergency, even to a relatively late date in Jewish history (*see* Jer. 7^{31}). Possibly one of the reasons for telling this story was to explain that the Hebrew Tribes realized that human sacrifice was not worthy of their religion much earlier than neighbouring peoples. The call to sacrifice Isaac was a test of Abraham's willingness to keep his side of the Covenant and obey what he believed to be the will of Yahweh. He could not withold anything from God, for all things were His and He had a right to demand them. But, since all hopes of founding a divine race depended upon Isaac producing descendants, the prospect of his premature death seemed to destroy the hope which had sustained Abraham. It must have looked to him as if God were not going to fulfil His side of the Promise. His faith, however, was equal to the strain, and in the event he realized that Yahweh had not failed him. The provision of the ram made it clear that He was continuing His care of His servant and would secure the fulfilment of His purpose through Isaac.

(48)* *Gen.* 24. ISAAC'S MARRIAGE

This chapter tells of the way in which the divine providence guided Abraham's servant and provided a mother for the Chosen Race. Underlying this beautifully told story, we are perhaps intended to see recorded the fact that more Semitic tribes, represented by Rebekah, migrated from Mesopotamia and, in Palestine, intermarried with descendants of the earlier migrations, represented by Isaac. Amongst Semitic people, marriage and the rearing of a family were regarded as a religious duty. Intermarriage was normal. For preference, a man chose one or more of his cousins and the marriage was negotiated by his agents, chiefly by his womenfolk. Costly gifts, or a dowry of money, had to be given in exchange for the bride. In most cases the groom was not allowed to see his future partner until after the marriage. The festivities were of an elaborate order and culminated when the bridegroom took his wife from her old home and carried her to her new one.

C. *Jacob*

(49) *Gen.* 27$^{1-40}$. THE DECEIVER

This story explains why the descendants of Jacob (the Israelites) became the Chosen Nation instead of the descendants of Esau (the Edomites), and why there was a never-ending enmity between the two peoples. We are shown Yahweh guiding Jacob through his many adversities and dangers, in order that the promise might be fulfilled through him. To many of us, Esau may seem to have been the more attractive character, for, in spite of his roughness of manner and his impetuosity, he was frank, lovable and generous. As Christians, we cannot but be shocked by Jacob's tricks and treacheries, though we must make allowances for the primitive level of life when these stories were first told. No one would be shocked then. Some of the Israelites, hearing for the first time of the theft of the birthright, might be inclined to commend it as a clever and astute move; and, in excuse for Rebekah, we may say that, to her way of thinking, once he had bought the birthright, Jacob had a right to whatever followed in consequence (Gen. 25²⁵⁻³⁴). In spite of Jacob's mercenary nature, and of the serious defects in his character, the Bible does show him to have been sensitive to the directions of God and obedient to His decrees as far as he understood them. As with so many Old Testament characters, his moral sense was only partly educated, and we realize how necessary it was for the fuller revelation of God's requirements to be made through Jesus Christ.

In later centuries, Israelite law decreed that the eldest son must be regarded as the head of the family after his father, and that the largest share of the property must come to him. In the age of the Patriarchs, it would seem that the father could exercise his own choice and appoint any one of his sons to succeed him. We notice that the inheritance of the divine promise is traced through younger members of the families, from Abraham, through Isaac and Jacob, to Joseph.

The 'blessing' was the ceremony in which the birthright was formally bestowed and, as with so many Israelite ceremonies, it was apparently sealed by the sharing of a special meal. It was as binding as the signing of a will is with us today. Indeed, to primitive thought, the very speaking of the words was thought to have a mysterious power of self-fulfilment. A blessing, properly uttered, carried with it good fortune for the recipient, just as a curse involved him in trouble and disaster. Once given, the blessing could not be withdrawn. Isaac might be bitterly disappointed at what he discovered he had unwittingly done, but he could not alter it. Esau had to be content with the promise of Edom for his inheritance, a country here regarded as dry and barren.

(50) *Gen.* 27⁴¹–28²². JACOB IN FLIGHT

Two reasons are given for Jacob's departure to Paddan-aran. For safety's sake he was compelled to flee from his brother's fury (27⁴¹⁻⁵); at the same time, at Rebekah's instigation, he was sent to the family of his uncle, Laban, to find a wife from amongst his kinsfolk. The character of the vision that came to him at Bethel (=House of God), may have been determined by the rocky district through which he was travelling and the stone terraces of the hillsides on which he had been looking during the daytime. Heaven did not seem far away and could be connected to the earth by means of a stairway, up and down which he saw angels walking. They symbolized a constant intercourse between God and man. We notice three important truths in this vision.

(a) Jacob was surprised to find Yahweh at Bethel. Probably Bethel was already a religious shrine but he had not connected it with the worship of Yahweh. Indeed, he had assumed that he had left Him behind when he departed from his old home. To flee from his family meant to flee from his God. Like all primitive peoples, he believed in a 'localized deity', whose presence and power were confined to the area occupied by the tribe that worshipped Him. To pass into other tribal territory was to come under the jurisdiction of other gods. According to this story, in the very dawn of Hebrew history, Jacob came to realize how wrong was this conception. Yahweh was at Bethel. 'Surely the Lord is in this place and I knew it not.'

(b) The Covenant Promise was repeated to Jacob (vv. 13–15), and he was given the assurance that, although he was leaving the land in haste, it would still be given to his descendants for their use. Meanwhile, he himself would be granted divine protection in his travels and a safe return.

(c) On his side, Jacob renewed his vows of loyalty to Yahweh and promised to give back to Him a tenth of what he received. This bargain seems to have been dictated by Jacob's mercenary nature in the belief that it would not be unprofitable to himself. Whether he fulfilled this promise, or how, we do not know.

(51)   *Gen.* 29. JACOB IN HARAN

Eleven sons were born to Jacob in Haran, and each became the ancestor of a Hebrew tribe: Benjamin was not born until after the return to Palestine. This sojourn in Haran, with the amassing of a family and flocks, suggests the formation of a federation of Aramean tribes for a further descent upon Palestine which will be indicated by the story of Jacob's return.

We may feel an un-Christian glee at the sight of the deceiver being himself deceived and cheated by his uncle, Laban. Jacob served seven years to obtain Rachel for his wife, only to be rewarded with Leah whom he did not want. A further term of seven years was demanded before he could get the one he loved, and a still further six years had to be endured to gather together sufficient flocks and herds to establish himself in independence as a sheep farmer. In Chapter 30, we are told of the tricks by which he managed to overreach the grasping Laban and to increase his own flocks more rapidly than had been expected.

(52)* *Gen.* 32¹⁻²¹. JACOB'S PREPARATION TO MEET ESAU

Chapter 31 tells of Jacob's resolve to return and seek a reconciliation with his brother. First he gained the approval of his wives, and with their help left Haran in haste, whilst Laban was busy shearing his sheep. Seven days later, his angry uncle caught up with him at Gilead, charging him with lack of courtesy in departing so abruptly, and with stealing his household gods. Rachel had hidden these in her baggage. Agreement was reached, however, and Jacob proceeded on his way.

The vision of angels (32¹) which he saw as he re-entered the Promised Land seemed to him a sure sign that Yahweh would protect him in the coming meeting with Esau. Naturally, Jacob was nervous and apprehensive. In case the attempt at peace should fail, he divided his company into two camps ('Mahanaim' =two camps) so that, if Esau attacked one, the other might escape. He also divided up the presents with which he hoped to win over his brother, intending that Esau should be surprised again and again as each new contingent of sheep, goats, asses, and cattle was brought before him. Thus his anger would have a chance of being melted before Jacob himself appeared. Although there is real beauty in Jacob's prayer to Yahweh, we notice no sign of regret for the past, no note of confession or repentance.

(53) *Gen.* 32²²⁻³². JACOB'S WRESTLING AT PENIEL

This incident is not easy for us to understand. In his famous hymn (M.H.B. 430), Charles Wesley used it as a picturesque description of a soul wrestling with God in prayer. The ancient story, as told in *Genesis*, is less simple. It seems to have been based upon the primitive idea that, before a human being could cross a river, he had to come to terms with the deity that presided over it. The Old Testament lifts this idea of a river god to a higher level. Jacob could not go forward with confidence until he had gained a knowledge of the bond that existed between Yahweh and himself. In his dream he found himself wrestling with a determined opponent. For a time neither could prevail, but, at length, Jacob was disabled. Then he realized that he had been striving with no ordinary human being, but with a supernatural antagonist.

When this knowledge came to him, he demanded from the victor a blessing, and the change in his name is meant to indicate that it was given. Moreover, he wanted to know the name of his opponent, for, according to primitive ideas, the possession of a name gave a man power over its owner. Consequently, Jacob's request was refused. He was not to know the personal name of his God. He himself was in the grip of Yahweh, for Yahweh had bestowed a name upon him, but he was not permitted to possess any power over Yahweh.

What happened at Peniel constituted a crisis in Jacob's spiritual history. The new name was, in truth, the token of a new character. Henceforth we are no longer conscious of the old deceitfulness and craftiness in him. Contrary to his fears, he found Esau friendly and ready to forgive the past. Indeed, although Esau had not altogether lost his suspicions of his brother, he suggested that they should travel along together in the future, but Jacob was not willing. He had obtained all he wanted. He and his family were now secured against what might have been a determined and relentless foe, and the way was open for the continued fulfilment of the divine promise to Jacob's descendants.

D. *Joseph*

(54) In our next *Study* we shall see that the people whom God had chosen to be a divine nation had to be rescued from a state of slavery in Egypt. How did they get there? The stories of Joseph are intended to provide us with the explanation. Some eighteen centuries before Christ, Lower Egypt was conquered by a people whose rulers are known as Shepherd Kings. They seem to have belonged to the same Semitic stock as the Hebrews. What more natural, then, in a time of famine, than for the wandering Israelites to move into Egypt seeking relief at the hands of their kinsmen. Probably they did not travel in a body, but in contingent after contingent as they were driven by hunger.

Unfortunately for them, the power of the Shepherd Kings was not permanent. After a régime of some 200 years, they were expelled. The Egyptian king who succeeded them saw that, in order to make his own position safe, it would be wise to take all power and freedom from the descendants of those who had settled in Egypt as friends of his predecessors. He, therefore, forced the Hebrews into slavery. Once more it looked as if Yahweh's purpose would be brought to nought. Nevertheless, He was in control all the time, making even the misfortunes of His children to serve His intention, working through the events of their history to achieve His will.

(55) *Gen.* 37. JOSEPH SOLD INTO EGYPT

Born in his father's old age, and of his best beloved wife, Joseph was marked out as his favourite son. The coat of many colours, which demonstrated that he was the heir, was, most likely, a long white garment, with flowing sleeves and edged with colours. It was worn only by persons of distinction and was obviously quite unsuitable as ordinary working attire. Besides that sign of superiority to his brothers, Joseph's own personal attitude gave them some justification for disliking him. There was a good deal of the prig about him: he was a treacherous tale-bearer; and his sense of his own importance was unbearable. Nevertheless, his character was not devoid of finer elements, and, as his life-story unfolds, we feel these qualities growing in strength and dominance. He possessed a high standard of moral integrity, a generous and forgiving disposition, and a very deep affection for his father and his younger brother.

In our first reading of the account of his sale to the Egyptians, it seems a straightforward narrative: but a closer reading reveals a number of difficulties and discrepancies. Did Judah persuade his brethren not to kill Joseph but to sell him to the Ishmaelites, or did Reuben, in the hope that he might be able to rescue him and bring him back to his father, get them to drop him into a pit where he was found by the Midianites? Who actually sold him to the Egyptians—the Ishmaelites or the Midianites? The explanation is that the story as we have it in *Genesis* is a mixture of two ancient stories, woven together with very little attempt to reconcile the differences between them. This chapter provides us with a good illustration of how the Biblical writers frequently went about their work, and will help us to understand the alleged 'contradictions' which exist in so many Old Testament narratives.

(56) *Gen.* 39. JOSEPH CAST INTO PRISON

In Egypt, Joseph became a slave in the household of an official whose name was Potiphar, where his ability and trustworthiness earned him the position of steward and manager. However, his refusal to commit adultery with his master's wife provoked her to bring a false charge against him, and he was flung into prison. During his two years there, his natural gifts of leadership brought him to the fore and he was placed in charge of his fellow prisoners. 'Whatsoever they did there, he was the doer of it.' He gained further distinction for himself as an interpreter of dreams (Gen. 40). The ancient world believed that dreams carried important but hidden messages to those who experienced them, and any who could unravel their meanings were much sought after. A court like that of Egypt had its own official interpreters, who were not always successful in their explanations.

(57) *Gen.* 41. PHARAOH'S DREAMS AND THEIR FULFILMENT

Troubled by strange and baffling dreams, the reigning Pharaoh, one of the Shepherd Kings, had Joseph brought from his prison to interpret them. He declared they were meant to forecast a period of rich harvests followed by seven successive years of scarcity. In Egypt, the crops depended upon the waters of the Nile, and, although there was a system of irrigation, a shortage of water at its source in the Abyssinian highlands could easily bring about famine conditions. Delighted to know the significance of his dreams, Pharaoh appointed Joseph to deal with the coming emergency, giving him the royal signet ring as a token of the favour and power bestowed upon him. He was also raised to the nobility and given the hand in marriage of a daughter of the priest of Om (Heliopolis). A scheme whereby he secured the control of all the land, except that owned by the priests, and imposed on it an annual tax of one-fifth of its produce, consolidated his position with the Pharaoh (47^{13-27}).

(58)* *Gen.* 42-4. JOSEPH'S MEETINGS WITH HIS BRETHREN

The coming famine threatened Palestine as well as Egypt, and Jacob sent his sons, except Benjamin the youngest, to buy corn from Egypt. It was not unreasonable that they should be regarded as spies, finding out how their kinsmen were faring with a view to a later invasion. Joseph deliberately decided to treat them as such. He seems to have felt that he was justified in inflicting upon them some degree of distress in return for their treatment of him, and only released them on condition that they returned with their remaining brother. Meanwhile Simeon was detained in

Egypt as an hostage. Possibly Reuben, the eldest, escaped this fate because of his kindlier treatment of Joseph at Dothan. When the others returned with Benjamin, they made haste to explain the money which had been returned in their sacks on their previous visit, for, otherwise, they might have been arrested as thieves. They knew that thieves who could not make compensation for what they had stolen were liable to be sold into slavery. The finding of the divining cup in Benjamin's sack exposed him to the same peril. The ancient world was full of magic and the divining cup was used to foretell the future. Fragments of gold and silver were thrown into it and the pattern of the pieces was supposed to predict the shape of things to come, as in the present day habit of reading tea-cups.

(59) *Gen.* 45. JOSEPH MAKES HIMSELF KNOWN

After the reconciliation with his brethren, they were sent back at Pharaoh's command to bring Jacob and their families to Egypt. Note not only Joseph's magnanimity to those who had caused him so much suffering, but also his firm belief in an overruling Providence. 'Be not grieved, nor angry with yourselves, that ye sold me hither: for God did send me before you to preserve life' (*v.* 5). 'So now it was not you that sent me hither, but God' (*v.* 8).

(60) *Gen.* 46–7. JACOB'S REMOVAL INTO EGYPT

Goshen lay alongside the Nile Delta on the eastern borders of the Egyptian Empire. Here Jacob and his family were given land and the status of free men and honoured guests. On the other hand, it would seem that they were not encouraged to mix with the Egyptians. For one thing, their occupation as shepherds made them an 'abomination' unto the Egyptians (46[34]), and prevented any terms of equality. The more important reason was that the distinctiveness of the Israelite stock must be preserved in order that the promise of Yahweh might be fulfilled through them. They were but sojourners in Egypt, waiting for the time when God should call them to make their home in Palestine. As a token of this hope, when Jacob died in Goshen his embalmed body was taken to Machpelah for burial, to lie side by side with the bodies of Abraham and Isaac in the land which their descendants were to inherit. When Joseph himself came to die, his body was buried in Egypt, but a promise was made that when his descendants moved to their new home, his bones should be carried with them.

We may notice that Jacob's blessing upon the two sons of Joseph, Ephraim and Manasseh (48⁸⁻¹⁴), marked them as the founders of the tribes which were to play such an important part in subsequent history.

E. *Religion in the Patriarchal Period*

(61)   A great difficulty in understanding what religion meant in the times of the ancestors of the Hebrew race comes from the fact that the stories which have been preserved about them were compiled and edited for us many centuries later. The editors always tended to assume that religion in the patriarchal period was much the same as in their own time, and that beliefs and practices which were part and parcel of their own lives had been in existence from the beginning. Thus they conveyed the impression that early religion was much more advanced than it could have been. We must allow for that tendency. At the same time, we must remember that religious ideas and customs often have a long history behind them, and Hebrew religion did not become a totally new thing under the guidance of Moses. Quite a lot must have been carried over from the patriarchal period.

(62)   The Hebrews were a Semitic people, related to the Arabs, and also to the Babylonians who were to influence them so much in the course of the centuries. They had many beliefs and customs in common with the Babylonians. Even in the pre-Mosaic period, they were not savages. They were nomads, wandering shepherds; but unlike most nomads, they did not keep to well defined tracks in their search for pasturage, but ventured into new territories.

(63)   They took the existence of supernatural beings for granted; gods were everywhere. They recognized them in the storm, in trees, in fountains, wherever they came unexpectedly across the means of living, wherever something unusual happened. An oasis in the desert across which they travelled might be the garden of one god, and a boulder that gave them protection from the sun and wind, the home of another. Doubtless fear played a large part in their religion. Gifts had to be made to turn away the anger of the gods, or at least to secure the continuance of their goodwill. The Patriarchs shared this belief in many gods. We cannot know for certain how far they believed in a special tribal

god of their own, or how far they merely accepted the local gods of the tribes through whose territory they passed. The editors of *Genesis* would have us believe that the Israelites were bound to Yahweh from the beginning and that Abraham, Isaac, Jacob and Joseph were in a covenant relation with Him. Of that, we cannot be sure.

(64) At each place of settlement, however temporary it might be, the Hebrews set up an altar, or used an altar they found already there (Gen. 12[8], 13[15], 28[19], 33[20]). Some vision, some gift or help, revealed to them the presence of a god. The altar was in most cases a mere shrine, and the priest the head of the family or clan. Religion was a family affair and its rites were family occasions. Happy events, a marriage, the weaning of a child, the visit of a welcome guest, were also religious feasts. In hours of sorrow, there were fasts. Religion imposed upon the wanderers certain duties which ought to be paid to their ancestors, to other tribes, to their children and their children's children. The desire for offspring, the effort to perpetuate the family name, so strong amongst the Hebrews from the beginning, suggests something more than the normal instinct of procreation. To produce a family and to hand on the spiritual heritage of the tribe was also a high religious duty. Though we can never get a firm answer to our question, we are tempted to ask whether the primitive Hebrews actually worshipped their ancestors as in ancient China.

(65) Idols and images were in common use (Gen. 31[35], 35[4]). We should expect this to be so at this early stage. It took a long period of spiritual discipline and growth before men were able to worship God without any visual aid. In the patriarchal times, it is not surprising that people did not distinguish between the image which was only a symbol of the presence of a god and the invisible reality which it represented. They thought the sacred thing possessed in itself something of the power of the god for whose sake it was revered. At some stage, articles were manufactured to represent deities and fashioned into some sort of a likeness which could be carried about; but in the earliest days the image would be an upright stone, perhaps carved in an unusual shape. Sacrifices for the most part were sacred meals that were meant to unite the worshippers with their god. Upon occasion, the Hebrews seem to have offered human sacrifices, but they were amongst the first of the nomadic tribes to repudiate the practice (*see para.* 47).

(66) The custom of circumcision came to have a religious significance. The rite had a long history. In later times it was practised upon all males of a week old and became one of the distinctive marks of a Jew. In the first place it may have been instituted for hygienic reasons, but it became, as with other peoples of the east, a rite of initiation into the full membership of the tribe. At some point in Hebrew history it was linked with the idea of the Covenant and symbolized the bond that united the Hebrews with Yahweh their own God.

(67) Thus we must think of the religion of the Patriarchs as being simple, even in some respects crude. As they have come down to us, the stories of *Genesis* breathe a sublime faith in Yahweh but that belonged largely to the final editions. Yet even the simple forms of religion, which seem to us to be authentic patriarchal practices, are not to be despised. Out of them grew the rich and intimate fellowship with God which is the great contribution of Judaism to the life of mankind.

TEST QUESTIONS

(Send answers to TWO *questions to your tutor)*

1. Give the story of Abraham so as to illustrate the statement, 'Abraham believed God'.
2. Write a character study of Jacob.
3. Outline the main incidents in the life of Joseph to illustrate the theme of Gen. 45^5.

Study Three

Moses and the Exodus

(68) We come now to the more solid rock of history. Our information about Moses has, it is true, to be gathered from the writings of the Old Testament itself, for there are no other contemporary accounts of his life. Possibly some of the incidents attributed to him have a legendary element about them, but in the main we can regard as reliable the outline of his career and the most important events in it as given to us in the Bible. Were we to doubt the existence of Moses, or his outstanding achievements, the story of the Hebrew people would not make sense, and the very foundations of the Biblical message would be irreparably weakened.

(69) Moses was the great *deliverer* who rescued the Children of Israel from the bondage of Egypt. Throughout the Old Testament we meet with a constant sense of wonder and gratitude as men recall this amazing achievement. It was the result, in the first place, of the providence and power of God, and it was only right and proper that the fulness of the praise should be given to Him. Still, it was recognized that Yahweh required a human instrument for the accomplishment of His purpose, and Moses had been chosen for the task and had wrought a marvellous service.

(70) The story of the deliverance from Egypt was one that no Israelite would have invented, for it focussed attention upon the lowliness of their national origins. The Hebrews were a proud people, amongst the proudest who have ever walked the earth, and it would have suited their purpose to have hidden anything discreditable in their ancestry. Had it been possible they would have concealed the fact that their nation had sprung from a rabble of uncouth slaves down in Egypt. But the truth was too firmly established in their tradition. Slaves their fathers had been, and slaves they would have remained but for the divine intervention.

(71) Moses possessed in a very high degree the qualities of a great *statesman*. In a very real sense, he laid the foundations of the Hebrew nation. He took a rabble of slaves and infused into

them the beginnings of a spirit which would cause them, through long centuries and much adversity, to remain an indestructible nation right down to the present day. The sense of national identity and unity did not come all at once, of course, but he carried the various tribes, with their own family loyalties and clan customs, to the east of the Jordan under his leadership, and left in their hearts a spirit which in due course would make their descendants a truly remarkable race. Two things he gave them in his wisdom and out of his dependence on divine direction—a common code of laws and a common ritual of worship.

(72) The world probably thinks of Moses first and foremost as a *lawgiver*. The Ten Commandments have proved to be not only a sound basis for the conduct of desert wanderers, but an equally sure foundation for the most complicated and advanced civilization. The Covenant which bound Yahweh and His people together was ethical in character. Some of the laws it laid upon the Israelites may seem to be concerned to a large degree with the correctness of religious rites and ceremonies, and there is still much in them that falls short of the moral standards accepted by those whose conscience has been awakened by Christ; yet the ethical quality is there all the time, and must not be overlooked. God's people were required to do what they believed to be right. The first Hebrew tribes may have thought of Yahweh to a large extent as the God of battles, who would give them support against their foes or help them fight their way to a new home; but it began to be felt, even in those early days, that defeat might not be due to weakness on His part, but to their failure to keep His laws.

(73) Though the Old Testament does not use the title, we may prefer to regard Moses as a *prophet*. Long before that unique series of prophets who played such a prominent part in Hebrew history and religion, Moses stood before his fellows as a revealer of God, sent to share with them the knowledge of Yahweh and His demands which had been divinely disclosed to him. All his life and work were rooted in his own faith in Yahweh as a Living and Redeeming God. In the Book of *Exodus*, we begin to see Biblical religion taking on its fundamental characteristics. Under Moses' guidance, the Covenant became the very heart of religion. The nation, even in its childhood, was led to look upon its God as a Living God, active in history, controlling the rise and fall of nations, achieving His purposes through the various crises of the human story. With the remembrance of the part He had played

in their own deliverance from Egypt, they entered upon their course with the sobering thought that they were a nation specially singled out by His will and called into being to be the instruments of His purpose.

(74) In the chapters we are to study, we are watching the birth of something great, in fact the mightiest religious movement the world has ever known, and we shall go on to see how it grew from that beginning to the rich and wonderful thing it is. The greatest tribute we can pay to Moses is to say he was so entirely the servant of God that he was able to give to a collection of crude and primitive peoples, who had grown weary of their wandering life and who asked chiefly for bread and a place in which to live in peace, a sense of God and of a divine vocation which they never lost, and which made possible, in the fulness of time, God's supreme self-disclosure in Jesus Christ.

A. *The Call of Moses*

(75) Exactly how the descendants of Jacob became slaves in Egypt we do not know. Evidently a time came when the Egyptians' debt to Joseph was forgotten, and his descendants came to be looked upon with fear rather than gratitude. There were grounds for such a fear. Should any foreign power threaten Egypt, they might make use of the Israelites as an exceedingly useful fifth column. Their numbers were so strong that the Egyptian authorities could not afford to overlook them. When the dynasty of the Shepherd Kings came to an end, some subsequent Pharaoh, so we must surmise, changed the status of the Hebrew people. Instead of being guests, they found conditions of slavery imposed upon them. To rescue them from that humiliation and oppression, God determined to call a deliverer and fit him for his mission.

(76) *Exod.* 1. ISRAEL IN EGYPT

The steps to render the Israelites harmless were probably taken in the reign of Rameses II (1292-1225 B.C.). Forced labour was demanded from them, with the intention of breaking their spirit and leaving them neither time nor energy to get up to mischief. At the same time, Pharaoh solved his problem of the shortage of labour for his extensive programme of fortifications, munition stores and granaries alongside the Nile, not far from the modern Suez Canal.

In spite of the almost unendurable conditions of their servitude, the Israelite population continued to increase, and a more drastic attempt had to be made to keep their numbers within bounds. Their midwives were ordered to kill every male child at birth. The midwives whose names are mentioned were probably only two out of a much larger number, but they are singled out because they disobeyed the order. To counteract any such leniency, a further order decreed that all Hebrew male children should be thrown into the Nile, and the Egyptians were given power to see this savage command carried out.

(77) *Exod.* 2. THE EARLY LIFE OF MOSES

Yahweh was looking after Israel. The child Moses was saved from destruction, adopted by an Egyptian princess, and brought up at the royal court. Escaping in this way the hardships of slavery, he was educated in the ways of leadership, whilst his capacity for sympathy preserved a sense of kinship with his fellow Israelites in their oppression. To prevent one of them being bullied by an Egyptian, he made a practical intervention; but when his concern for the unity of the tribe led him to come between two Israelites whom he found fighting, this action was not so welcome. Clearly, his previous interference had been talked about, and there was more than a possibility that reports of it would reach the court. To avoid the punishment that would have followed, Moses fled to Midian where he found a wife and a home. The years he spent with Jethro were years of preparation for the work of deliverance that awaited him. The memory of what he himself had seen happening to his fellow Hebrews in Egypt burned in his soul like a fierce fire, and made him ready to receive the divine summons when it came.

(78) *Exod.* 3$^{1-10}$. THE REVELATION OF THE BURNING BUSH

The 'back' of the desert was the west, facing the setting sun, just as the east was referred to as the 'front'. Here, as he led his flock, God spoke to Moses, not, of course, with an ordinary human voice, but in the secret places of his soul. Scholars have tried to explain the phenomenon that Moses saw. The simplest explanation is that, in the glaring sunlight of the desert, a mimosa bush had all the appearance of being on fire. Whatever explanation we may give, the important thing is the interpretation of the vision. Moses saw something unusual and realized it was a sign that God had a message for him. In the Bible, fire is frequently regarded as a token of the presence of God. As the divine presence made itself felt, Moses knew that, as a mortal man, he must take off his shoes as a mark of reverence and awe. He does not seem to have felt he was in the presence of any strange and unfamiliar deity, but rather that the God of his fathers was disclosing Himself. Already that God had made Himself known in history and would continue to give guidance and power to Moses as He had to the Patriarchs.

(79) *Exod.* 3¹¹–4¹⁶. MOSES' HESITATION

Having received such an exacting call to leadership, it was perhaps only natural that Moses should begin to raise difficulties, though God had an adequate answer to each one of them.

(*a*) Moses argued he was not fit for such a task, but God assured him that He knew what He was doing and promised to be with him (3¹¹).

(*b*) He did not know the proper name of God, and, without such knowledge, he did not feel that he possessed the divine authority and power, nor would he be able to tell the Israelites whom they were to serve and worship. In answer the divine name was disclosed to him (3¹⁴. *See para.* 80).

(*c*) He had no personal credentials with which to overcome the disbelief he was sure to encounter amongst the Israelite slaves. God replied by giving him power to work three signs (4¹⁻⁹).

(*d*) He was slow and halting of speech. This may very likely have been so, and it would be a serious handicap. Moses was, however, reminded that God had the power to give him the eloquence he needed, and, as a practical way out of the difficulty, Aaron was appointed to be his spokesman, although the authority of leadership was to remain with Moses (4¹⁰⁻¹⁶).

(80) *Exod.* 3¹⁴. THE DIVINE NAME

God revealed His name to Moses as JAHVEH or YAHWEH. The RV margin gives us a clue as to its meaning: 'I will be what I will be.' The God of Israel was a God who was living and active, who was always working out His purpose and revealing His will through the history of His people. In later times, this name came to be regarded as too sacred to be uttered by mortal man, even by the priests. When they came to it in their reading of the scriptures, they dared not pronounce it, and, in its place, they substituted a more ordinary name for God. Until the sixth century A.D., only consonants were used in Hebrew writing (*see para.* 15). But when vowel signs began to come into use, the scribes fixed the vowels of this word for 'my Lord' to the consonants of His proper name. Thus we get a mixed or 'hybrid' word—'Jehovah'. We may still find it convenient, especially in public worship, to use this as the personal name of the God of Israel rather than the more correct Jahveh or Yahweh. In the Revised Version, the word LORD, in capitals, indicates the presence in the ancient scriptures of the sacred and unspeakable name YAHWEH, whilst Moffatt translates it as the 'ETERNAL'.

B. *The Escape from Egypt*

(81)   In order to accomplish the rescue of his fellow Israelites, Moses found himself faced with a twofold task. He had to secure the loyalty of the Hebrews to his proposals, which called upon them to take great risks and show no little courage; and at the same time he had to secure the consent of Pharaoh to their departure. Again and again, the attitude of the Israelites was what we should expect in slaves—suspicious, hesitant, over-cautious, lacking in initiative and without self-discipline. Moses had great difficulty in getting them to face up to the challenge of the deliverance. On the other hand, although Pharaoh might realize that the presence of the Israelites in Egypt carried with it certain dangers for him, he preferred to have them under his eye, and did not relish the prospect of losing his supply of cheap labour. Some of the methods by which Moses secured the ultimate liberation of the slaves do not commend themselves to a Christian conscience, but, once again, we must make allowances for the moral standards of the time. The great truth is that God was at work, shaping the destiny of His chosen race.

(82)*   *Exod.* 4²⁷–6¹.   THE CHALLENGE TO PHARAOH

When the Israelites were persuaded to respond to the leadership of Moses and Aaron, they requested permission to make a pilgrimage into the wilderness in order to offer their sacrifices. Their case was that these could not be presented in the correct way on Egyptian soil, since they involved the killing of animals which the Egyptians held sacred. Pharaoh was obstinate in his opposition. He denied all knowledge of Yahweh as the God of the Hebrews, and pretended to believe that their petition was merely an excuse for a holiday. Obviously he realized its true significance, for he proceeded to make any escape impossible by imposing more difficult conditions of forced labour. The supplies of chopped straw, with which they caked together the mud of the Nile to make bricks, was stopped. Under divine direction, Moses was compelled to take more drastic steps for, if he failed to get their release from Pharaoh, the Israelites would lose their faith in the adventure to which he was persuading them.

(83)* *Exod.* 7¹–10²⁹. THE PLAGUES

We do not need to study in detail the series of plagues recorded in these chapters and which the Old Testament interprets as being specially sent by Yahweh in order to force Pharaoh's hand. The Hebrews in those early days had no difficulty in supposing that He deliberately inflicted such catastrophes upon the enemies of His people. We Christians find it hard to accept such a naïve explanation and would prefer to think that the Egyptians' confidence was shaken by a series of disasters which fell upon them in quick succession, and which we should trace to their natural causes.

The plagues were, in fact, the kind of misfortunes that could easily happen to a people who lived so close to the Nile—the river running red as blood with the silt it carried along; multitudes of frogs in the streets and houses after a flood; swarms of gnats and mosquitoes hatched out in the swamps; diseases that struck men and cattle; hailstorms laying low the crops and locusts that ate them; sandstorms shutting out the light of the sun; epidemics of malaria carrying death into what seemed to be every house in the land, not even excepting the royal palace. For such mishaps our inclination is to look for natural causes and explanations; the Israelites had no difficulty in attributing them to the direct intervention of Yahweh to punish those who opposed His will.

Stricken in this way, the Egyptians decided that their sorrows were due to the presence of aliens in their midst. Moses took advantage of their embarrassments and made them serve the purposes of Yahweh. Pharaoh at last decided that there could be no health or happiness for his people until the dangerous influence was removed and reluctantly gave permission for the slaves to go.

(84) *Exod.* 11. THE FINAL PLAGUE

The death of the firstborn finally broke Pharaoh's resolution not to let his slaves go, and led to their deliverance. It is chosen for our reading because it gave rise to the religious ceremony of the Passover which took a central place in the ritual of Israelite religion.

(85) *Exod.* 12$^{21-28, 43-51}$. RULES FOR THE PASSOVER

We can be reasonably sure that, at first, the celebration of the deliverance consisted of a simple memorial meal. Later it became more elaborate, and, after the settlement in Canaan, many Canaanite ideas were incorporated. There were two main features:

(*a*) Blood was sprinkled on the top and the sides of the doors to denote that the house was consecrated and those within specially protected.

(*b*) A hurried meal was partaken, consisting of roasted flesh, unleavened bread and bitter herbs. The flesh must not be eaten raw because the blood, as the current of life, was regarded as too sacred. The bitter herbs, probably endive or wild lettuce, suggested the bitterness of the bondage. The unleavened cakes were a kind of flat biscuit which could be quickly baked. The meal was to be eaten in haste and trepidation, the guests clad ready for their departure, and no particle of the food was to be left for a later meal. The over-ruling thought was the promise of Yahweh to 'pass over' Israel and spare it from disaster.

This account of the Passover comes from the oldest of the strands which are woven together to make the Pentateuch—the 'J' document (*see para.* 442 (*a*)).

(86) *Exod.* 12$^{29-42}$. THE DEPARTURE FROM EGYPT

This account of the journey from Egypt does not suggest the same sense of speed and urgency. *Verse* 35 indicates a more leisurely and organized escape. The Egyptians were to be despoiled by their ex-slaves according to a deliberate plan. Once again, we must bear in mind the standards of the time as we pass judgement upon the proceeding.

(87) *Exod.* 13$^{3-10}$. RULES FOR THE FEAST OF UNLEAVENED
BREAD (MAZZOTH)

Probably in origin this was an agricultural feast to celebrate the beginning of the barley harvest, and one which the Israelites adopted from the Canaanites after the settlement. It fell at the same time as the Passover and was combined with it. Again, the accent is on the haste with which the Israelites left Egypt. They had no time for the leaven to work in their bread. In later times, the Passover and the Mazzoth together became the most important of the annual festivals of the Jews. In Exod. 12$^{1-20}$ we have a set of regulations for the combined observance of the Hebrew Passover and the Canaanite Mazzoth (Unleavened Cakes) drawn up by the priests during the Exile (document P; see para. 442 (d)), and they show the ritual that was practised at this later period.

(88) *Exod.* 13$^{1-2,\ 11-16}$. THE DEDICATION OF THE FIRSTBORN

All the firstborn males, both of human beings and of animals, were to be regarded as sacred and dedicated to God as a sign of gratitude for the great deliverance. Since the ass was regarded as unclean in the ceremonial sense, it could not be eaten or sacrificed, but its firstborn must be redeemed by the substitution of a lamb. If not redeemed, it must be strangled.

(89) *Exod.* 13^{17}–14. THE PURSUIT

Fleeing from the scene of their oppression, the slaves made their way across the northern inlets of the Red Sea into the Sinai Peninsula, probably avoiding the normal caravan routes. Yahweh was their guide, and a pillar of cloud by day and a pillar of fire by night symbolized His presence. Some people think the cloud and the fire were the flames and smoke of Mount Sinai which marked the destination Moses had in mind. Once more, the interpretation rather than the explanation is the important thing. It meant that Yahweh was directing His people and every Israelite could be aware of it (13$^{17-22}$). Naturally, Pharaoh did not accept the escape of his slaves without an effort to recapture them. The Egyptian army was called out, but in attempting to follow the fugitives across a stretch of swampy ground was destroyed. Many attempts have been made to explain what happened; the Israelites attributed their deliverance to the intervention of Yahweh (14$^{1-31}$).

(90) *Exod.* 15. MOSES' SONG OF TRIUMPH

Scholars believe that this is a very ancient poem, though they

D

do not think it was actually composed by Moses. Probably those who first told the story of the Exodus put a song of triumph into the mouth of Moses, and this was added to in later centuries. You will notice that, whilst it begins with a celebration of the defeat of the Egyptians (*vv.* 1–13), it goes on to speak of the establishment of the people in Canaan when their enemies were the Philistines and the Edomites (*vv.* 14–16). There is even a reference to the Temple (*v.* 17) in Mount Zion which was not built until a much later date (*see para.* 173).

(91)★   *Exod.* 16–17⁷.   MURMURINGS IN THE WILDERNESS

These chapters help us to understand why the entry into the Promised Land had to be deferred. Moses was compelled to wait until a new generation of Israelites had arisen, who no longer shared the slave mentality of their fathers, but knew how to make use of their freedom. In the desert, the escaped slaves found it difficult to obtain food and drink and, by contrast, saw their previous life in Egypt in bright and idealistic colours. The manna and the quails which Yahweh provided formed an adequate diet, though somewhat dull. We are told that quails still abound in this region and can easily be caught in the evening after a long flight. The manna may have been a kind of biscuit such as Arabs make from the juice of the tamarisk plant. Shortage of water led to a revolt, but Moses was able to satisfy their need by smiting the rock with his rod.

(92)★   *Exod.* 17⁸⁻¹⁶.   THE FIGHT WITH AMALEK

Briefly we are told of the first clash with the native tribes of the lands through which the Israelites were journeying. Amalek was determined to block the road to Palestine. Apparently the incident happened towards the end of the wilderness wanderings. Moses is an old man; his two companions, Aaron and Hur, who support the hand in which he holds the rod are also aged; and Joshua is already acting as commander of the Israelite forces.

(93)★   *Exod.* 18.   JETHRO'S ADVICE

Moses was able to convince his father-in-law, Jethro, of the presence of Yahweh with the Israelites, and to persuade him to join with him in the adventure. In return, Jethro proposed a scheme to relieve Moses of some of the heavy burden of administering justice amongst the Hebrew people. It was no longer possible for him to act as the sole judge of all disputes. Hence-forth, although the right of deciding the principles of justice was to be left in his own hands, the detailed application of them was delegated to a number of carefully chosen deputies.

C. *Moses at Mount Sinai*

(94) The Israelites set forth on their long and arduous journey to the Promised Land, inspired and sustained by the belief that they were doing so in response to the call of the god of their tribes, Yahweh. At this period of their history, and for a long time afterwards, it never occurred to them that Yahweh could be more than their tribal deity. He belonged to them in the same way as Chemosh belonged to the Moabites and Melkart to the Edomites. They believed in Him without questioning the right of their neighbours to believe in other gods. Each people was under an obligation to be faithful to its own god. In practice they accepted their duty with varying degrees of loyalty. On occasion, and for what seemed to them sufficient reasons, they paid their homage to each other's deities. Israel was little better than its neighbours. Although they were bound to Yahweh, the Hebrews from time to time paid their respects to other gods and worshipped them alongside of Him.

(95) Not until the time of the great prophets, Amos and his successors, did the idea begin to take hold of them that Yahweh might be more than the god of their nation; that He was in fact the only true God and that beside Him there could be no other. At that stage of religious thought, we have what is known as 'monotheism', the belief in one God, and one only. The view that each nation ought to be faithful to its own god, though accepting the existence of other gods for other peoples, is known as 'monolatry' or 'henotheism'. This was the state of affairs in the time of Moses. To us this may seem a strange conception, but we must remember that, whatever its defects, it registered an advance upon 'polytheism', which allowed each tribe to worship many gods (and goddesses) at the same time.

(96) At Mount Sinai, the Children of Israel were formally declared to be the People of Yahweh, chosen to fulfil His purposes and bound to Him by the closest of ties (19$^{1-25}$). In the time of

the Patriarchs, it was assumed that there was a Covenant relationship between God and them; at Sinai that relationship was made explicit and its terms set out clearly. The Covenant set out the terms on which fellowship between God and man could take place. Yahweh pledged Himself to give providential guidance and protection to His people; Israel had to give Him complete loyalty and set itself to obey His will in all things (*see para.* 44). The choice of Israel to be God's Nation was a pure favour on Yahweh's part; nevertheless, although the obedience that Israel would give in return was likely to be brittle and unsure, He would not go back upon His choice.

(97) The idea of the Covenant was to play the central part in the religious thought of the Hebrew people. Moses laid down for them in the simplest terms what Yahweh required of His chosen race. In course of time, as we shall see, the Covenant had to be renewed and its conditions revised. A revision of extreme importance was that which we know as *Deuteronomy*, where a wholesale attempt was made to reform the religious and moral life of the nation (*see para.* 264). Even more important were the ideas of Jeremiah, who came to see that an entirely New Covenant was needed, of a much more spiritual character, based, not upon Israel's obedience to a legal code, but upon an inward bond of fellowship between God and man (*see para.* 298). The perfect Covenant relationship, however, was not to be found in Old Testament times at all. It could not be created until the coming of Jesus Christ; until, by His death and resurrection, He brought God and man together in a Covenant of Grace.

(98)   *Exod.* 20¹⁻²¹.   THE TEN COMMANDMENTS

Israel's obligations to Yahweh were expressed in ten demands, which could be ticked off on the fingers of the hands. The first five are concerned with religious obligations. Israel must:

1. Have no other god but Yahweh
2. Worship no graven image
3. Make no wrong use of the divine name
4. Keep the Sabbath
5. Honour parents. This counted as a religious duty since religion had to be passed from generation to generation, and the teaching ministry of the elders required an attitude of respect from those who were taught.

The second five deal with social and moral issues, and fitted the sort of crimes that must have been common amongst desert peoples.

6. No murder
7. No adultery
8. No stealing
9. No perjury

10. No covetousness. This last commandment transcends the legalistic and external point of view and deals with man's inward motives. We recognize covetousness as the root of nearly all moral delinquency.

(99) We should expect the Ten Commandments to bear the imprint of pre-Christian days. For instance, they take for granted the existence of other gods than Yahweh; they have in mind a primitive and pastoral community with a much simpler way of life than in the time of Christ, let alone in ours; they shock our modern point of view when they list a man's wife amongst his possessions along with his ox and his ass. Still, only a fool would despise them. Wise and clear-sighted thinkers have always recognized that even an advanced civilization is likely to go to pieces if it ignores their guidance. They are, indeed, valid for all men and for all time. They are not merely moral regulations devised by men to give a structure of decency and security to society; they enshrine nothing less than the will of God and set forth the directions of the Creator for the lives of those whom He has created. Certainly we are taught by Jesus to interpret the Ten Commandments at a deeper level than a mere slavish obedience to their letter. But He did not set them aside. He took them for granted. They made the relationship between religion and morality absolutely firm. We in the twentieth century are still to be guided by the principles and spirit behind them or we shall find ourselves in trouble and confusion.

(100)* *Exod.* 20²²–23³³. THE BOOK OF THE COVENANT

This compilation of laws and regulations, in its present form, was probably drawn up for the direction of the Israelites at a later and more settled period than that of Moses, but the ideas derive from him. The underlying principle is that adequate compensation must be given for damage done. It is summed up in the phrase 'An eye for an eye, a tooth for a tooth'. In the New Testament, Jesus specifically called attention to this principle and tried to carry His hearers to a higher level. They must seek to love those who did them wrong. Although the Book of the Covenant falls short of our Christian ideals, it does show an advance on the savage and unregulated life of early Hebrew history, bringing to an end the unrestrained and indiscriminate vendettas and feuds that vexed primitive society, and applying some sort of a limit to the pursuit of revenge. Those who had suffered, or those who took up a quarrel on behalf of sufferers, were not to exact from their enemies more than the equivalent of what they had endured. It may still seem crude to us, but it was a real preparation for the still higher Christian conception of brotherhood and forgiveness.

(101) *Exod.* 32. THE GOLDEN CALF

During Moses' absence on Sinai, the Children of Israel set up a clamour for a visible representation of Yahweh. They wanted a leader they could see. Aaron felt compelled to give way to their pressure and demanded from them their gold, out of which he manufactured a golden calf to be carried with them on their travels. There was always a tendency for the Israelites to fall back on this particular form of idolatry. Bull worship was a widespread Mediterranean cult and was prevalent in Canaan. The bull-calf provided a natural symbol of life and vitality such as would appeal to simple peoples, and it had its place in the worship of many of Israel's neighbours. Even centuries later, the Hebrews were guilty of this kind of unfaithfulness to Yahweh, and the charge against Jeroboam I was that he set up golden calves in the northern half of Israel to prevent his subjects looking towards Jerusalem as their religious centre (1 Kings 12$^{12, 33}$). As we can imagine, Aaron's concession to the people aroused the deep anger of Moses, and he returned from the Mount to stamp out this apostasy with ruthless determination. At the same time he pleaded with Yahweh to forgive His people for their rebellion.

(102) *Exod.* 33. THE ORGANIZATION OF WORSHIP

We are shown here a picture of Israelite worship. Moses knew the immense value of a common ritual, however simple, in preserving tribal unity and loyalty to Yahweh. The Tent of Meeting was a very simple affair of goatskin, erected outside the camp, and it would seem that the people were commanded to put off their ornaments in order to make possible its erection. Moses used to visit it from time to time in order to consult with Yahweh, but the people were only permitted to watch from afar. The only attendant was Joshua. Within the Tent was the sacred Ark, a box of acacia wood, containing the two tablets of stone on which were written the Ten Commandments, and it symbolized the presence of God. Although Yahweh was invisible, the Ark seems to have been regarded as in some special sense His dwelling place. There was a great yearning amongst the people for an assurance of the divine presence, but not even Moses was allowed to see Him. Even he was only granted a distant vision of Him as He passed by, the 'afterglow' of God, the sign that He was ahead of them, leading them on although out of sight.

(103)* *Exod.* 34. A SECOND ACCOUNT OF THE GIVING OF THE COMMANDMENTS

It is not easy to fit this account into its proper chronological place. It is an older account than that of Exod. 20, but the editors of *Exodus* have used it to tell us of the renewal of the Covenant, and a second giving of the Commandments after the lapse into idolatry. The description of Yahweh's character (*vv.* 5–9), may be taken as an answer to the request for a vision of His presence in Chapter 33. The writers point out that, when he discovered the erection of the golden calf, Moses had broken the tablets on which the Commandments had been originally inscribed, and the Covenant was therefore made null and void. It had to be renewed after intercession on Moses' part, and a number of religious rules were added to the Ten Words.

D. *On the Threshold of the Promised Land*

(104) Apparently Moses made a long stay of some thirty-seven years at the Oasis of Kadesh on the borders of Palestine. We must assume that the Israelites were not yet strong enough to carry out the invasion.

(105) *Num.* 13–14. THE VISIT AND THE RETURN OF THE SPIES

Two previous versions of this adventure have been woven together ($13^{1-17, 21, 25, 26a, 32a}$, $14^{1-10, 26-38}$, come from P; the rest is from the combination of J and E. *See para.* 442). This explains certain discrepancies in the account. The various Israelite tribes had not yet reached any real state of unity and it was necessary to choose a spy from each group (13^{1-16}). With its hills and its valleys, its plains and its deserts, Palestine is such a varied land that both the optimistic and the pessimistic reports could contain a great amount of truth. The majority of the spies were stricken with fear when they contemplated the sons of Anak, giants in size (v. 28); only the more courageous, Caleb and Joshua, realized the potentialities of the land, and brought back specimens of its fertility (vv. 23f.).

The gloomy report almost provoked another revolt amongst the Israelites, with an attempt to displace Moses and Aaron from their position of leadership (14$^{1-10}$). Once more Moses had to intercede with Yahweh on behalf of the people, and this time he appealed to the divine pride. If the Israelite adventure came to nought, Yahweh would be discredited in the eyes of the Egyptians! Israel, therefore, must be punished, but in such a way as not to lower God's reputation (14$^{11-19}$). The present generation would have to perish in the wilderness, but the Promise would be fulfilled to their children. They in due course would enter and possess the land (14$^{20-5}$).

The first to perish, with appropriate justice, were the pessimistic spies (14$^{26-39}$). In sheer panic, the people attempted to make an invasion of Palestine, but it was premature, and ended in disaster. They were not allowed to carry with them the Ark, with its assurance of the presence of Yahweh, and the inhabitants of the land, the Amalekites and the Canaanites, quickly repulsed them (14$^{40-5}$).

TEST QUESTIONS

(Send answers to TWO *questions to your tutor)*

1. Show how the life-story of Moses, before his return to Egypt, may be seen as a preparation for his later work.
2. Why do we regard Moses as a great religious leader?
3. What is the value of the Ten Commandments for today?

Study Four

The Settlement in the Promised Land

(106) From one point of view, we may regard this confused period of Hebrew history as the completion of the mighty act of deliverance from the bondage of Egypt. Moses was not permitted to carry his liberated slaves over the borders of the promised land; but the Exodus could not be regarded as fully accomplished until Palestine had been conquered and a settlement made there by the Israelites. From another view-point, we are dealing with a period of necessary preparation before the Israelites could be regarded as being in any real sense a nation rather than a collection of nomadic tribes. This is the dark age of Hebrew history. Its conditions gave rise to the monarchy which, whatever its weaknesses, did give unity and strength in the land.

A.   The Invasion of Palestine

(107) The Book of Joshua tells us, with a wealth of detail, of the entry into Palestine. We may look upon it as the 'official' history, based upon a number of old documents compiled by various writers at various times, and edited to illustrate the two great truths of the Covenant. Yahweh is shown to be taking care of His people in every kind of peril and guiding their affairs; at the same time, we are reminded that He required from His chosen people an unbending loyalty and an unquestioning obedience. Whenever either the people or their leaders failed to fulfil their side of the Covenant, disaster befell them; on the other hand, their faithfulness was always rewarded with success.

(108) *Joshua* gives the impression that the conquest was swift and sure, that all the Israelite tribes acted together in a common effort, and that the whole of the land fell under their domination. According to this 'official' version, the original inhabitants of Palestine were exterminated and the country divided amongst the various tribes. However, there is a second account of the

invasion preserved for us in Judges 1, believed to come from a very old document and to give a much more accurate picture of what happened. It suggests that the Israelites acted in separate tribes, or in groups of tribes, rather than in unison, and that the conquest was neither speedy nor thorough. Individual tribes settled where they could get a foothold, and formed a series of pockets in the land which was still largely possessed by the original Canaanites.

(109)   Until the rise of the monarchy, it would not be right for us to think of the Israelites as a single united nation or one that had gained for itself a new and permanent home in Palestine. What hold they had upon the country was always precarious. In some respects, they possessed a sense of unity. They had a common ancestry and shared a common religion; yet the separate tribes were only loosely linked together. Sometimes they joined together in their exploits or to ward off an invader, but rarely, if ever, did they all manage to combine at the same time and for the same purpose.

(110)   They fell into four distinct groupings:

(a)   The tribes of *Judah*, *Simeon*, and *Levi* settled in the southern hill-country of Palestine, making their capital in the city of Hebron. This was a somewhat isolated group, separated from the sea on the west by the Philistines, hemmed in on the east by the Dead Sea, and hindered in any close dealings with their fellow Hebrews in the north by the Canaanite city of Jerusalem which none of the tribes was able to capture.

(b)   The followers of Joshua (*Ephraim*, *Benjamin*, and half the tribe of *Manasseh*), settled in the central highlands, cut off from their fellow Israelites on north and south by the Canaanites. These tribes had two centres—Shiloh and Shechem.

(c)   A further group (*Dan*, *Naphthali*, *Asher*, *Zebulon*, *Issachar*) made their home in the north, in the district which later became known as Galilee. The plain of Esdraelon divided them from the Joshua group.

(d)   Some of the tribes remained on the east of the Jordan (*Reuben*, *Gad*, and the other half of *Manasseh*), and seem to have spread themselves rather thinly over a fairly wide area.

(111)   *Josh.* 1–4.   THE CROSSING OF THE RIVER JORDAN

Since Moses was only permitted to see the Promised Land from afar and not to set foot on it, the leadership of the Israelites was passed on to Joshua, who had acted as his personal attendant.

He had also been one of the two spies who brought back an optimistic report of Canaan (1¹⁻¹⁸). The invaders found the river Jordan forming a deep rift in the land and constituting a formidable natural obstacle to their progress. At the time of their arrival it seems to have been in flood. The one town in the valley which appeared to be strong was Jericho, but two spies, helped by an innkeeper of doubtful character, Rahab, reported that the news of the coming invaders had already filled its citizens with fear (2¹⁻²⁴).

The Ark, symbolizing the presence of Yahweh, was to enter the river first, and remain there until all the Israelites had passed over (3¹⁻¹³). As soon as it took up its position, the stream ran dry and the invaders were able to cross dry shod (3¹⁴⁻¹⁷). Two cairns of stone were erected to commemorate this first stage of the conquest—one on the western bank and the other in the centre of the stream, sufficiently high that, when the waters returned to their normal level, its head would be just visible above them, and excite the curiosity of those who saw it (4¹⁻²⁴).

(112) *Josh.* 5¹⁰–6²⁷. THE CAPTURE OF JERICHO

Contrary to the fears of the Israelites, the town of Jericho put up no effective opposition. We can well believe that the enervating climate of the Jordan valley, at this point over 1,000 feet below sea level, had sapped the vitality of its inhabitants and caused them to make an easy surrender in face of the ferocity of the invaders from the desert. In view of their discoveries, modern excavators who have been digging at Jericho suggest that the city walls fell outwards as if they had collapsed owing to an earthquake. In any case, after its capture, Joshua pronounced a curse upon the site (6²⁶), and the city lay in ruins, with no attempt to rebuild it, until about 850 B.C.

The Israelites proceeded in their efforts to occupy Canaan with a ruthless savagery. No Christian conscience can condone their wholesale slaughter of their foes. In many respects they were dropping away from the high level of religion and morality to which Moses had lifted them, and entering upon the Dark Ages of their history. In their ignorance, they believed that the extermination of their enemies was the only way to preserve their religion in its purity. To have lived side by side with those who worshipped other gods, so they argued, would have led to a contamination of their own life and faith. Events were to prove how true this was, but that is no justification of their behaviour.

Moreover, they were sure that when people like the Amalekites offended the divine justice, it was the will of Yahweh that they should destroy them.

As a matter of fact, their fierce policy did not succeed. They were not able to accomplish the total destruction of the inhabitants of Canaan. They had to settle down alongside them, and the risk of having their faith in Yahweh degraded had to be met by other ways than that of annihilation.

(113) *Josh.* 7–8. THE CAPTURE OF AI AND ACHAN'S SIN

When they had crossed the Jordan, the invaders found themselves confronted by rough country rising to 3,000 feet above them, and their enemies were in strong positions on the tops of the hills. Three passes led up to the plateau. Joshua decided to make an attack by means of the northern one, in which lay the town of Ai. The first attempt was a failure and ended in a disastrous panic (7^{1-5}).

Seeking the reason for this catastrophe, Joshua discovered that Achan had been guilty of disobedience at the capture of Jericho and that the Israelites were now being punished for his offence (7^{6-26}). As the 'first fruits' of the conquest of Palestine, Jericho had been 'devoted' to Yahweh (6^{17}). That meant a 'taboo' had been placed upon it. Everything in it belonged to Yahweh; nothing was for the use of ordinary mortals. To make sure that this was so, no living thing in the city was to be saved alive, and no property found there was to be taken away by the invaders. What could be destroyed was to be burned; the rest was declared untouchable. Achan defied this ban. He kept back part of the spoil for his own purposes and hid it in his tent. According to the ideas of the time, not only Achan himself, but all the members of his family were regarded as being corporately responsible for what Achan did, and corporately liable to punishment. With our modern emphasis on individualism, this Hebrew attitude is not easy to understand, but it is important for us to make the attempt, for it plays a big part in the Old Testament, and is one of the outstanding differences between its world and ours.

Once the cause of the trouble had been removed, the town of Ai soon capitulated (8^{1-35}). The news of its fall spread fear amongst the neighbouring hill-towns, and some of them, like Gibeon, hurried to make terms with the invaders (9^3). Nevertheless, the Israelite conquest of Palestine was by no means as thorough as the Book of Joshua would lead us to think.

(114) *Josh.* 24. THE NATIONAL DEDICATION AT SHECHEM

In his farewell address, Joshua recalled the events of Israelite history, and set them forth as the work of Yahweh. Therefore the people must have no other gods (*vv.* 1–14). As an example, Joshua and his family affirmed their own loyalty, an affirmation which recognized that their ancestors had worshipped other gods, and that other people still did (*v.* 15). But Yahweh alone was to be the God of Israel and the consequences of failure to observe this loyalty would be serious. In response to Joshua's appeal and warning, the people agreed to put aside the foreign gods which they were evidently still worshipping, and the Covenant was renewed (*vv.* 16–25). To commemorate this dedication, a great stone of witness was set up (*vv.* 26–8).

B. *The Exploits of the Judges*

(115) The settlement in Palestine brought the Israelites in conflict with various neighbours. We note four groups:

(*a*) The *Ammonites, Edomites, Moabites*. These were Semitic tribes, as the Hebrews were, and lived in the east and south-east of Palestine. From time to time they raided Palestine and sought to bring it under their control (*see para* 43).

(*b*) The *Midianites* and *Amalekites*, nomads from the deserts, who swept down upon the Israelites, especially at harvest time, to raid their crops.

(*c*) The *Canaanites*, the original inhabitants of the land, who were by no means exterminated by the Israelite invasion. For a time, they proved a nuisance. They were especially strong around Jerusalem (a city which remained uncaptured until the time of David) and in the plain of Esdraelon. In the end, as the result of much intermarriage, they merged with their conquerors and became part of the Hebrew race.

(*d*) The *Philistines*, in origin a European, not a Semitic, people. They probably came from Crete and settled in Palestine alongside the Mediterranean. This coastal strip proved too restricted for them and they made repeated attempts to move further inland. They were a more civilized people than the Israelites and more accomplished in the arts of war. Consequently they proved a very difficult and formidable foe. We gain some idea of their strength and ability when we remember it was they who gave their name to the whole of the land—Palestine.

(116) *Judges* 2[16-23]. THE RISE OF THE JUDGES

In *Judges* we have a series of pictures of Israel's early life in Palestine. Until the coming of the monarchy, the people were divided by tribal and geographical distinctions. There was no centralized power. Yet there remained, even though for periods it seemed to vanish from sight, a tradition of political and religious unity. Yahweh was worshipped at many local shrines and altars, but the sanctuary which contained the Ark had a pre-eminence over all the others.

The 'Judges', who were raised up to deliver Israel from her foes, did not hold sway over the whole of the land; they were the champions of their own particular tribe, rallying their kinsfolk to resist some specific enemy, though on occasion calling for the help of neighbouring tribes. In spite of their title, they were warriors rather than lawgivers, although it would seem that any leader who was recognized as a man of Yahweh might be called a 'judge', for the list includes Eli who was a priest, and Samuel who was a prophet. There is no indication that any of the Judges were formally appointed to wield power; rather they seem to have risen to leadership by popular support and enthusiasm.

Nevertheless, behind their individual and tribal exploits, we can detect a common theme. First, by adopting the worship of the Canaanite gods, Israel was disloyal to Yahweh and brought about punishment in the form of one or other invader who for a period exercised supremacy over God's people; then, when the people repented, Yahweh raised up a deliverer who overthrew the foe in His name.

(117) *Judges* 4–5. DEBORAH AND BARAK

The Canaanites of the plain of Esdraelon were particularly strong under their king, Jabin (*see* Josh. 11[1-9]), and his commander-in-chief, Sisera. Inspired by an Israelite prophetess, Deborah, two groups of Hebrew settlers, north and south of Esdraelon, were rallied under Barak in an attempt to break the Canaanite power. The Hebrew tribes were obviously still disunited. The more distant tribes of the north failed to respond to the summons, and we notice there is no mention of Judah and Simeon in the south. On the other hand, it is taken for granted that they all belonged to Yahweh and ought to have come to His help (4^{1-6}).

Unlike the Hebrews, the Canaanites possessed horses and chariots, which, though most effective on level ground, were apt to be an encumbrance amongst the hills. Barak, therefore, concentrated his forces on the spur of Mount Tabor, whilst the enemy gathered in the valley below (4^{7-10}). Suddenly a heavy storm broke, the Kishon valley was flooded, and Esdraelon became a perilous swamp (5^{20-1}). The horses and chariots of Canaan were unable to manœuvre quickly in the waters, and presented the Israelites with a great opportunity to sweep down upon them (4^{12-16}). Sisera was forced to flee on foot. Seeking shelter in the tent of the woman Jael, he met with a savage end (4^{17-24}). His murder was a contravention of the nomadic laws of hospitality which decreed that Jael should have protected her guest, at least until morning-light; but, because her deed was such a valuable contribution to the cause of Yahweh, it was applauded, not condemned, and her patriotism was extolled.

There are two accounts of this episode with certain discrepancies between them, e.g. the manner of Sisera's death. The poem in Chapter 5, known as Deborah's Song, is older than the prose account in Chapter 4.

(118) *Judges* 6–7. GIDEON

At least two different traditions have been woven together in these chapters, giving rise to a number of discrepancies. The main events in Gideon's career are, however, clear:

(*a*) His exploits were directed chiefly against the Midianites, whose raids in the south were plaguing the tribe of Manesseh to which Gideon belonged. Fear of them caused him to thresh his wheat in hiding (6^{1-6}). He felt himself called to be the champion of his people (6^{11-24}). Though his motives may have been partly patriotic (6^{13}), and partly a thirst for revenge because of his brothers' murders (8^{19}), he was also sure that he had been divinely chosen, and his assurance was confirmed by a sign.

(*b*) His first act as leader of the resistance was one of religious penitence and loyalty. He destroyed the Baal and the Asherah which his family had been accustomed to worship alongside Yahweh (6^{25-32}).

(*c*) Having sought a second assurance of his divine call, and having received the sign of the wet fleece, he called upon the men of his tribe to follow him, and summoned Ephraim to seize the

fords of Jordan. For this task, Gideon got too many volunteers.
The majority of them were happy to accept his suggestion that
they should stay at home, whilst a further test reduced the
number to 300. The significance of this test is obscure. It may
have indicated that those who cupped the water in their hands,
rather than get down on their knees, were alert men whose eyes
were watching all the time for any sign of the Midianites on the
high land; the kind of men who were prepared to put their own
personal comfort on one side (6^{33}–7^8).

(*d*) With this picked band, and encouraged by a dream he
overheard being related in the enemy's camp, Gideon attacked
the Midianites at night, and, skilfully using torches and trumpets,
gave them the impression that they were being raided on three
sides. They were thrown into panic, and the forces of Gideon
won a decisive victory ($7^{9 \cdot 25}$), the tradition of which was in after
centuries enshrined in the phrase 'the day of Midian' (Isa. 9^4).

An attempt was made to crown Gideon king, but he resisted it
on the ground that Israel could have no king but Yahweh. In
Chapter 8 we read that his son was not so scrupulous, and un-
successfully tried to create a monarchy and put himself on the
throne.

(119)* *Judges* 13-16. SAMSON

Although more space is devoted to Samson than to any of the
other leaders of this book, he does not fit into the characteristic
pattern of the Judges. He was the local Danite hero, the Hercules
of the Old Testament, who carried on a feud with the Philistines
which was personal rather than patriotic, a series of acts of private
vengeance. The stories have little religious value but may serve
as a warning against the misuse of physical strength and as an
illustration of the unconscious processes of moral degeneration.

Samson was under a Nazirite vow (*see* Num. 6), which appears
to have been taken for him before his birth. Some of the Israelites,
as a sign that they intended to resist the corrupting influences of
an agricultural life, and to preserve the integrity of their religion
amidst the Baal-worship of their new home (*see paras.* 120-1),
resolved to maintain after their settlement certain characteristics
of their old nomadic ways of life. For instance, they wore their
hair long as if they were still wanderers in the desert, and refused
to drink wine because it was the fruit of the vine and was the
product of a settled agricultural existence.

It seems pretty clear that Samson must have betrayed these

vows long before his association with Delilah. He had mixed with the Philistines, married a Philistine woman, and accommodated himself to their manners and customs. Like the Canaanites, the Philistines were farmers and worshipped the gods of fertility. Samson was no hero of the faith, ready to suffer rather than break his loyalty to Yahweh and the vows of the Nazirites. He stands out merely by reason of his unique physical power. Thrilling stories were associated with his amazing strength, in many of which we are bound to deplore the vindictiveness of his spirit. His final downfall was contrived by a Philistine woman, Delilah, and he ended his days in the power of his enemies.

C. *Samuel the Prophet*

(120) We have already begun to see that the Israelites had to struggle both to maintain their position in the Promised Land and to preserve the fulness of their religious faith and allegiance. As they mingled with the Canaanites, lived side by side with them and often linked themselves by marriage, they were tempted to join with them in their worship. There must have seemed to them compelling reasons for doing so. They were no longer wandering shepherds without a settled home. They had taken to tilling the land and living on its produce. They had built for themselves houses of stone, huddled together in little villages protected from any possible marauders by thick walls of mud. The question must have arisen in their minds: How far was Yahweh still able to help and succour them in their new conditions of life? True, He was their tribal God and they were bound to Him by the Covenant. In the past, He had guided them in their trials, protected them through strange adventures, brought them success in their warfare. But was He able to make their fields bring forth in abundance? Would He give increase to their flocks and bless them in their new agricultural pursuits?

(121) Many of the Israelites were not quite sure about the answer to such questions. They noticed that the Canaanites, who were more used than themselves to a settled life in villages and fields, had their own ways of worship. In each locality they paid their respects to the gods of the district, whom they called Baals. Their shrines were on every hill and by every spring and in every field. They also brought their homage to female deities, goddesses, wives of the Baals, represented by a sacred pole or

Asherah. These, said the Canaanites, were the powers that brought increase to the land. Anxious for success in their new way of life, the Israelites began to think that it might be a good policy to pay tribute to the Canaanite deities. They did not entirely desert Yahweh. Perhaps many of them argued that they were not really being disloyal to Him. They merely added the worship of the Baals to their existing worship of Yahweh.

(122) The result of this was not only a religious decline amongst the Hebrews, but also a degeneration of their moral life. At the pagan shrines, the ritual was frequently of a low ethical order. Preoccupation with the fertility of the land led the worshippers to indulge in much drunkenness and sexual licence, the symbol of the fertility they wanted for their land. Still, in spite of this, the worship of Yahweh was not allowed to disappear or to be merged in the religion of the land, and there were brave spirits who protested against what was happening, and loyal souls who kept the faith of Moses alive in its integrity. Amongst these, the leaders of the loyalist movement, were the prophets, the first of whom we are now to consider.

(123) Samuel may be regarded from three points of view:

(a) He was the last of the Judges. In this respect, he was not famous, like his predecessors, for military exploits against Israel's enemies, but for the more matter-of-fact duties that the title suggests. He went on circuit, to Bethel, Gilgal, Mizpah, settling disputes and arbitrating in the name of Yahweh.

(b) He was a priest, dedicated to God from his birth and serving at the shrine at Shiloh. He wore the distinctive garments of the priesthood, the 'ephod'.

(c) He was the first of the prophets. There was, we are told, no 'open vision' in Israel, that is to say, no open declaration of Yahweh's will. Samuel was commissioned to remedy this state of affairs. In the name of Yahweh, he summoned all the tribes to abolish Baal-worship and at Mizpah he called upon them to offer sacrifices to Yahweh.

(124) The prophets, who from this point played an increasingly powerful part in Israel's life, were holy men on fire with zeal for Yahweh. Unlike the priests, they did not form an hereditary class in Hebrew society, but each received his personal and individual call to the office. At times the prophets were solitary figures, walking alone; at other times, and particularly at the beginning of the prophetic movement, they seem to have gathered themselves together in groups or schools. Frequently their

religious and patriotic excitement took such a hold upon them that they broke into dervish-like dances and chanted choruses that to those who heard must have sounded impressive, even if not intelligible. The prophets began as a set of men whose business was to stir up and keep alive the Israelite's loyalty to his nation and religion, and some of the activities of the first prophets do not seem to rise much above the enthusiasm of recruiting sergeants in the wars against Israel's enemies. But out of this strange phenomenon in Israel's life was to develop the unique line of great prophets of later history, whose voices were raised so fearlessly in criticism of their nation's policy, and whose vision of God's character and demands, and insight into His ways, have left the whole world permanently enriched.

(125) One of the principal tasks that Samuel had to undertake was the institution of the kingship in Israel. In theory, the Israelites belonged to a 'theocracy', that is to say, they were a people under the direct rule of God. So far, all attempts to create a monarchy had been suppressed on the ground that a human king would detract the loyalty of his subjects from their divine sovereign. The time came, however, when it was seen that a leader in possession of the power and authority that neighbouring peoples gave to their kings might have very great advantages for Israel.

(a) A king would bring about internal unity and order. So long as justice was dispensed by elders whose authority only extended to their individual tribes, so long as there was no common code which all accepted, there was bound to be a great deal of disorder in the land. 'There was no king in Israel; every man did what was right in his own eyes.' There was need of a supreme authority with wide and absolute legislative powers.

(b) A king would provide the necessary military leadership. Unity and strength were needed against Israel's external enemies. A king would be able to call upon all the tribes to support his campaigns. He would possess a personal 'guard', under the command of a captain, which could undertake relatively small expeditions, but, on more desperate occasions, he could summon the 'host' made up of fighting men from all Israel. The Philistines were proving a much tougher proposition than Israel's other foes. Constant warfare had to be waged against them, and there are hints in the Old Testament that they managed at times to impose their will upon the Hebrews (1 Sam. 13[19-23]).

(126) Driven by these considerations, the Israelites realized

that the creation of the monarchy was an urgent necessity, and that in the circumstances it was not bound to be regarded as an act of disloyalty and treachery to Yahweh. Provided the one who was chosen for the office proved to be obedient and faithful, and kept the nation's religion sound and dealt effectively with the abuses that threatened the Chosen People, he might be regarded as the servant of God. Hence the choice must be made by a prophet as the representative of Yahweh, and the appointed king be given to understand that he held his position only on condition that he accepted the prophetic direction. This is implied in the act of anointing performed by the prophet. Whilst this, no doubt, represented the attitude of the majority of Israelites, there were not wanting those who, from the beginning, looked upon this innovation with dismay, and predicted that it would lead to trouble.

(127) 1 *Sam*. 1–4¹ᵃ. THE BIRTH AND CALL OF SAMUEL

The Hebrews regarded a childless woman as a disgrace and under the divine disapproval. Hence the birth of Samuel, to a woman who had had to accept the fact of barrenness, was a singular work of Yahweh's favour, and it was only natural that in return Hannah should dedicate her son to the service of God. Note the detailed description of family life in early Israel, and the recognized procedure for a family sacrifice and a sacred meal at a sanctuary (1¹–2¹⁰). Samuel became assistant to the priest, Eli, who was in charge of the central shrine of Shiloh in the territory of Ephraim. The temple there was a small building of stone and in its inner chamber the Ark was kept. Here Eli slept to guard it, whilst the boy Samuel occupied the outer court which was open to all worshippers and where the great religious festivals were held. After he had answered the call of Yahweh, Samuel was commissioned to announce the fall of the house of Eli. Hophni and Phinias, the sons of Eli, were declared unfit to inherit the priestly office. Their particular offence was their refusal to be content with the portion of the sacrifices allocated to them by the worshippers (2¹²⁻¹⁷). It is clear that they were slack generally and responsible for sexual immorality at Yahweh's shrine (*see para.* 122).

(128) 1 *Sam*. 4¹ᵇ⁻²². THE LOSS OF THE ARK

The deaths of Hophni and Phineas were brought about by a great Philistine victory, the shock of which also killed Eli. His house was brought to an end, and probably the shrine at Shiloh was destroyed. To the Israelites, the worst feature of the catastrophe was that the Ark, which Eli's sons had carried into battle to bring them good fortune, was taken captive by the enemy (4^{11}). Thus the symbol of Yahweh's presence with His people was taken away. To the Philistines, however, it brought anything but good fortune. In their city of Ashdod, a plague of bubonic fever broke out which was attributed to the presence of Yahweh, whose home they assumed it was. In the end they decided to get rid of the cause of their troubles by solemnly returning the Ark, first to Beth-shemesh, and then to Kiriath-jearim where it remained until the time of David.

(129) 1 *Sam.* 9^1–10^{16}. AN OLD ACCOUNT OF THE ESTABLISH-
MENT OF THE KINGSHIP

This account is based on court records and oral traditions. In search of his father's asses, Saul consulted Samuel, who is here described as a 'seer', one possessing the gift of second sight. The prophet recognized in his visitor the very man for whom the country was waiting, and privately anointed him for the kingship (9^{1-27}). As an assurance of this call, he gave him three signs.

(*a*) A messenger would report that his father had found his lost asses but was sorrowing now for his missing son. This was an indication to the coming king that under his rule people were to matter more than property (10^{1-2}).

(*b*) Pilgrims with food would give Saul out of their provisions sufficient to keep him from starvation. This was a token that Yahweh would provide Saul with all that was really essential for his office (10^{3-4}).

(*c*) Saul would join a company of prophets in their ecstatic music and dancing, and thus proclaim his faith in Yahweh in the face of an enemy stationed in the Hill of the Lord (10^{5-6}).

After Saul had experienced these signs, and understood their significance, God would give him another heart and make him a suitable person for the kingship.

Obviously, in this old account, the kingship is regarded as a blessing, and Samuel is shown to be in full approval of Saul as the gift of God.

(130) 1 *Sam.* 8, 10^{17-24}. A LATER ACCOUNT OF THE ESTAB-
LISHMENT OF THE KINGSHIP

The tune is changed entirely. Probably this version was

written some 300 years after the other, and it is undoubtedly coloured by Israel's bitter experience of what monarchy could mean for the nation. The election of Saul is set forth as a defiance of the will of Yahweh, an insult and a repudiation of the divine sovereignty. We are told that the prophet opposed it with all his power, and warned the people that kingship would involve them in forced labour, military conscription, and heavy taxation. In spite of these strong words, the tribes insisted on having their way, and Saul, having been chosen by lot, was acclaimed by the people at Mizpah.

(131)* I *Sam.* 12. SAMUEL'S FAREWELL ADDRESS

When Samuel formally abdicated from the office of Judge, and handed over his authority to the newly appointed king, he used the opportunity to review the history of Yahweh's dealings with them, and to contrast His goodness with their ingratitude. This was especially seen in their insistence on having a king. Samuel's address echoes the terms of the Covenant, declaring that in the future Israel's obedience will bring them rich rewards, but disobedience will most surely carry with it punishments (*vv.* 1–15). A thunder-storm at harvest time (March or April), when rain did not normally fall in Palestine, was taken to be a confirmation of Samuel's words. The people confessed their sins, and Samuel made intercession for them (*vv.* 16–25).

(132) From this Dark Age of Israelite history, the people of Yahweh emerged with their religion still alive and not without vigour. That it should be so is an amazing thing in view of the circumstances. The chapters we have selected for our study have not been very edifying, and must have brought home to us how far the general level of life and religion had fallen from the noble ideas and principles set forth by Moses. Yet the more we ponder over this period, the more amazing it seems that the isolated and relatively small groups of settlers in Canaan did not adopt entirely the ways of their new home and merge themselves completely into the life of the older inhabitants. They were prepared to accommodate themselves to their new surroundings up to a certain point, but no further. There must have been a tough element of conservatism or puritanism in them that kept them from losing their identity.

(*a*) Certain groups, like the Nazirites, made it their business to resist 'modern' fashions in food, dress, and even personal hygiene. They looked back to their desert life as being simpler and more religious, and they were determined not to let its ideals slip away entirely (*see para* 119).

(*b*) The priests played their part in preserving Israel's true religion. At first, the sacrifices and ceremonies of religion were carried out by the heads of families who officiated at the pre-scribed sacrifices. But a class of professional priests arose who either wandered from place to place offering their services (*see* Judges 18⁴), or attached themselves more permanently to some particular family or tribe. Their duties were both to offer the sacrifices and also to consult the oracles to discover whether the future was favourable for some family or tribal enterprise. This priesthood tended to be hereditary, and thus the priests came to be the guardians of the various traditions and rituals associated with their own special locality.

(*c*) The prophets, though their ecstatic utterances seem strange to our western thought, were more than merely enthusiastic patriots whipping up the zeal of the Israelites against their enemies. Their patriotic fervour was based on their faith in Yahweh. Thus, in those dark days, their fiery energy helped to maintain and stimulate Israel's true religion.

(*d*) Ultimately we are bound to acknowledge that it was none other than the providence of Yahweh Himself that preserved the identity of His people and kept alive their faith in Him.

TEST QUESTIONS

(*Send answers to* TWO *questions to your tutor*)

1. Write a summary of the life and work of Joshua.
2. What was the general state of Israel in the period of 'the Judges'?
3. Why was Saul appointed king of Israel? Why are there two accounts of this, and what are the differences between them?

The Three Kings of a United Israel

A. *The Reign of Saul*

(133) Saul had many fine qualities which ought to have made him an outstanding success in the kingship. Attractive and commanding in personal appearance, he had courage and energy, a high sense of devotion to his task, and considerable military skill. When he came to the throne, the condition of the Israelite tribes had sunk to a very low ebb, and they were in danger of extinction as a result of the attacks of the Ammonites in the east and the Philistines in the west. The Philistine menace was indeed very serious. An exploit by his son Jonathan (1 *Sam.* 14), quickly restored some measure of confidence in Israel, but all through his reign Saul needed to be on guard, and it was from the Philistines that in the end he met his death. His campaigns against them were probably more numerous than the Old Testament records suggest.

(134) Saul certainly realized that the enemy could only be dealt with effectively if the various Hebrew tribes acted together in a unity. To a very large extent, he succeeded in making himself the central rallying point, and for most of his reign he continued to beat off the Philistine raiders. In the end, they decided to attack him from the north. When they brought about his defeat at Gilboa, on the plain of Esdraelon, he was probably still trying to secure the loyalty of the most northern Hebrew tribes.

(135) In some respects, the Old Testament hardly does justice to the first king of Israel. His achievements were overshadowed by his quarrel with the prophet Samuel and by the growing power of young David. We can well believe that the melancholia, which developed as the years went on, was due to this double strain. In this study our readings are mainly concerned with his relationship with his rival, David.

(136) 1 *Sam.* 15¹⁻³⁵ᵃ. THE REJECTION OF SAUL

There are two accounts of Saul's rejection; this is the older one.

It is intended to explain the breach between Samuel and the king. From this time forward, we must note the two authorities in Israel—the prophetic and the royal. Theoretically, we might say that the prophet looked after the religious affairs of the nation, and the king its secular concerns. But who was to define the boundary between the two spheres? In any case, the prophet claimed that the word of Yahweh which was entrusted to him must govern the monarch's policy and activity, since Yahweh had the right to control all life. Hence there were frequent clashes between prophet and king, for monarchs did not readily accept the direction of those who spoke in the name of God. They were apt to call it interference.

Saul very quickly came into collision with Samuel. The prophet decreed that the tribe of Amalek should be 'devoted' to Yahweh. This meant that it must be destroyed entirely; no prisoner, no booty, no spoil was to be taken (see para. 113). Saul disobeyed this order, spared the life of their king, Agag, and chose the best of the spoil for himself. It is not suggested in the account that his motive might have been one of compassion; it is rather a lack of restraint on his part, a refusal to recognize in the decree of the prophet the higher authority of Yahweh. This was a real weakness in his character. In the event, Samuel himself proceeded to do the grim work of butchering the foe. He refused to accept the king's confession, and looked round to find his successor.

1 Sam. 13$^{1-15}$ gives a later account of the breach between prophet and king. Here Saul was condemned because he insisted that he had the right to offer sacrifices in an emergency, whilst Samuel claimed that he alone could undertake the office. For the king to do so was a usurpation of the divine authority, which had been bestowed only upon the prophets.

(137) 1 Sam. 15^{35b}–16^{13}. THE ANOINTING OF DAVID

Three stories tell us how David came on the scene, this and the next two readings. It is not possible to harmonize all the details, and we must think of them as three independent traditions which were included, without revision, in our Book of Samuel. The first account says that, after the rejection of Saul, Samuel was sent to find a successor and chose a son of Jesse at Bethlehem, where he anointed him. If this were the case, it is hard to understand how the news was kept from Saul. Moreover, in the narratives that follow, David himself shows no consciousness of having been appointed to take Saul's place; Saul alone is the Lord's anointed.

Possibly the point of this tradition is the desire to connect Samuel with the one who in later days was regarded as having fulfilled the prophetic ideal of kingship.

(138) 1 *Sam.* 16$^{14-23}$. DAVID'S INTRODUCTION AS A COURT MUSICIAN

In the hope of being able to charm away Saul's black moods (*see para.* 135), David was brought to court on the recommendation of one of the royal officers. The experiment was successful and a friendship sprang up between the Bethlehem shepherd and the king.

(139) 1 *Sam.* 17–18^5. DAVID'S INTRODUCTION AS THE SLAYER OF GOLIATH

There are discrepancies in this well-known story. Scholars say that it was probably made up of two separate accounts of the incident which differed in many details, and that the interweaving did not get rid of all the inconsistencies. For convenience, we may separate these stories:

(*a*) 17$^{1-11,\ 32-54}$. This is the older account of the Philistine challenge. Once more Israel was at war with its old foe, and the Philistines offered to settle the issue by single combat. Goliath, their counterpart of the earlier Hebrew Samson, was thought to be invincible. David, an armourbearer in Saul's camp, accepted the challenge and slew the champion. This version of the story follows the previous reading (*para.* 138) without difficulty.

(*b*) 17$^{12-31,\ 55-8}$, 18$^{1-5}$. This account says that David was at home in Bethlehem, and not in the camp. He was sent with supplies for his brethren who, although men of Judah, had attached themselves in service to the Benjaminite, Saul. Hearing Goliath's proud boast, he volunteered to meet him. When the giant had been defeated, David was introduced to Saul and the Royal Court where, up to this point, he had evidently been a stranger. Jonathan, the king's son, and he entered into a covenant of blood-brotherhood, symbolized by their exchange of garments. Clothes were thought to carry with them something of the personality of those who had worn them, and in this way they proclaimed the closeness of their friendship.

(140) 1 *Sam.* 18$^{6-30}$. DAVID'S POPULARITY; SAUL'S JEALOUSY

Saul was not without grounds for his attitude. The public looked upon the handsome young musician from the court as a

popular idol and thought no less of him after Saul had removed
him to the lower rank of the 'captaincy of a thousand' (v. 13).
The friendship between him and Jonathan could become extremely dangerous to the king. Nevertheless, Saul was compelled
to give David the hand of his daughter, Michal, in marriage,
though he seems to have hoped that the conditions he imposed
would result in David's death (vv. 17–27). How far the son of
Jesse had designs upon the throne and was using these alliances
with the family of Saul to advance his position, we cannot say. It
is quite likely that the king suspected he had some such plan in
mind.

(141)   1 Sam. 19^1–20^{42}.   DAVID'S FLIGHT FROM COURT

The further successes of David against the Philistines increased
the royal jealousy and made the position at court intolerable.
Saul determined to be rid of a possible rival. True to the
covenant of blood relationship into which he had entered,
Jonathan would not take part in his father's intrigues and, when
all attempts at a reconciliation were seen to be in vain, warned
his friend of the danger. When David's wife knew that her father
was intent on murder, she put in her husband's bed a teraphim
to mislead him. This was an image in human form; the 'pillow of
goat's hair' was possibly something like a mosquito curtain (vv.
1–17).

David was driven to seek refuge with Samuel at Ramah, where
parties of soldiers sent to arrest him succumbed to the psychic
influence of the prophets. Even Saul himself could not resist the
power (vv. 18–24). Before finally branding himself as an outlaw,
David sought out Jonathan and made one further attempt at
conciliation. His friend offered to find out Saul's mood and to
communicate a message to him; in return, David pledged himself
to show favour to Jonathan's family when he reached the throne.
On the first day, David's absence was attributed to ceremonial
uncleanness. On the second, the king was told that David had
gone to hold a sacrificial feast with his family at Bethlehem. The
anger of Saul at this news suggests that he may have feared that
a rebellion was already beginning. In any case, it was now clear
to Jonathan that his father was resolved upon his friend's death,
and next morning he gave the promised signal (20$^{1.42}$).

(142)   1 Sam. 21–2.   DAVID AT NOB

For safety, David made his way to Nob, in the territory of

Benjamin. After the destruction of the shrine at Shiloh (*para.* 128), the priests had made a new home for themselves and were under the authority of Ahimelech, possibly a great-grandson of Eli (1 Sam. 14³). When David arrived, without arms and without provisions, he persuaded the priest to allow him and his men to eat the bread which had been made sacred by being offered to Yahweh (Jesus quoted this incident in Mk. 2²⁵⁻⁶). Ahimelech presented him with the sword of Goliath (21¹⁻⁹).

For a period, David seems to have sought refuge at the Philistine court of Achish at Gath, but, when he was recognized, he feigned madness and escaped (21¹⁰⁻¹⁵). Making his way to the Cave of Adullam, some twelve miles south-west of Bethlehem, he was joined by a number of fellow-clansmen, together with some bankrupt debtors who were afraid of being sold into slavery. From this centre, they went to the rescue of villages and cities threatened by the Philistines (22¹⁻⁵). Saul, furious at the priests at Nob for their support of David, massacred the whole community, and only Abiathar, one of the sons of Ahimelech, was able to escape and flee to David (22⁶⁻²³).

(143) 1 Sam. 24.   DAVID SPARES SAUL'S LIFE

In the course of his pursuit of David, the king entered a cave at Engedi, not knowing that David and his men were concealed in its further recesses. Although his followers would have persuaded him otherwise, David refused to lift his hand against the Lord's Anointed, merely cutting off a strip of his cloak to prove he had had him in his power. Even this sacrilege troubled his conscience, and he explained to Saul what he had done, protesting his loyalty. Touched by his rival's magnanimity, the king prayed David not to destroy his family when he came to the throne.

(144)* 1 Sam. 25.   DAVID AND ABIGAIL

In return for the protection he and his followers had given to many of the Israelite farmers against the Philistines, David tried to exact from them tribute in order to maintain his army. Such a levy had no precedent. But David was already king in everything but name, and he alone seemed strong enough to protect Israelite property. Nabal, a wealthy sheep-owner, refused to contribute the provisions that were demanded of him, and treated the request with churlish contempt. But for the wise intervention of Nabal's wife, Abigail, who realized the justice of David's claim, the outlaws would have wiped out all Nabal's family. Moved by her tact and charm, David acted with restraint and generosity. He felt she had saved him from a great sin. When, shortly afterwards, Nabal died, David took her to wife.

(145)* 1 *Sam.* 31.   DEATH OF SAUL AND JONATHAN

The Philistines moved their horses and chariots from the coastal plain into Esdraelon. Their object may have been to prevent Saul from securing the services of the northerly tribes for a mass resistance, and then to move southwards to attack the main body of the Israelites. The two armies met on the slopes of Mount Gilboa (28$^{1-4}$). On the night before the attack, Saul, much harassed and full of fear, went to Endor to seek out a witch in the hope of getting a comforting message about the outcome of the battle. She called up the shade of the prophet Samuel, whose message was but a repetition of his prediction of Saul's defeat and death, and David's triumph (28$^{5-25}$). When it was clear that the fight on Gilboa was going against him, Saul followed the custom of Eastern kings and ordered his armour-bearer to kill him. Jonathan also met his death in the conflict (31$^{1-13}$).

B.   *The Reign of David*

(146)   The defeat at Gilboa was a serious matter. The first king of Israel, from whom so much had been hoped, had been killed in battle, and all western Palestine lay exposed to the raids of the Philistines. The gravest threat was to the southern tribes, especially to that of Judah, of which David was a member. Although his own people acknowledged him as king and crowned him at Hebron, in all probability what power he possessed was accorded to him by the Philistines, and he was required to do their bidding.

(147)   Meanwhile, Saul's son Ishbosheth (or Ishbaal), made an attempt to win for himself his father's throne, but he was unable to make any headway even in his own territory of Benjamin. With a few loyal supporters, he retired to Mahanaim, beyond Jordan, where he founded for the time being his own little kingdom (2 Sam. 2^8). It looked as if there would be a long and determined trial of strength between himself and David. However, his uncle quarrelled with him and transferred his

loyalty to the son of Jesse. Both Abner and Ishbosheth were conveniently assassinated—we do not know whether David had anything to do with it—and the double event enabled David to proclaim himself Saul's successor without appearing to be disloyal to the house of Saul. The tribe of Benjamin was able to offer him its allegiance without any loss of self-respect.

(148) Once secure in the kingship, David proceeded to recruit and train an effective military force. For all normal purposes, a little standing army under Benaiah (in effect the King's body-guard) was sufficient. In times of emergency, and to carry out raids upon Israel's enemies, this needed to be reinforced by men called from their ordinary occupations. Joab was placed in command of this militia. In order to ascertain the names of those upon whom he could call for this service, and also with the purpose of taxation in mind, David ordered the compilation of a register of all his subjects. The Hebrews did not yet sufficiently appreciate the value of a centralized government to accept this without protest. Even Joab advised against it. But David would not draw back. When, therefore, a pestilence broke out in the land, it was regarded as a divine punishment (1 Sam. 24).

(149) Although this caused dissatisfaction within the nation, the reign of David was, on the whole, one of peace and security. The Philistines, or the Moabites, or the Edomites, might from time to time offer noisy threats, but there was no longer any serious likelihood of their being able to overrun the land and wipe out the Hebrews. Israel had become a strong nation and must now be treated with respect.

(150) The common effort against the Philistines drew all the tribes together and made them a unity. During the reign of the first three kings, Israel was one politically: in David's reign it was more united than at any time in its history. The capture of Jerusalem, the establishment of the Ark there, and the proposal to erect a temple to Yahweh gave a sense of religious unity that went deeper than any political bonds. By David's time, the native Canaanites had largely ceased to be a separate element in the community. They had lived side by side with the invaders, intermarried with them, fought with them against common enemies; their two languages had gradually become assimilated until now they spoke the same tongue; thus, in the end they lost their identity and became one with the Hebrews. The Israelites, therefore, became a people of mixed blood, but the Hebrew type persisted. Those who merged with them worshipped the God

of the Hebrews, Yahweh, and regarded themselves as equally bound to Him in the Covenant relationship. This does not, however, mean that Canaanite influence in religious matters had ceased; on the contrary, it was to have very serious effects in the days to come. But it was certainly not predominant.

(151) *2 Sam.* 1¹⁷⁻²⁷. LAMENT FOR SAUL AND JONATHAN

The Second Book of Ṣamuel is almost certainly based upon contemporary records and may actually be quoting from them in many of its narratives. David's Lament was taken from the ancient 'Book of Jasher'. Jasher means 'upright', and probably refers to the faithful Israel whom Yahweh had prospered; and the book was a collection of songs about the early victories of Israel. According to *vv.* 1–16, the news of the deaths of Saul and Jonathan was brought to David by an Amalekite who claimed to have killed the king at his request (cf. 1 Sam. 31⁴). Instead of receiving a reward for his alleged services, the Amalekite was promptly put to death. The poem in which David commemorated the passing of his enemy and his friend is one of the most touching in all literature. All bitterness has been purged from David's mind, and, in the case of Saul, nothing remains but the memory of the late king's greatness.

(152) *2 Sam.* 5¹⁻¹². THE CAPTURE OF JERUSALEM

The Israelite tribes of the north came to realize the need for strong leadership and sent their chiefs to acknowledge David as the king of all Israel. To the Philistines, this was the signal for alarm. Afraid that they would have to deal with a united country, they immediately resumed their attacks. For a time David was compelled to flee from his capital at Hebron and take refuge in the Cave of Adullam, from which he waged guerilla warfare. Once he had managed to rally round him sufficient resources, he drove the Philistines from the tribal territory of Judah. Though these wars are recorded in 5¹⁸⁻²⁵, it seems likely that they took place before the capture of Jerusalem and prepared the way for it.

Jerusalem was a Canaanite fortress, built on a rock, three sides of which fell away sheerly. None of the Hebrew tribes had been able to capture it. David saw that it would make an excellent capital for the whole country. It had a central position, yet was not in the possession of any one of the tribes, and it ought to be possible to secure the loyalty of all of them to it. Under Joab, a party of men climbed up to the city from the Virgin's Well. (The account here should be compared with that in 1 Chron. 11⁴⁻⁸). Once he had gained possession of it, David set to work to make it a worthy capital. By a trade agreement with Hiram of Tyre, he got both materials and advice. Skilled foremen came to supervise the labour of the slaves whom David had captured in his wars.

(153)   2 Sam. 6.   THE BRINGING OF THE ARK TO JERUSALEM

Since the bond that united the Israelite tribes was fundamentally a religious one, David realized the wisdom of transferring the Ark from Kiriath-jearim to his new capital. This course would also wipe out the reflection upon Yahweh's honour and power caused by its capture by the Philistines. Previously the Ark had had its home at Shiloh in the territory of the northern tribes; now it would stand between north and south, and help to hold them together (vv. 1–5).

One of the drivers of the cart on which the Ark was being carried from Kiriath-jearim put out his hand when the oxen stumbled, and touched the sacred object. The shock of realizing that he had broken a 'taboo' brought about his instantaneous death (vv. 6–7). The incident was interpreted as a sign that Yahweh did not want to go to Jerusalem and the Ark was left at a neighbouring house. The householder, Obed-edom, is described as a native of Gath, and was presumably a Philistine who for some reason or other had been admitted into the privileges of the Israelite race. Since he was not a true Hebrew, it was assumed that the presence of the Ark would not affect him. In point of fact, he escaped all calamity and prospered (vv. 8–11). Whereupon David concluded that Yahweh was no longer displeased, and, after three months, the journey was resumed. The entry of the Ark into Jerusalem was greeted with unrestrained dancing which was thought to be pleasing to Yahweh. It was led by David, clad only in the linen ephod of the priest, to the disgust of his wife, Michal, who expressed her disapproval in forthright terms (vv. 12–23).

(154)   2 Sam. 7.   DAVID AND THE TEMPLE

When the Ark reached Jerusalem it was placed in a tent. David proposed to build a Temple, a house of cedar to contain the Ark, and the prophet Nathan assured him of the divine approval of this suggestion. It seems, however, that Nathan was misled, and

Yahweh sent him to the king to say that He did not desire a house of cedar for Himself, but that, on the other hand, He proposed to build a 'house' for David. That is to say, He promised to secure the permanence of David's dynasty. He would continue to be gracious to the Hebrews and the line of David should not cease.

(155) 2 Sam. 11 2-27. DAVID AND BATHSHEBA

Christians regret this sordid episode in David's life, but he has a right to be judged by the standards of his own day, and not of ours. A despotic king, such as David, claimed privileges. In any case, polygamy was the general practice at the time, and, no doubt, many acts of treachery took place under war conditions without shocking men's consciences. Uriah was not a Judahite, but a Hittite, one who had married into the Hebrew race. To cover his intrigue with Bathsheba, David devised a scheme for him to be sent home on leave, in the hope that the child that was coming would be presumed to be his. Uriah's religious scruples stood in the way. A sexual taboo was in force in time of war and he refused to break it. Whereupon, David arranged with his commander-in-chief for Uriah to be killed in the next battle.

(156) 2 Sam. 12 1-15. THE REBUKE OF NATHAN

The heart of David's sin was his abuse of his royal authority. He had used for personal pleasure and advantage the power that had been entrusted to him by Yahweh for the benefit of the divine community. The unique feature of this episode is that a man of God dared to rebuke a monarch to his face. The quick sense of social justice which David showed in his championship of the poor man in Nathan's parable, is a commendable quality in his character, and his readiness to apply its meaning to his own conduct and to confess his own wrongdoing lifts him in our estimation. In spite of the divine forgiveness, the consequences of this sin were serious. The child died, but the family troubles and feuds which vexed the king's later years had their beginning here.

(157)* 2 Sam. 12 16-25. THE BIRTH OF SOLOMON

Though David pleaded with God for the life of Bathsheba's child, the prayer was not granted. To the astonishment of his court, the king accepted the situation and threw aside his mourning. Another son was born, Solomon. Verse 25 suggests that his training was put into the hands of the prophet Nathan.

F

(158)   *2 Sam.* 15¹⁻¹².   ABSALOM'S REBELLION

The sons of David's various wives quarrelled amongst themselves and plotted against their father, so that the last years of his reign were greatly disturbed by civil war. His third son, Absalom, spent some years in exile, having been banished for the murder of his brother Ammon (13¹⁻³⁹). David recalled him and restored him to power, but only (14^{23-4, 28}) in a half-hearted way. For two years he refused to see him. On his side, Absalom proceeded to curry favour with the people and assumed the marks of the successor to the throne—appearing with horses, a chariot, and runners. He insinuated doubts about the quickness and the fairness of the king's justice. Finally he raised the standard of revolt at Hebron, whither he had gone under pretext of having a vow to fulfil. From this old capital, he summoned his friends to rally round him. Amongst them was Ahithophel, the grandfather of Bathsheba, who probably wanted to avenge the disgrace in which David had involved his family.

(159)*   *2 Sam.* 15¹³-16¹⁴.   DAVID'S RETREAT FROM JERUSALEM

Caught off his guard, and perhaps suspecting the loyalty of its citizens, David fled from Jerusalem with his bodyguard of 600 hired soldiers, all apparently Philistines, under Ittai. He refused to take the Ark with him, for he did not mean his absence to be prolonged, and persuaded Hushai to return to Jerusalem to offer friendship with Absalom and to counteract the influence of Ahithophel.

(160)*   2   *Sam.*   16¹⁵-17²⁹.   ABSALOM'S   OCCUPATION   OF
JERUSALEM

In Jerusalem, Hushai sought a way into the new court which Absalom had established, and pretended to have transferred his loyalty. In the position he won, he tried to gain time for David to collect the troops that were required for the final test of strength. As a sign of the complete break between Absalom and his father, Ahithophel suggested that he should take over the royal harem.

(161)   *2 Sam.* 18¹-19^{8a}.   THE DEATH OF ABSALOM

David had gathered a small but very efficient army. The forces of Absalom were larger but not so well trained. The two armies met in the difficult hill-country of Ephraim. Absalom himself ran into a detachment of the king's men, and, riding at full speed upon his mule, his hair got caught in a branch, so that he was held fast in the heart of an oak. David's commander, Joab, slew him, covered his body with stones, and sent a messenger to break the news to the king.

(162)* 2 *Sam*. 19^{8b-43}. DAVID'S RETURN TO JERUSALEM

Recalling the benefits he had brought them, the people demanded the restoration of David, whilst the king himself used the situation to bind to himself the men of Judah amongst whom the rebellion had started. They made their way to the Jordan and they too invited David to return. Shimei, who had cursed David (16⁵⁻¹⁴), made his peace. Saul's property was divided between Ziba and Mephibosheth. Barzillai, who had been David's host during his exile, escorted his guest to the river Jordan, but declined the invitation to accompany him to Jerusalem. After this, the men of Judah and a contingent from Israel, not by any means at peace with each other, carried the triumphant king back to his capital.

(163) THE IMPORTANCE OF DAVID

Whatever his faults, David was a very great king. The Children of Israel, in succeeding generations, came to look upon him as their ideal. His weaknesses were the weaknesses common to the rulers of his time. His sin with Bathsheba, the murder of Uriah, and the abuse of his royal authority were the kind of things any eastern monarch would have done without a second thought. A king was a despot, and had a right to his own way. In any case, we must set against David's offences his humble acceptance of Nathan's rebuke. His family quarrels, culminating in the rebellion of Absalom, were not merely due to weakness in his character, but much more to the prevalent custom of polygamy. Few eastern rulers, with their harems, escaped such problems.

(164) By the light of his own age, and indeed by the standards of later and much more enlightened ages, David was a great and good king, bringing unity to the tribes and a very large measure of peace from their external enemies. He treated the poor with consideration and was ready to champion their cause against the rich. To those who had wronged him, he could show an amazing spirit of forgiveness and generosity. Above all, he was a loyal follower of Yahweh who made religion the centre of the nation's life. If he did not fulfil his desire to build a Temple, he prepared the way for the later achievement of his son. Throughout his career, he was willing to acknowledge that the power he exercised came from Yahweh, that he was the subject and servant of

Yahweh, that he was as much under obligation to give obedience to the will of Yahweh as the meanest member of his land.

(165)   THE IDEA OF THE MESSIAH

So deeply did David's reign strike into the imagination of the Hebrew people that, as the centuries passed, they could only hope and pray that Yahweh would send them a second David. Only so did it seem they could be delivered from their foes and rescued from their confusions. Hence arose the idea of the Messiah. God, they anticipated, would send them one like unto David, of the very stock of David, anointed by Himself and appointed to be their deliverer. He would be their king and judge, a prince who would bring them peace, a saviour who would lift the people from their oppressions. In its details, this hope took many different forms, and it will recur frequently as we read the rest of the Old Testament. After each difficulty and disaster it gained in strength and clarity. At length it was fulfilled in a way that men had never anticipated in any of their dreams. Jesus came; and those whose eyes could see recognized Him, different as He was from their expectation, as God's Messiah, the true Son of David.

C. *The Reign of Solomon*

(166)   Solomon was one of David's younger sons, the child of Bathsheba. Although Adonijah, the eldest son of the royal house, assumed the position of heir-apparent, the monarchy was not regarded as necessarily an hereditary office. Bathsheba realized that Adonijah was the popular candidate, but persuaded the failing king to name Solomon as his successor. Backed by the royal bodyguard and his father's preference, Solomon had little difficulty in securing the crown after David's death. Such leaders as might have given support to his rival, he dealt with ruthlessly. Joab was put to death, Abiathar the priest was banished to Anathoth, and, later, Adonijah was killed by Benaiah (1 Kings 1-2).

(167)   It looked as if Solomon's glory was going to outshine that of David. Israel seemed on the edge of her greatest political power. Her near neighbours, Moab, Ammon, Edom, Aram, had to acknowledge Solomon's overlordship, and, where there

were possible rivals on his borders, he made alliances with them. By a trade treaty with Hiram of Tyre, he obtained a share in the commerce of the Mediterranean, and Hebrew sailors made expeditions to far countries. A port on the Red Sea, Ezion-geber, gave him an outlet in the opposite direction. Where caravans used the land route that crossed his territory, he was able to levy dues, and he himself developed a considerable traffic in horses, buying them from Asia Minor and selling them to Egypt (1 Kings 10^{28-9}). At home, Solomon embarked upon vast building schemes, especially an ambitious scheme to beautify Jerusalem. The Temple, the Royal Palace, the barracks, and the various offices of State, were part of a grandiose conception.

(168) It is probable, however, that the glory of Solomon's reign has been overrated, that some of it was the reflected glory of his father's achievements, and that it lasted only for a short time. The general opinion is that the empire began to disintegrate fairly soon in his reign. The Old Testament tells us of some of his failures, but it places these stories together later in the account of his kingship. We ought rather to think of the unity and strength which David gave to Israel slowly breaking up, owing to the extravagance of Solomon's personal and public schemes and the presence of outside enemies.

(169) Certainly Solomon does not seem to have inspired the devotion that was given to his father. His luxurious way of life isolated him from the common people, and his policy bore hardly upon them. The Northern Tribes had to supply forced labour for three months of the year and to work under Phoenician craftsmen. By dividing his kingdom into twelve new districts, not on a tribal basis, and appointing officials to get this labour and to collect taxes, he caused great discontent. Hiram of Tyre came to his help and provided him with material and advice, but in return Solomon had to send enormous quantities of food-stuffs to Tyre. Later Hiram demanded gold, and, in the end, Solomon had to pass over to him twenty Galilean cities. He also lost during his reign the dependencies of Edom and Syria, and when he died the country was full of discontent and the treasury empty.

(170) The greatest weakness, in the eyes of the Old Testament writers, was Solomon's lack of any deep religious interest. His building of the Temple tends to obscure this, until we remember it was only meant to be an appendage to the Royal Palace. His foreign wives easily led him into disloyalty to Yahweh.

He allowed the gods of Egypt and of surrounding nations to have a place in Jerusalem and he himself seems to have been content to regard Yahweh as one amongst a collection of deities.

(171) 1 *Kings* 3. THE GREATNESS OF SOLOMON

After a note of Solomon's alliance with the royal family of Egypt, the practice of worship at high places is explained (*vv.* 1–3). As these became regarded in later days as a menace to the purity of Hebrew religion (*see para.* 263), it must have been embarrassing to discover that they were in common use in Solomon's time and accepted as regular sanctuaries of Yahweh. The building of the Temple did not bring them to an end; indeed there was no attempt to abolish them until the reign of Hezekiah. We are given to understand that Solomon acknowledged their existence, though deploring them. His sacrifice of 1,000 burnt-offerings at the beginning of his kingship was not offered at the Jerusalem altar, but at Gibeon, a high place, although he returned to the Holy City to make his peace-offerings before the Ark (*vv.* 4, 15*b*).

In a dream, God gave him an opportunity to ask for the gifts he wished for his high office. To his credit, he rejected riches and honours and long life, the customary marks of an eastern monarch —though when he became established he showed how deeply he cared for these things—and chose instead wisdom to undertake his tasks. Maybe this wisdom was a kind of practical shrewdness, rather than a capacity for balanced and mellowed judgements (*vv.* 5–15*a*). His dealings with the two harlots who disputed the possession of a child shows that kind of an insight into human nature and that sort of ingenuity in solving problems (*vv.* 16–28).

(172)* 1 *Kings* 5. THE ALLIANCE WITH HIRAM

Solomon's friendship with Hiram was mutually important and had benefits for both Israel and Tyre. Vast stores of timber were provided from Lebanon, but the price Solomon ultimately had to pay was heavy.

(173) 1 *Kings* 6[1-13]. SOLOMON'S TEMPLE

The Temple was not much bigger than an English parish church (90 feet by 30 feet in area and 30 feet high). As with all ancient temples, it was not intended to be a place in which a congregation would assemble, but the shrine or abode of a god. Though it was recognized that Yahweh exercised His power throughout the length and breadth of Israel, the Temple was meant to be in a special sense His dwelling place. It was divided into two parts, the Temple proper, and a small inner shrine in which the Ark was kept, surrounded by darkness as a symbol of the mystery of God. The whole was set in a spacious courtyard where the Israelites gathered to celebrate their feast days. Much of the ritual took place in the open air, especially at the great altar of sacrifice. Although the Temple contained the Ark with the cherubim, no image of Yahweh was permitted. In this way, the Hebrews expressed their belief that their God could not be seen or represented in any adequate way, and the manner was prepared for still higher conceptions of Yahweh as a spiritual deity whose presence could not be localized.

It is doubtful whether the Temple was very popular at first. The mere fact that it was an innovation would be sufficient to make many people suspicious. Moreover, the relays of Israelites brought into Jerusalem to contribute their compulsory labour towards its building deeply resented the indignity. But in course of time it caught their imagination and came to dominate their religious thought and aspiration. Though built chiefly as a royal chapel, and not half as costly as Solomon's own home, its position raised it above that of the palace and the public buildings associated with it, and it reminded the people of the supreme place of Yahweh in their lives. It brought home to them, every time they saw it, or thought of it, the Covenant which existed between Yahweh and the nation. They came to believe it was the token of God's providential care and that, so long as it remained inviolate, their nation would be safe. No blow to their faith was ever so severe as the fact that, in the time of the Exile, it lay in ruins and decay.

(174) 1 *Kings* 10¹⁻¹³. THE VISIT OF THE QUEEN OF SHEBA

Rumours of Solomon's greatness reached Sheba, in south-west Arabia. Its people were known by the Israelites as exporters of gold and their queen journeyed to Jerusalem to inspect the Hebrew capital and to listen to the wisdom of its king. The present she left behind suggests that her real purpose was to pay tribute money to Solomon. His great wealth probably came from a number of vassal states, and this chapter gives some idea of his magnificence and wealth.

(175) *Kings* 11[1-13]. THE DECLINE OF SOLOMON

The compiler of *Kings* traced Solomon's downfall to the multitude of his foreign wives. Since polygamy was not itself frowned upon, and it was no doubt a wise policy for the king to form alliances with other countries by his various marriages, the heart of the condemnation would seem to be that he allowed them to bring their own religions to Jerusalem and practise them. The effect upon the worship of Yahweh by the ordinary people was bound to be bad. Consequently, the divine punishment had to fall upon Solomon, though, for the sake of his father David, the division of the kingdom was postponed until after his death.

TEST QUESTIONS

(*Send answers to* TWO *questions to your tutor*)

1. What did Saul achieve as a King? Why is he regarded as a failure?
2. How far would you describe David as 'a man after God's own heart'?
3. What did Solomon do for Israel (*a*) for good, and (*b*) for ill?

Study Six

The Prophets of Northern Israel

A. The Division of the Kingdom

(176) Unity had been imposed upon the various groups of Israelite tribes by the strong hand of David, and maintained to a very large degree by Solomon, but, beneath the surface of the community's life, there was still a great deal of division. The Northern Tribes resented the pre-eminence of Judah. For all its magnificence, the new capital of Jerusalem had not yet secured the loyalty of all the Hebrews. As Solomon's reign proceeded, with its heavy taxation and its vexatious system of forced labour, both occasioned by his grandiose schemes, a smouldering discontent began to spread in the north. Men disliked intensely having to leave their own farms to take part in the royal programme, especially at times when their own crops were due to be sown or garnered. Their treatment reminded them of the slave conditions of their ancestors in Egypt.

(177) Even during the lifetime of Solomon, a revolt broke out in Ephraim, led by one of the king's overseers, Jeroboam (1 Kings 11$^{26-40}$). The rebellion was put down, and Jeroboam took refuge in Egypt, where he waited till the time was ripe for a more successful movement. The feeble Rehoboam, who ascended the throne after his father's death, had not sufficient sense to listen to the advice of the elder statesmen who pleaded with him to make some attempt to lighten the people's load. He handled the deputation headed by Jeroboam with incredible stupidity, bluntly announcing a policy which would increase the burdens of his subjects. The ten Northern Tribes took this as a signal for them to revolt, and declared Jeroboam as their king.

(178) An important part was played in this revolt by the prophet Ahijah. His grounds for supporting Jeroboam were chiefly religious. A native of the ancient shrine of Shiloh, he no doubt resented the selection of Jerusalem as the religious capital of Israel, and would have preferred Shiloh to have been restored to its earlier dignity. Moreover, he stood for the simplicities of

Yahweh worship, as practised in the times of Saul and David, over against the oriental display of Solomon's reign. It seemed to him that David's son had failed to use his power to govern on behalf of Yahweh and according to Yahweh's will, and that by consolidating his position by a series of marriage-alliances, he had brought a corrupting influence into the religious life of Israel.

(179) The business of a prophet was to recall even kings to a sense of their proper responsibility to God. With all his faults, David had been wise enough to listen to the rebuke of Nathan and accept it. Solomon was less responsive. It was pretty clear that the weak Rehoboam was still less likely to give heed to any divine message. Ahijah, therefore, concluded that such an unsatisfactory situation justified him in supporting Jeroboam and in assuring him of the support of ten of the tribes, even before the king's death.

(180) 1 *Kings* 12$^{1-24}$. THE STORY OF THE REVOLT

The one wise thing that Rehoboam did was to get himself crowned at Shechem, one of the oldest sanctuaries in the land and connected with the names of Abraham, Jacob, Joseph, Joshua, and Gideon. According to 14^{21}, Rehoboam had reached the mature age of forty before coming to the throne, but one manuscript of the Greek Old Testament (*see para.* 448) says that he was only sixteen, which would perhaps explain his behaviour. No doubt he believed he was acting as a worthy son of the despotic Solomon.

(181) THE NORTHERN KINGDOM

In later centuries the revolt of the ten tribes was looked upon as the worst misfortune that ever befell the royal house of David. The northern half of the kingdom, with the trade route between Damascus and Egypt passing through it, was much bigger and richer than the south. It could indeed be called a land of corn and wine and oil. Jeroboam determined to detach the loyalty of his people from everything connected with Southern Israel. To stop religious pilgrimages to Jerusalem, he revived the old shrines of Canaanitish worship at Dan and Bethel. The presence of Yahweh there was denoted by a metal image of a bull, giving a clear indication to us that Yahweh worship was getting close to the native worship of fertility (the Baals; *see para* 121). The priesthood at these shrines was drawn from all the ten revolted tribes.

(182) The compilers of 1 and 2 *Kings*, who could not have completed their work until a generation after the fall of Jerusalem in 586 B.C., were interested in religion rather than the narrower field of politics, and judged the various monarchs of North and South Israel by their attitude to religious issues. All those of the north were, in their opinion, 'bad kings'. They made Israel to sin after the fashion of Jeroboam, by encouraging the worship of Yahweh at Bethel and under the form of a bull, and by permitting the moral evils that accompanied such worship. In the south, the test of the kings was their attitude towards the 'high places' and the sanctity of worship at the Jerusalem Temple. Only two of the Judean monarchs earned praise for doing what was right in the eyes of Yahweh—Hezekiah and Josiah—though several others came near to the high standard required by the editors of *Kings*.

B. *Elijah*

(183) In the Books of Kings we have stories concerning both the northern and the southern halves of Israel, arranged according to the reigns of the various kings. We may find that the attempt of the editors to keep the two histories in step somewhat confusing. It will be easier for us to deal with the Northern Kingdom first and, instead of taking it reign by reign, to look at it through the eyes of those outstanding men, the prophets of Yahweh.

(184) In the period of Samuel and Saul, as we have seen (*para.* 124), the prophets were bands of patriotic enthusiasts, stirring the nation from its apathy and recalling it to its loyalty to Yahweh. This meant, in particular, a summons to a relentless warfare against His foes. Their intense excitement disturbed their mental balance, and their behaviour passed into frenzy. With the passage of time, however, they slowly changed in character and became more what we should expect of men of religion. They came to see that their chief function was to criticize and oppose whatever failed to accord with their vision of Yahweh's character and demands. In speech they became exceedingly forthright and fearless, and they did not hesitate to declare even in the highest places the messages God laid upon their consciences.

(185) Solomon's building of the Temple did not please them, and they began to form themselves into groups, the 'Schools of the Prophets', which shunned city life in preference for the countryside, which seemed more natural to them. They looked back to the sterner and more bracing conditions under which their ancestors had wandered in the deserts, and set out to re-capture what they could of the simplicity and sincerity of those days. Some of them, inconsistent though it may seem, learned to write, but writing gave them the power to perpetuate stories of their national history. These they coloured with their own personal convictions and they became in effect powerful sermons preaching their point of view. To such unknown groups we owe the ancient documents J and E (*see para.* 442). In course of time the more outstanding prophets began to make notes of their own pronouncements, which were preserved for the benefit of later generations.

(186) We owe a great debt to these prophetic schools. From them emerged a unique line of inspired men, most of them solitary and highly individualistic, who asserted their independence of the schools and proclaimed the vision that had been given to them of Yahweh, His nature and demands. Nowhere else in religious history is there anything to be compared with this succession of Hebrew prophets. They were a salutary force in Israel, proclaiming divine truths that people had forgotten or never comprehended, and fearlessly doing battle with everything that threatened to corrupt the purity of religion or to frustrate the purpose of Yahweh. In the next few readings, we see Elijah's valiant fight to preserve Yahweh worship from the corrupting influences of the Baals.

(187) 1 *Kings* 16$^{29-34}$. THE REIGN OF AHAB

Following a familiar policy, Ahab formed an alliance with Tyre and cemented it by marrying a daughter of the royal house. It was with Jezebel, rather than with Ahab, that Elijah fought. She brought to Northern Israel her own religion, that of the Tyrian Baal, Melkart, and tried to force it upon the Hebrew people. Ahab does not seem to have been unwilling, and built for her a special temple and a special altar; but he was not pre-pared to make a wholesale surrender of Yahweh worship. It seemed to him that the cult of Melkart could very well be com-bined with the traditional Israel religion. No doubt to the ordin-ary people this was a welcome proposal. They certainly found

Melkart attractive; he reminded them of the Canaanite Baals, towards which they had always been drawn because of their promise to give fertility to the land. Jezebel also encouraged the worship of the female deity, Ashtart or Ashtoreth, which was an ancient cult of the countryside, and it seems certain that the 'new' worship was largely sexual in character.

(188) This mixing of religions (which we call 'syncretism') was likely to have a twofold effect:

(a) It would cause Hebrew religion to slip back into polytheism, instead of developing from monolatry towards monotheism.

(b) It would lower the level of moral life, and obscure the truth that Yahweh's demands upon His worshippers were ethical; that He required personal and social righteousness.

(189) Jezebel's adherence to Melkart was by no means a formality. She was a fanatic. She set out to make converts wherever she could, and did not hesitate to persecute those who stood out for an undivided allegiance to Yahweh. But she met her match in Elijah the Tishbite.

(190) 1 *Kings* 17. ELIJAH AND THE DROUGHT

Rugged, fearless, and lonely, Elijah suddenly stepped on to the scene from the wild highlands of Gilead. The schools of the prophets had raised their voices in protest at Ahab's religious policy, and Obadiah had had to come to the rescue of some of them (18[4]). The Nazirite party no doubt also stood out against Baal worship. But the situation needed a champion of Yahweh's cause, and he was found in Elijah, who realized that Israel must be challenged to make up its mind for or against polytheism. He began by announcing that a period of drought was a punishment sent by Yahweh. Had Baal really been able to give fertility to the land, as his prophets and followers maintained, he ought to have been able to bring the drought to an end and restore plenty to the land. But only Yahweh could do that. Whatever the Baal worshippers might say, Elijah knew that Yahweh, and Yahweh alone, was the source of plenty, and the giver of sustenance to Israel. During the famine, Elijah himself was provided for, first by a river-course east of Jordan, later by a widow of Zarepath.

(191) 1 *Kings* 18. ELIJAH ON MOUNT CARMEL

For his contest with Jezebel's priests, Elijah chose a ridge of land jutting out towards the queen's home territory. With characteristic courage, the prophet was carrying the warfare as

near to the enemy's country as he could. Through the agency of
Obadiah, the Tyrian prophets were gathered together in the
presence of representatives of the nation. The god who answered
by fire was to be the god of Israel. 'How long are you going on
limping between two opinions?' The pouring out of water was the
current ritual act which accompanied prayers for rain. When a
storm broke, it seemed as if Elijah had gained a complete victory.
The people shouted their acceptance of Yahweh. Elijah ordered
a slaughter of the Tyrian priests, and Melkart further demonstrated his powerlessness by his inability to save them. The
drought came to a swift finish, the little brook at the foot of
Carmel bursting its banks, so that Ahab in his chariot barely
managed to reach his summer palace at Jezreel in safety.

(192) 1 *Kings* 19$^{1-12}$.   ELIJAH'S FLIGHT TO HOREB

Though the last chapter suggests a resounding victory for
Yahweh, Jezebel's influence in Israel was not diminished. The
surviving followers of Baal were in all probability able to find
some way of explaining the end of the drought as the work of
Melkart and not Yahweh. It seemed to Elijah that, in his fight
with the queen, she was likely to get her own way. Scared for his
very life, he fled beyond Ahab's jurisdiction and passed through
the neighbouring territory of Judah to the wilderness beyond.
Finally he reached Horeb, the holy mountain on which Moses
had entered into the Covenant with Yahweh. Here it was
revealed to him that he had been entertaining wrong expectations
about the divine activity. He had looked for Yahweh to work out
His purpose through extraordinary means, through wonders
instead of through quiet, normal events. God, he discovered,
was not in the fire or the earthquake or the tempest, but in the
silence. The 'still small voice' means literally, 'a sound of gentle
stillness', and it indicated that Yahweh was at work when nothing
unusual seemed to be happening.

(193) 1 *Kings* 19$^{12-21}$.   ELIJAH'S COMMISSION

As a consequence of this revelation, Elijah was bidden to do
three things, each of which had a significance that does not lie
on the surface:

(*a*) He was to anoint his successor, Elisha. Contrary to his
despairing outburst, he was by no means the only loyal follower
of Yahweh left. There were 7,000 in Israel who had not bowed
the knee to Baal, and they would require a leader when Elijah

was no longer able to carry on. We notice here the beginning of
the idea of a godly Remnant in Israel, a faithful minority at the
heart of the nation (*see paras.* 242–4).

(*b*) Elijah was to anoint Jehu to be king over Israel. Thus
Yahweh was getting ready a man whom He would use to overthrow the house of Ahab and rid the country of the menace of
the Tyrian Baal (2 Kings 9–10^{31}).

(*c*) Elijah was also to anoint Hazael to be the king of Aram
(=Syria). The inner meaning of this is that Yahweh's authority
was not confined to the territory of Israel, as was generally
supposed. In order to fulfil His purposes, He would make use of
members of other nations. Hazael was to be an instrument with
which Yahweh would chastise Israel.

(194)   1 *Kings* 21.   NABOTH'S VINEYARD

This was the last clash between Elijah and Jezebel. With the
dramatic suddenness which is characteristic of him, the prophet
reappeared in Samaria to denounce the king for his part in the
affair of Naboth's vineyard. An Israelite farmer owned a piece
of land which Ahab wanted for an extension to the Palace garden,
but he refused to sell it on the ground that he held it in trust from
his fathers and was under obligation to pass it on to his descendants intact. As far as Ahab was concerned, that would have been
the end of the matter, for the king was prepared to abide by the
Israelite laws regarding private property (*vv.* 1–4). But Jezebel
was not content. She arranged for Naboth to be accused falsely
of blasphemy and treason, and the mob was incited to stone him
(*vv.* 5–16). In spite of his appearance of being horrified at the
deed, Ahab was deemed by Elijah to have been fully guilty of
committing it, and doom was pronounced upon him and his
family. Though Jezebel had persuaded her husband that, as king,
his power was absolute, the prophet insisted that Ahab was the
servant of Yahweh and under obligation to use his power according to the divine laws. These were ethical in character. The
worship of Yahweh required a far higher standard of conduct
from its followers than Melkart worship (*vv.* 17–29).

(195)*   2 *Kings* 2$^{1-15}$.   THE TRANSLATION OF ELIJAH

The prophetic guilds warned Elisha, already consecrated as
the Tishbite's successor, that the time for Elijah's departure was
at hand. As a parting gift he asked for a double share of his
spirit (the share of the firstborn), but Elijah's reply shows how

difficult it is to transmit a spiritual office. The chariots of fire were a symbol of Yahweh's presence.

C. *Elisha*

(196)   When the prophetic bands, whom we have seen supporting Elijah in the final scene of his life, saw that Elisha could use his mantle with miraculous effect, they elected him their leader. He proved a very different type of prophet from his predecessor, for there was little about him of the old rugged solitary. On the contrary, he mixed with the rank and file of ordinary folk, kept company with the schools of prophets, and not infrequently appeared at the royal court in the role of adviser and friend rather than of judge and critic.

(197)   A number of stories grew up around his name which suggest that he possessed either miraculous powers or a medical knowledge in advance of his day. Even if we regard some of them as legends, they do at any rate bear testimony to the esteem in which he was held. Some of the tales associated with him are brutal and cruel, but others reveal a sense that mercy and kindness are part of the divine demand upon men.

(198)★   2 *Kings* 4⁸⁻³⁷.   ELISHA AND THE SHUNAMMITE WOMAN

This is a useful picture of everyday country life in ancient Israel. In return for hospitality, and moved by sympathy and compassion, Elisha restored to life the son of his benefactors.

(199)★   2 *Kings* 5.   ELISHA AND NAAMAN

In the kindly consideration of the Israelite maid for her foreign master, we see the Old Testament at its best. The period was apparently one of peace in Northern Israel, and there is a clear suggestion that Israel had become the vassal of Syria. The King of Israel obviously feared that when his overlord sent Naaman to him to be cured, he was trying to pick a quarrel with him. Elisha seems to have been living at Samaria. His treatment of the Syrian seemed so offhanded that Naaman's pride was aroused and he almost missed his cure. When he had been restored, however, he acknowledged himself a convert to the worship of Yahweh out of gratitude; though there remained the difficult problem of how to practise the new faith on his return to Syria.

He found a way out by carrying back with him a load of Israelite soil, for he believed that the Hebrew God could only be worshipped on Hebrew territory. At the same time, he asked for a dispensation when his official duties compelled him to prostrate himself in the house of Rimmon. Elisha's words are not necessarily a granting of this. The injunction 'Go in peace' simply means 'Farewell'; it does not indicate approval.

Elisha's servant, Gehazi, determined to get the gift which his master had refused, and was afflicted with Naaman's leprosy. Possibly the infection was carried in the Syrian's clothing.

(200)* *2 Kings* 6⁸⁻²³. ELISHA AND THE SYRIANS AT DOTHAN

(200)* *2 Kings* 6$^{8-23}$. ELISHA AND THE SYRIANS AT DOTHAN

The prophet took a leading part in this war with the Syrians. The Syrian king devised a series of ambushes to waylay the forces of Israel, but, on each occasion, Elisha was able to reveal the secret. It was, therefore, resolved to capture him. At Dothan, ten miles north of Samaria, the attempt seemed likely to succeed; even Elisha's servant thought the position to be hopeless. He did not know that the prophet was defended by horses and chariots of fire. In response to Elisha's prayer, his enemies were stricken blind and led away to Samaria, though on their arrival the prophet ordered that they should be treated with kindness.

D. *Amos*

(201) Although the Old Testament has little good to say of the Northern Kingdom of Israel, from other sources we have evidence that it had some very successful kings and developed a vigorous life of its own. Jeroboam II (782–743 B.C.) was a monarch whose power and glory were excelled only by those of the early Solomon. He raised the political prestige of his country to a very high level and gave it great economic prosperity.

(202) There was, however, another side to the picture. There was much moral and social evil in the land. Great wealth and luxury were to be seen on all sides; but there was also deep poverty. The well-to-do landowners were set on gathering into their own hands all the land they could obtain, and this meant dispossessing the original tenants and reducing them to the level of serfs. The richer these landowners became, the more self-indulgent they grew, and the less they cared about the sufferings

of their unfortunate brethren. Commercial activity grew by leaps and bounds, and with it the assumption that money could secure everything that people wanted. The rich had a right to take what pleasure they desired, and where. If they were brought to the courts of law, they were powerful enough to secure any verdict they wanted. None of the ordinary rules of personal and social morality applied to them!

(203)   Religion ceased to be a power making for righteousness. It was the sure conviction of these Israelites that they were under the special protection of Yahweh and no ill could befall them. Throughout the land there was a spirit of smug self-satisfaction. True, the ceremonies of religion continued—for it was obviously wise to keep on the right side of Yahweh; but they were devoid of any reality. Often, indeed, they were accompanied by that sexual immorality which the Israelites had always been prone to incorporate into their worship from the practices of the native Canaanites.

(204)   Nevertheless, doom and disaster were lying in wait for Israel. The prosperity of Jeroboam II was in a large measure due to the period of peace that he was permitted to enjoy; but that peace was the result of the weakness of the Assyrians. If you look at a map, you will see that the little states of Palestine lie between the vast empires of Egypt and Assyria. These empires were rivals for the domination of the ancient world, and the tension between them (or between Egypt and Assyria's successor, Babylon) was to become the most influential factor in Hebrew politics for many years to come. Israel, Judah, Syria, and their neighbours were in the dangerous position of being buffer-states. In any collision between the two great empires they were bound to be involved. Even when things were comparatively quiet, the great empires manœuvred to get these little states under their thumb; in their turn, the leaders of the Palestinian countries not infrequently succumbed to the temptation to play one power off against the other.

(205)   With the help of Ben-hadad of Syria, King Ahab of Israel had managed to stem the advance of the Assyrians for the time being, though in the reign of Jehu they got as far as Damascus. Israel escaped invasion, but had been compelled to pay tribute. In the period of Jeroboam II, Assyria was pre-occupied with troubles nearer home, and Israel allowed itself to be lulled into a false sense of security. Once the civil strife in Assyria was quietened, its threat would appear again, and it was not the kind

of threat that any small nation could despise. Amongst all the empires of the ancient world, Assyria was conspicuous, not only for her military skill, but for her cruelty and savagery. But whilst Israel as a nation might choose to forget the danger, Amos the prophet was on the alert. As he looked ahead, it seemed to him quite certain that Assyria would be the instrument Yahweh would use to punish His guilty people. Disaster, he predicted, would come from the north, from beyond Damascus, and the fate of Yahweh's people would be captivity in a strange land.

(206) Amos was the first of the 'great' prophets of Israel. Though descended from the schools of the prophets, they became so different from them as almost to belong to another category. They were unique individuals, living in close communion with God, and with a deep insight both into the divine nature and into the movements of their own days. In season and out of season, they proclaimed the will of Yahweh as they understood it, and shared with their fellows the self-disclosures He made to them. Inevitably they were forced into becoming critics of their contemporaries. They had to speak God's word, regardless of the worldly position of their hearers or the coolness with which it was received.

(207) On the other hand, the schools of the prophets tended to degenerate, and their members became mere place seekers, speaking the easy and pleasant word which would offend none. They became known as 'false' prophets, and stood in contrast to those true prophets whose vision of truth had to be delivered in Yahweh's name, regardless of the consequences it involved for themselves.

(208) The home of Amos was in the south, in the village of Tekoa belonging to Judah. He describes himself as a shepherd and a husbandman, a dresser of fig trees (Amos 7^{15}; sycamore = fig tree). He has many points of similarity with Elijah. Both were rugged characters; both give the impression of standing aloof from the community they condemned; both were offended by the complicated civilization of city life, small though their cities were compared with ours; both preferred the simplicities of their own agricultural background.

(209) No doubt Amos travelled to sell his wool and went north to Bethel, the chief religious centre of the Northern Kingdom where Jeroboam I had erected one of his golden bulls. What he saw shocked him to the core. Returning to the loneliness of his desert home, he had time to brood upon the state of Israel,

until at length the fire of God that burned in his bones found utterance. Amos 8⁹ suggests that the prophet witnessed an eclipse of the sun, and that this somewhat terrifying event may have been one of the factors that led him to speak out. Scholars have calculated that this was in June 763 B.C., some twenty years before the Assyrian power began to revive. Amos is the first of the prophets whose actual words have been preserved for us. Probably some time about 750 B.C. he retired from his public ministry and went back to Tekoa, where he wrote down the notes of his preaching and teaching.

(210) *The message of Amos* had three main themes:

(*a*) As a God of righteousness, Yahweh demanded righteousness from His people. Ritual and ceremony, if divorced from just and honest dealings of man with man, meant nothing to Him. Religion was ethical, and social justice was an essential part of it. Alas! in Israel the very ceremonies of worship were being used to cover up unethical practices. To sleep in the Temple overnight might be an act of piety, but not if it were used to retain a creditor's cloak which, by the humane law of the time, ought to have been given back to him for his own use at sundown! To observe the Sabbath was an excellent thing; but it became a mockery if it merely gave unscrupulous merchants an opportunity to plan more trickery (5²²⁻⁴)!

(*b*) The selection of Israel as Yahweh's chosen nation, if understood properly, had thrust upon the people a very heavy burden of responsibility. Yet too many Israelites saw in it nothing but a pledge of divine protection, and forgot that they had to fulfil their side of the Covenant agreement. To the prophetic mind, the fact that they were a chosen people gave them no excuse for moral slackness, but meant that more was expected of them. Indeed, they had less excuse than others for disobeying God's laws, and, if they failed, must bear a greater punishment (3²).

(*c*) The Day of Yahweh, for which the nation was looking, would prove to be a Day of Darkness, not of Light. The nation anticipated it as the time when all the purposes of Yahweh would be triumphant, and when still greater prosperity and joy would come to them as His chosen race. The prophet bluntly warned them that they were wrong. Unless there was a general repentance and reformation, it would be a time of judgement and disaster. As he looked with deep insight into the life of his times, Amos realized that a community like Israel, split into two sections, the very rich and the helpless poor, was a nation already being corrupted from within, and one which would be quite unable to stand up to the threat of a powerful foe such as Assyria (Amos 5¹⁸).

(211)   *Amos* 7¹⁰⁻¹⁷.   AMOS AT BETHEL

This is the only narrative concerning Amos that has survived, and it would seem to refer to an incident early in the reign of Jeroboam, before he was fully settled upon the throne. Suddenly Amos appeared in the midst of the worshippers at Bethel and proclaimed his message (*vv.* 10–11). Not unnaturally, his words were taken to be disloyal to the new king and he was challenged by Amaziah, the official guardian of the sanctuary, who described Amos as a 'seer', a member of the prophetic schools. (A 'seer' was one whose business was to enquire the mind of Yahweh on behalf of ordinary men and women who wanted direction in their everyday affairs. He made use of the 'lot' which said 'yes' or 'no' to whatever was proposed.) Amos was bidden to cease his prophetic proclamation and to return and deliver it to his native country of Judah; his reply was a warning of disaster (*vv.* 12–17).

(212)*   *Amos* 1–2.   AMOS'S JUDGEMENT OF THE NATIONS

The message of Amos begins with a series of judgements on the countries neighbouring Israel, and we can imagine the great joy with which the citizens of Samaria listened. Each opens with a traditional formula, 'For three transgressions, yea, for four', and the country concerned is charged with an offence of an unpardonable character. Damascus has been guilty of cruelty in time of war, Gaza of inhumanity, Tyre of taking part in slave traffic, and Edom, Ammon and Moab of vindictiveness. Notice that Amos takes it for granted that Yahweh is the God of these peoples as well as of the Israelites, which is a step towards the full idea of monotheism (1³–2³). After pronouncing judgement upon the sister nation of Judah for its godlessness (2⁴⁻⁵), the prophet turns his attention to Israel itself. The Northern Kingdom is denounced for its crimes in 2⁶⁻¹².

In their greed, they have oppressed the poor and obstructed the course of justice, selling the honest man for silver and the needy for a pair of sandals (i.e. 'an old song'), trampling into the earth the heads of the poor, thrusting aside the humble (2⁶⁻⁷ᵃ); they have indulged in immoral worship at the shrines of the Baals (2⁷ᵇ); they have retained garments taken in pledge, contrary to the regulation of Exod. 22²²⁻⁷, and have used them to lie upon in their immoral worship (2⁸ᵃ); they have made use of the fines they have received to purchase wine for these sacrifices, much of which they have drunk themselves in the feast that, according to the practice of the day (*see* Exod. 32⁶), followed the offering (2⁸ᵇ); they have silenced the prophets and corrupted the Nazirites who sought by word and example to call them back to a simpler and purer way of life (2¹²). All this is aggravated by their ingratitude to Yahweh who has shown them favour after favour (2⁹⁻¹¹).

(213)   *Amos* 3¹–4³.   THE DENUNCIATION OF ISRAEL

The two opening verses of this passage state explicitly one of the themes that underlie the whole of his preaching (*see para.* 210 (*b*)). The prophet goes on to declare that his judgements are certain because they have most surely been inspired by Yahweh. Nothing happens without a cause. Two people will not meet in the desert unless they have an agreement to do so; a lion will not roar unless it has taken its prey; a bird will not be caught unless a trap has been laid for it; a trumpet will not be blown in the city unless there is danger. In the same way, a prophet would not utter threats of doom unless they had been laid upon his conscience by Yahweh (*vv.* 3–8). A further denunciation is directed especially against Samaria, the capital, the centre of luxury and oppression. Amos predicted the invasion and overthrow of the land. Indeed the very heathen are summoned to testify that justice no longer reigns in the city (*vv.* 9–15). Finally the women of Samaria are indicted as the cause of their lords' excesses (4¹⁻³).

(214)   *Amos* 6¹⁻⁷.   THE GODLESS RICH

A nation which has allowed the wealthy to override all the principles of decency and justice ought to reflect upon the fate of other cities, such as Calneh, Hamath, Gath. Is Israel bigger or better than these city-states? But no warning seems to touch the people of Yahweh. Instead of listening to the prophet, the idle and godless upper classes sprawl upon couches and beds of ivory, feeding daintily and singing coarse songs. There will have to come an end to all this, and it will be a terrible one. The rich, as the chief offenders, will be the first to be carried away into exile.

(215)*   *Amos* 8⁴⁻⁷.   A FURTHER LIST OF CRIMES

Holy days are regarded with impatience. They stop business, though they provide opportunities for thinking out further sharp practices. The ephah was a measure of about eight gallons. The custom apparently was to give short measure and charge high prices. When the buyers came to weigh out the price for the goods they were buying, weighted shekels were used.

(216)* *Amos* 9[11-15]. A VISION OF HOPE

For the most part, Amos's words were full of gloom, but he ends on a more cheerful note. The contrast is so great that some commentators have felt that these verses could only have been added at a later date, perhaps after the return from the Exile. Yet there is no reason why Amos should not have glimpsed the mercy of God, and finished his ministry in the hope that, if Israel repented, Yahweh would give her teeming seasons, peace, and prosperity, and a return from captivity.

E. *Hosea*

(217) Shortly after Amos had retired, a second great prophet appeared on the scene. Hosea belonged entirely to the Northern Kingdom and exercised his ministry during the last years before the fall of Samaria (721 B.C.) and possibly in the days that immediately followed. Jeroboam II died in 741 B.C. A period of great unsettlement followed; king followed king in quick succession; many of them were murdered by their successors. Meanwhile the Assyrian menace drew nearer and became more pronounced. Pul (or Tiglath Pileser III) had seized the Assyrian throne and realized that, to consolidate his power and to advance his plans, he must keep Palestine in subjection. In 738 B.C. he compelled Israel to pay him tribute and to cede some territory in the north and east (*see* Hosea 5[13]). Nevertheless there were statesmen in Samaria who believed that by intriguing with him they might avoid his aggressive attention. Others turned in hope to his rival, Egypt. Hosea knew quite well that by neither expedient could Israel be saved.

(218) Hosea is one of the few prophets to invite us to enter his private life and his inner experiences. In his case, the whole of his ministry and message is coloured by the unhappiness of his domestic situation. The two accounts of his ruined home life, given in Chapters 1 and 3, can be interpreted in various ways. Some scholars think that we have two accounts of the same

event; others that they refer to two different women. The generally accepted view, though it is not beyond dispute, is that the two chapters record two stages in Hosea's relations with the same woman.

(219) Gomer was a bad character. The prophet may not have been aware of it when he married her, but it soon became obvious. She was frequently unfaithful to him. Three children were born; then she left him to go after her lovers. Yet in spite of the way she had treated him, Hosea found that he still loved her, and could find no contentment of spirit until he had brought her back home. Only so could the deep quality of his love be satisfied. At the same time, her faults were far too serious to be condoned. What Hosea had to do was to find a way of winning her from her fickle lovers, to devise some sort of discipline that would make a better woman of her.

(220) Out of this grievous experience, the prophet came to a deeper vision of the relationship between Yahweh and His people. God used it as a means of disclosing to Hosea the quality of His love. Israel was the wife of Yahweh, but she had played falsely by Him, especially by her readiness to turn to the Canaanite Baals. Yet Yahweh could not cut her off entirely; His love could only satisfy itself when it found a way of restoring her. First, however, she must be punished and reformed, and there seemed no other way of doing that than by the painful discipline of suffering. The disasters which Hosea saw coming upon the nation were to be accepted as part of the divine process of redemption. Thus, whilst Hosea shared to the full the insistence of Amos on the righteousness of Yahweh's character, and His consequent demand for justice and truth amongst men, he put his own special emphasis on God's mercy and love.

(221) The words of Hosea are not easy for us to read. We are unable to say what circumstances called forth many of his utterances and they are not preserved for us in the order in which they were delivered. The Hebrew text is often so corrupt that it is impossible to translate it correctly. A commentary is needed to guide us through the many difficulties. Nevertheless we can get a pretty clear picture of what the prophet had to say to the people of his day, and has to say to us.

(222) *Hosea* 1 and 3. THE TRAGEDY OF HOSEA'S MARRIAGE

The two chapters come from different pens, the first being part of a biographical account of Hosea's life, the second written by himself. It is best to take them in sequence as describing two stages of his experience. Most scholars think that Gomer was not unfaithful until after her marriage, though a few believe she had originally been a religious prostitute at one of the Baal shrines. The names given to Hosea's children were symbolic and part of his message to the nation. 'Jezreel' (1⁴) reminded them of the cruelty which had put the house of Jehu on the throne, of which dynasty Jeroboam II was the third representative; vengeance for that cruelty would be required—'God sows' (see 2 Kings 10¹¹). 'Lo-ruhamah' ('I will no more have mercy') in v. 6, and 'Lo-ammi' ('Ye are not my people') in v. 9, explain themselves. We should note in 2⁹ the argument of Hosea that Israel had run after the Baals for the very gifts that were bestowed upon men by Yahweh—this unfaithfulness was stupid and unnecessary. In Chapter 3 we are told of the buying back of Gomer, although this seems to have been an unlawful practice at that period (see Jer. 3¹). The discipline which Hosea finds it necessary to impose upon her suggests that Yahweh will recover and restore His faithless nation, but that the way of redemption will involve the bearing of suffering.

(223)* *Hosea* 4¹⁻¹¹. THE CHARGE AGAINST ISRAEL

The denunciations and pleadings of this chapter cannot be arranged in order, but they give us the spectacle of a nation in decay and corruption, due to its desertion of Yahweh. Punishment must fall upon both the priests and the people. There is much in this passage which reminds us of the words of Amos and the situation he had to face. It brings home to us the truth that Hosea did not contradict his predecessor; he supplemented his vision and message.

(224)* *Hosea* 6. ISRAEL'S FALSE PENITENCE

The opening three verses are words of contrition which Israel was forced to utter by reason of her troublous situation. Yet in spite of their beauty, we have to assume this plea was rejected. Yahweh knew that in the hearts of the people there was no real penitence and tells them their words were shallow. What He wants from them (and from Judah) is not sacrifice but 'chesed' (the word means 'dutiful love', something more than 'mercy'); not offerings but the knowledge of God (v. 6). Israel, in spite of her apparent penitence, is still sinful and unfaithful, and cannot expect to receive any remission of her punishment (vv. 7–10).

(225)   *Hosea* 11¹⁻⁹.   THE DIVINE FATHERHOOD

The prophet, throughout Chapters 4–13, makes use of two principal images. Sometimes Yahweh is Israel's Husband; sometimes Israel's Father. In this section we begin with the idea of Fatherhood. Yahweh's tenderness for His child is endless. He called Israel from Egypt to be His son, though he has proved a disloyal son going after the Baals. The more Yahweh has called to him through the prophets, the more he has wandered away. Yet it was Yahweh who taught him to walk, Yahweh who protected and healed him (*vv.* 1–3). Then the metaphor changes. Yahweh has treated Israel as a humane master would treat his oxen, leading them gently and when necessary easing the yoke (*v.* 4). Going back to the former figure of speech, we are told that punishment must fall upon the ungrateful son (the word 'not' in *v.* 5 should be omitted). Israel must go again into bondage, a bondage like that of Egypt, and its cities will be destroyed (*vv.* 5–7). Nevertheless, Yahweh cannot bear the thought that His chosen people should be destroyed like the cities of Admah and Zeboiim (*see* Deut. 29²²⁻³). He is God and not man, and His love and mercy must be satisfied (*vv.* 8–11).

(226)   *Hosea* 14.   THE DIVINE MERCY

The prophet makes a passionate appeal to Israel to repent and confess its sins. The people reply by declaring they will no longer put their trust in foreign alliances (Asshur = Assyria), or in idols, the work of their hands (*v.* 3). Yahweh therefore assures them of His forgiveness (*vv.* 4–7). His anger is turned away, and a new era of Yahweh's forgiveness is reaffirmed. God is to be an evergreen fir-tree which refreshes by its shadow and sustains by its fruit. In fact, however, Israel did not repent, and Yahweh had no justification for exercising such a forgiveness towards the Northern Kingdom. But the insight Hosea had derived from the tragedy of his married life carried him into further truth. However faithless Israel might be, the love of Yahweh would not change. There would be a restoration of His people, for His love could not be satisfied with less; but it could not take place until the nation had endured the purifying experience of suffering. That alone could bring about moral and spiritual regeneration (*vv.* 8–9).

F. *The End of the Northern Kingdom*

(227)   Both Amos and Hosea had predicted the coming doom of the Northern Kingdom. It seemed to them to be not far off. For the time being, Assyria might be quiet and unaggressive, but before long it would be sure to become a menace once more. Its ambitions could not be realized without a trial of strength with its formidable rival, Egypt. Under the influence of its neighbour Syria, Northern Israel precipitated the crisis. The leaders of the two small countries knew that, if Assyria chose to march against the Egyptians, its armies would have to pass through their territories. Their plan was to form a defensive alliance and to persuade the Southern Kingdom of Judah to join it. Judah was not willing. But Syria and Israel deemed the situation so serious that they sent their armies to compel Ahaz to act with them (the Syro-Ephraimite Invasion. *See* 2 Kings 16¹⁻⁹ and *para* 239). In despair, the leaders at Jerusalem turned to Assyria for help. Tiglath-Pileser was only too willing to seize the chance of intervening in the affairs of Palestine. He attacked Damascus, the capital of Syria, and Pekah, the king of Israel, was killed. In his place, the Assyrians put a puppet king on the throne, Hoshea, whose business was to rule on behalf of his overlords.

(228)   As time went on, however, Hoshea began to feel his strength, and decided to play the dangerous game of plotting with the enemies of his master. It was not long before the Assyrians found out that he was mixed up with the Egyptians in intrigues against them, and then they moved quickly. Tiglath-Pileser was now dead and Shalmaneser reigned in his stead. His armies moved once more into Palestine, and Hoshea, with his advisers, was shut up in the siege of Samaria which lasted for three years. By the time it was raised, 722 B.C., Sargon had taken the place of Shalmaneser, and was determined to take whatever steps were necessary to prevent any such trouble in the future. The Northern Kingdom had met its doom.

(229)   The custom of the day was for a conqueror to deport the leaders of a captured country, in order to prevent their attempting to recover its independence. Israel, therefore, was bereft of all its leaders and its potential leaders, and only those were left behind who were judged unlikely to cause any trouble. The captives were carried away, either to Assyria itself, or to one

of its dependent territories, and allowed to settle there. In such a case, it was usually not long before they became merged in the alien population to which they were sent and lost their own national identity. It was so with the leaders who were deported from Samaria. We describe them as the Lost Ten Tribes, and lost those tribes certainly were. They were absorbed beyond recovery in some other race, and no convincing evidence can support the claims, made in various parts of the world, that their descendants have been discovered today.

(230) We shall see how different, how unique, was the fate of the Southern Kingdom when its turn to be conquered came (*see Study Nine*). In spite of a similar deportation, one perhaps even more severe in character, a large number of the inhabitants retained their racial distinction and their descendants emerged from the Exile with their sense of nationality unimpaired. No wonder this was attributed to the overruling providence of Yahweh, working out His purpose through His chosen people.

(231) To take the place of the deported Israelites, captives from other territories in the Assyrian Empire were brought into Samaria. Naturally they carried with them their own religious beliefs and practices, but they were not unwilling to pay their respects to the god of the land in which they had been compelled to settle. Indeed, a priest of Yahweh gave them instruction, preparatory to their offering of homage to Israel's God. Before long, they began to intermarry with the poor and harmless Hebrews who had been left behind, and in due course they all became in effect one people. Nevertheless, they remained heartily disliked by the inhabitants of the Southern Kingdom. These orthodox Jews would not acknowledge them as kinsmen, and viewed their religion with the greatest suspicion. The tension was still present after the return from the Babylonian Exile, when Nehemiah strove to re-establish the Kingdom of Judah (*see paras*. 356–7), and even in the time of Christ the enmity had not abated. The Jews had no dealings with the Samaritans.

(232)* 2 *Kings* 17. THE FALL OF SAMARIA

It is suggested that this chapter should be read through for its description of the events referred to in the preceding paragraphs (227–31). The reasons given by the Old Testament for the collapse of the Northern Kingdom are religious. It had permitted the building of high places and the erection of pillars and asherim throughout the land. Idolatry was rampant, especially the 'worship of heaven', which was a recent development, a copying of the Assyrian worship of the sun and moon. Children were made 'to pass through the fire', which means that the new gods demanded child sacrifices, and, in the stress of these difficult times, it unhappily seems likely they were offered. At the root of all the trouble, Northern Israel walked in the 'sins of Jeroboam', who had divided the Kingdom, and, by his revival of the shrines o Bethel and Dan, encouraged a way of worship that rivalled the worship at the Temple in Jerusalem.

TEST QUESTIONS

1. Describe the part played by Elijah in the religious history of Israel.
2. (a) What were the chief points in the teaching of Amos? (b) In what respects did the message of Hosea (1) resemble and (2) differ from that of Amos?

Study Seven

Prophecy and Reform in Southern Israel

(233) After the division between Rehoboam and Jeroboam, the Southern Kingdom of Judah settled down to a relatively peaceful existence for over 200 years. In size it was no larger than the county of Yorkshire. Like its neighbour, it lay on the route between Assyria and Egypt, but it was not exposed to quite the same perils. On the one hand, its northern borders were protected by Israel; on the other, after the disastrous invasion of its territory by Pharaoh at the beginning of the period (1 Kings 14[25]), Judah had the sense to live at peace with Egypt. On the whole, the descendants of David gave the country good government, and both king and people remembered their covenant with Yahweh. True, the desire to conciliate the native gods of Canaan was not absent, but the matter never became as serious an issue as it did in Samaria. The Temple at Jerusalem exerted a healthy influence in the land, and was a constant reminder of the bond that linked the nation to Yahweh.

A. Isaiah—His Call and Message

(234) The public ministry of Isaiah covers the last forty years of the eighth century B.C. (roughly 740–700), and was exercised under the successive kingships of Jothan, Ahaz and Hezekiah. From a distance, Isaiah witnessed the decay and collapse of the Northern Kingdom and did not fail to read its warning lessons. Unlike the prophets we have considered so far, he moved easily amongst the aristocracy of Judah. A man of the city rather than of the countryside, he knew intimately the merchant princes and their pleasure-loving wives, and became the friend and adviser of kings and politicians. Often he was their critic. Part of his ministry, as he conceived it, was to bring pressure upon the policies of the nation, especially in regard to their relation to international affairs.

(235) *Isa. 6.* THE PROPHET'S CALL

Isaiah gives us his own account of how his ministry began. Uzziah was a 'good' king, under whose guidance Judah had wealth and power, and was not without some degree of culture. 'Their land also is full of silver and gold, neither is there any end of their treasures; their land also is full of horses, neither is there any end of their chariots' (Isa. 2⁷). But the king was a victim of leprosy. The prospect of his death—it happened in 740 B.C.—awakened a solemn mood in the young Isaiah as his thoughts turned to the future. He knew that, in spite of the glories of Uzziah's reign, Judah had not kept itself entirely free from the evils that were ruining Northern Israel, and that the same degrading influences were affecting its religion. A customary visit to the Temple brought to him a decisive spiritual experience.

(*a*) Isaiah saw a vision of Yahweh in His glory, high and lifted up. Although in some sense it was thought that Yahweh was localized in the Temple, Isaiah realized it was too small to contain Him. Moreover, the impression of His majesty and power was increased by the presence of superhuman beings, who were not able to behold His splendour with naked eyes, but had to be veiled, and who waited only to do His will (*vv.* 1–4).

(*b*) The holiness of God brought home to Isaiah in the strongest possible way his own personal imperfections and the fact of his identification with a sinful nation. He dwelt in the midst of a people of unclean lips and shared to some extent their pollution. Yet the holiness of Yahweh was also redemptive. The prophet's lips, wherein lay his sinfulness, were cleansed by means of a live coal taken from the divine altar, and he was assured of forgiveness (*vv.* 5–7).

(*c*) The consequence was something which is unique amongst the prophets of Israel. Instead of being pressed into the service of Yahweh, as the others were, in spite of personal reluctance and a sense of inadequacy, Isaiah volunteered to be sent to do the work in the world that so obviously needed to be done (*v.* 8).

(*d*) The task before the prophet was indeed difficult. The political horizon was darkened by the advance of Assyria, yet the danger was by no means fully realized. Isaiah would find that his ministry would seem to have the opposite effect upon people to that for which he hoped. It would increase their spiritual dullness: they would resent his words and harden their hearts: their obstinacy would make it impossible for them to receive the divine truth. The puzzled volunteer was compelled to ask how long this would go on. The answer was, 'Until the existing Israel has been annihilated'. Still, there was yet a ray of hope and comfort. As a felled tree retains a spark of vitality and can begin to grow again, so in Judah there would be left some indestructible element that God would be able to use (*vv.* 9–13). Here, so it seems, is a hint of the prophet's doctrine of the righteous remnant (*see para.* 242–4).

(236) THE SOVEREIGNTY OF YAHWEH OVER ALL NATIONS

The prophets were slowly leading the Hebrew people to the conception of monotheism. Though Elijah did not question the existence of other gods than Yahweh, on Mount Horeb he was told that Yahweh was the master of Syria as well as Israel (*see para.* 193(*c*)). Amos pronounced his judgements on the little nations around Israel in the name of Yahweh, implying that they too were under His control (*see para.* 212). Hosea even suggested that the great Assyrian Empire could be used by Yahweh to punish His chosen people for their sins (*see para.* 226). Isaiah carried the thought even further. All the nations belonged to Yahweh and could be used by Him. According to the old ways of thinking, the rise of Assyria could be interpreted as a sign that its gods were stronger than the gods of the countries it challenged and overran. Isaiah was not prepared to accept that notion. In his view, Yahweh was the God of Assyria also, and was using it as His instrument, the razor with which He would shave Israel (Isa. 7^{20}). His sovereignty extended over all the nations.

(237) THE HOLINESS OF YAHWEH

Following in the steps of his predecessors, Isaiah proclaimed the righteousness of Yahweh. He also stressed His holiness, which is not quite the same thing. It expresses the idea that Yahweh is altogether *different* from man. He is separated, not only by reason of His utter and absolute righteousness, but by His very being. Man was His creature and could only approach Him with awe, indeed with dread. Up to this point, Yahweh's people had approached Him with care, but not with the utter submission which Isaiah felt to be fitting. They must realize that He possessed a mysterious and incalculable power and could, if He wished, crush them into nothingness; therefore they should come near to Him with awe. He was the Almighty Creator, they but His puny creatures. Isaiah drove home this truth in word and life. As in the inaugural vision in the Temple, Yahweh is always high and lifted up, and man a sinful creature in the presence of the absolute being of God.

(238) *Isa.* 5¹⁻²⁴. THE PARABLE OF THE VINEYARD

Early in his ministry, Isaiah used this parable to confront the nation with a vision of the sorrow in the heart of Yahweh caused by its ingratitude and rejection of Himself. The parable may have been used as a song at some public festival and was intended to win the sympathy of the audience. Just as the vineyard must be abandoned to the wild beasts, so Israel, if she did not repent, must be left to the mercy of the nations round about.

Isaiah goes on to enumerate the sins of the upper classes of Judah; each passage is introduced by the word 'woe!' The wealthy landowners have absorbed the small properties of the peasant, and are becoming dissatisfied and spiritually blind. They are hardened in their sins and have lost their sense of moral distinctions. The politicians of Jerusalem are astute and self-satisfied, but unaware of the danger in which their country stands. The judges are corrupt and incapable. In a word, even the presence and influence of the Temple have failed to prevent in Judah the sins that were bringing about the downfall of the sister Kingdom.

B. *Isaiah and the Syro-Ephraimite Confederacy*

(239) This was the first of two crises in the life of Judah which brought Isaiah into public prominence. Syria and North Israel (Ephraim), tried to compel their southern neighbour to join them in a defensive alliance against the growing menace of Assyria (*see para.* 227). Judah was not willing to throw in its lot with them, and in consequence was attacked by Pekah of Israel and Rezin of Syria (734 B.C.). The two kings marched against Jerusalem and besieged the city until, in despair, King Ahaz was driven to appeal to Assyria for help. By his appeal to Tiglath-Pileser he had succeeded in making his country a vassal of the Assyrian Empire.

(240) Unlike his prophetic predecessors, Isaiah moved with ease amongst the politicians of his day and was at home in the royal court. In this emergency, he proffered his advice to the king, counselling him to have nothing to do either with Assyria or any other foreign power. The Syro-Ephraimite invasion, he

H

assured him, would come to nothing. Pekah and Rezin were not worth bothering about—'two tails of smoking firebrands'—'fagends' (Isa. 7⁴). As a politician, Isaiah was wise enough to see that what hope of safety Judah had, depended upon its lying low and not getting mixed up in any foreign entanglements. As a prophet, he based his attitude upon his religious confidence. Judah was Yahweh's people and it ought to trust Him to bring about its deliverance. Any attempt to bolster up its position by relying upon the help of other nations was a denial of His sovereignty. Isaiah did not regard the armies of Syria and Ephraim as having been chosen by Yahweh for the purpose of chastising His own people; he could, therefore, exhort Ahaz and his court to trust in the divine protection and walk humbly before Him. To appeal to Assyria was to trust in the machinery of politics rather than have faith in God.

(241) *Isa.* 7¹⁻¹⁷. ISAIAH'S INTERVIEW WITH AHAZ

Amid the general panic caused by the threatened siege of Jerusalem by the armies of Pekah and Rezin, the prophet was bidden by Yahweh to meet Ahaz as he was inspecting his defences. He was to promise him deliverance, but only on condition that he put his faith in Yahweh. 'If ye will not believe (have faith), surely ye shall not be established' (*v.* 9). With him, the prophet took his son, called Shear-jashub, a name which was intended to be a symbol. Its meaning is 'A remnant shall return', (that is, to Yahweh), and it had probably served as a text for many of Isaiah's earlier discourses. On this occasion, the presence of the boy was intended to remind the king of what the prophet had said. It suggests one of Isaiah's characteristic doctrines— that, whatever happened, there would remain at the heart of the nation a loyal core (*see para.* 242).

If Ahaz wanted a sign of Yahweh's determination to defend His people, he could have it. The king refused to make any request, whereupon, in the name of Yahweh, Isaiah himself offered a sign. A young woman standing by ('virgin' =any woman of marriageable age), was to bear a child. In spite of the surrounding state of alarm, when he was born she would give him a name that would express her faith in the deliverance which she was sure was about to come. The name 'Immanuel' meant 'God with us'. By her attitude Ahaz was to know that there were braver hearts in Israel than his own. Before the child should be old enough to make an intelligent choice between good and evil,

that is to say in four or five years' time, the two kings of whom
Ahaz was so terrified would have lost their power.

(242) ISAIAH'S DOCTRINE OF THE RIGHTEOUS REMNANT

As we have seen above, this is one of Isaiah's dominant ideas.
It was not an entirely new way of thinking, though he gave it a
place in his teaching it had not received before. Elijah had been
made aware of a loyal nucleus of righteous souls at the heart of
a nation that had been disloyal to Yahweh. There were 7,000 in
Israel who had not bowed the knee to Baal.

(243) The prophetic teaching made the rise of such a doctrine
natural, and, perhaps, inevitable. Yahweh's covenant was with
the whole nation. But the more the prophets insisted upon the
righteousness of His demands, the higher the standard of conduct
this required of His people, the less likelihood there was of the
nation as a whole fulfilling their side of the agreement. Any hope
of a loyal obedience must be transferred to a minority within the
nation. How far this line of thought took hold of Isaiah can be
seen in his naming of his son, Shear-jashub (*see para.* 241). It
became the theme of many of his addresses and probably took
a far greater place in his thought than the records suggest.

(244) It is possible that, at the time of the Syro-Ephraimite
invasion, Isaiah hoped that Judah as a whole might repent and
turn to God, and thus would become the Righteous Remnant of
the whole family of Israelites. The Southern Kingdom would
then escape the judgement of Yahweh. When this hope failed,
he pinned his faith to a loyal core within Judah itself. He himself
gathered together a band of disciples and committed his teaching
to them, which we may regard as an attempt on his part to create
and maintain the Remnant (Isa. 8[16-18]). In later studies we shall
see how this idea of a Saved Remnant became also that of a
Saving Remnant, in the thought of Isaiah of Babylon (*see paras*
326ff.), and had its influence upon Christ's idea of the Kingdom
of God, a nucleus in the heart of the world through which God
would redeem mankind.

C. *Isaiah and Sennacherib's Invasion*

(245) The second crisis which brought Isaiah to the fore was
the siege of Jerusalem in 701 B.C. by the armies of Assyria. By
this time, the prophet had secured a position of some influence in

Jerusalem. He was in constant touch with the king and his advisers, and aware of the various intrigues that were taking place with neighbouring countries. He had his own distinctive point of view, which no doubt he pressed whenever there was an opportunity. All attempts to bolster up the strength of Judah by forming a series of foreign alliances was to him a denial of faith in Yahweh. He had no use either for those who sought help from the Assyrians, or for those who turned towards Egypt. The safety of the nation lay in repentance, and in reliance upon its God. 'In returning and rest shall ye be saved: in quietness and confidence shall be your strength' (Isa. 30^{15}). This was the policy he urged when the Assyrian menace rose to its height. Judah's best course was one of neutrality, for anything that Egypt had to offer to counter-balance the armies of Assyria would prove vain. 'The Egyptians are men and not gods: and their horses flesh and not spirit' (Isa. 31^3). Yahweh's might surpassed by far the power of every foreign promise of help, and Judah must put its trust in Him.

(246). 2 *Kings* 18$^{1-12}$.   THE ACCESSION OF HEZEKIAH

Hezekiah was now on the throne, in succession to his father Ahaz. He was the first king since David to receive the unqualified approval of the compilers of the Books of Kings. In matters of religion, he supported the better element in the nation and instituted a strenuous campaign to clear away the worship of idols. In some respects he seems to have anticipated the Reformation of Josiah (*see para.* 262), by suppressing the 'high places' and centralizing worship at the Temple. An old image of a serpent, which was reputed to go back to the time of Moses, Nehushtan by name, was broken in pieces. It is quite likely that, in these reforms, he had the backing of some of the citizens of Northern Israel who had escaped to Judah after the fall of Samaria, in the hope that by so doing they would be able to preserve their religious loyalty. We can well believe that they did not come empty-handed, but brought with them the records of the preaching of Amos and Hosea, and also still earlier documents giving accounts of the Patriarchs, the Judges, Samuel, and Elijah (including the document E; *see para.* 442).

(247)   THE PREOCCUPATION OF ASSYRIA

After the fall of Samaria, Sargon, who succeeded Shalmaneser on the Assyrian throne, seems to have decided that he had nothing to fear from Judah, though he cannot have been unaware that intrigues were going on with Egypt against him. At any rate, Hezekiah was left in peace until after Sargon's death in 705 B.C. Sennacherib, who followed him, was for the time being fully occupied in Assyria, dealing with trouble stirred up by Merodach-baladan (*Kings* spells it Berodach-baladan: the spelling of *Isaiah* in 39¹ is the correct one). This gave Judah the opportunity of undertaking even more serious plots with Egypt.

(248)   2 *Kings* 20¹⁻¹¹.   THE SICKNESS OF HEZEKIAH

Scholars agree that the events here recorded must have happened *before* Sennacherib's campaign (Chapters 18 and 19). 'The dial of Ahaz' evidently refers to a flight of steps which bore his name and served as a sun-dial. Probably when the shadows fell on each step, certain hours of the day were indicated. For the shadow to go backward was a reversal of the natural direction, and taken to be a sign that, contrary to what might be expected, Hezekiah was to recover.

(249)   2 *Kings* 20¹²⁻¹⁹.   THE VISIT OF MERODACH-BALADAN

As part of his attempt to stir up trouble for Sennacherib, Merodach-baladan used Hezekiah's recovery as a pretext for visiting him. Possibly in order to assure the visitor that he was ready to help him against Sennacherib, Hezekiah showed him his treasures. This disclosure of Judah's resources to an alien, and a potential enemy, earned from Isaiah a severe disapproval.

(250)   2 *Kings* 18¹³⁻19³⁷.   SENNACHERIB'S INVASION

To get a perfectly clear picture of Sennacherib's dealings with Judah is not easy. There are four accounts:

(*a*) A brief record, 2 Kings 18¹³⁻¹⁶.

(*b*) A longer account in which Jerusalem was threatened by the personal visit of delegates from Sennacherib, 2 Kings 18¹⁷⁻19⁹ᵃ.

(*c*) A further story in which Sennacherib's demands were carried in a letter, 2 Kings 19⁹ᵇ⁻³⁴.

(*d*) Sennacherib's own version of events which has been preserved for us.

Various attempts have been made to sort out the divergences in these accounts, but it is a matter on which there is no unanimous verdict. The reconstruction that follows here is not the only one that can be made.

It looks as if Sennacherib decided to subdue the strong places of Judah one by one. With his main army he laid siege to Lachish, whence he sent a detachment to Jerusalem under three Assyrian officials, the Tartan (commander-in-chief), the Rabsaris and the Rabshakeh (chief officials). The last acted as the spokesman. In order to demoralize the city, the Assyrians insisted on conducting their parley with Hezekiah in Hebrew, and, so that all the people could hear, the Rabshakeh insolently asked why the city was daring to resist Sennacherib. If it was because they trusted in Yahweh, they ought to remember that Hezekiah had been busy pulling down His altars at the high places. This was a plain sign that the king did not trust in Him. In any case, the Assyrians were far too strong to be defeated and Jerusalem had no real grounds for believing in the superior strength of Yahweh (2 Kings 18$^{17\text{-}37}$).

In spite of the reassuring words of Isaiah (2 Kings 19$^{1\text{-}9}$), it would seem that Hezekiah had to pay such a heavy tribute to the Assyrians that he was compelled to despoil the Temple (2 Kings 18$^{15\text{-}16}$). It is also possible that the enemy demanded in addition the surrender of the city, which the king refused.

For some reason or other, Sennacherib decided to move against Jerusalem a second time. Whether the tribute money had been withheld, or whether the Assyrian was alarmed by the appearance of an Egyptian army, hinted at in 19^9, we cannot say. This time he sent his demand for the surrender of the city in a letter. In the hour of his distress, with the Assyrians at his very gates, Hezekiah decided to consult Isaiah. The prophet assured him that Jerusalem would not fall and that the invader would return by the way he had come. For Yahweh's honour was at stake. He was making use of Assyria as His instrument, but Assyria was becoming too arrogant. In his mind, Isaiah identified Jerusalem with the remnant of Judah which he was sure Yahweh would save. Since His Temple was there, it would be preserved against all foes. This conviction gave rise to the belief in the inviolability of Jerusalem, a doctrine we shall meet again in time of Jeremiah (*para.* 291).

On the other hand, Isaiah predicted that disaster would befall the invader. That some calamity did come upon the Assyrian army is attested by Egyptian records, as well as in the Old Testament accounts. One account says that mice gnawed the bowstrings of the Assyrians and, since the mouse was the symbol of pestilence, this might be a way of saying that some sort of plague

broke out which compelled the armies to make their way home.
The Hebrew version simply says that an angel (= messenger) of
the Lord smote the Assyrian camp and destroyed many lives.

Note: A parallel account of events in the reign of Hezekiah is
also given in Isa. 36–9, but it is somewhat less detailed.

(251) *Isa.* 1¹⁻²⁰. YAHWEH'S CHARGE AGAINST HIS PEOPLE

Although this section is used as an introduction to Isaiah's
message, most scholars think it belongs to the time of Sennacherib's invasion. This is strongly suggested by the wretched state
of the country. The opening verse is a kind of title. In *v.* 2,
Yahweh begins to set forth His complaints against His people,
calling upon heaven and earth to listen. The sons He has brought
up have been guilty of rebellion and ingratitude, a sad contrast
to the faithfulness of the animal world (*vv.* 2–3). The prophet
proceeds to drive home the charge of rebellion and alleges that
the calamities that are vexing the land are sufficient evidence of
Judah's sinfulness. Nothing but the mercy of Yahweh has saved
them from a fate like that of Sodom and Gomorrah (*vv.* 4–9; *see
para.* 45). Israel still imagines that Yahweh can be propitiated
with religious ceremonies and ritual, whereas what He requires
is a moral reformation and righteousness in social and public
affairs (*vv.* 10–17). Finally Yahweh summons the nation to a trial
at law so that His righteousness may be indicated. Yet there is a
gracious invitation to forgiveness. 'Though your sins be as
scarlet, they shall be as white as snow; though they be red like
crimson, they shall be as wool.' Israel can have prosperity as a
reward of obedience, or destruction as the penalty of rebellion
(*vv.* 18–20).

(252)* *Isa.* 31. THE FUTILITY OF TRUST IN EGYPT

This chapter illustrates Isaiah's conviction of the uselessness
of turning to Egypt for help against the Assyrians. All the
material resources of Egypt are as nothing compared with the
power of Yahweh, and those who treat with her will only bring
trouble and evil upon Jerusalem (*vv.* 1–3). Yet Yahweh is determined to hold Judah in His grip, as a lion holds its prey, and He
will not allow the city to fall (*vv.* 4–7). In the end the Assyrian
invasion will be repelled by the personal intervention of Israel's
God (*vv.* 8–9).

D. *Isaiah's Messianic Prophecies*

(253)   In certain passages, Isaiah looks forward to the coming of a great deliverer, sent by Yahweh to bring about a golden age for Israel. The general belief was that the one who would rescue the nation from its embarrassments, and lift it to a new level of prosperity, would be a member of the house of David. In the centuries that followed, especially in periods of darkness, the hope grew stronger and stronger. Finally God did intervene in history to redeem mankind through Jesus. But the Messiah who came was not the Messiah who was expected. Nevertheless the early Christians realized that Jesus did in truth fulfil these Messianic aspirations, but at a deeper level and in a far richer way than had been anticipated.

The term 'the Messiah' means 'the anointed one'. Although in the following passages the *idea* of the Messiah is undoubtedly present, it is curious that Isaiah does not use the actual title. On the other hand, we shall find it used by the Second Isaiah to describe Cyrus the Persian (Isa. 45[1]; *see para.* 321).

(254)   *Isa.* 9[1-7].   THE COMING OF THE MESSIANIC KING

It is generally agreed that this passage comes from the time of King Ahaz, possibly when the Northern Kingdom had been invaded by Assyria (734 B.C. *See* 2 Kings 15[29]). There had been great slaughter and some of the Israelites had been carried into exile. Judah was faced with the question: Would its citizens suffer a similar fate? Isaiah replied with a vision of hope. Victory would be with Israel and not Assyria. The devastated land would rejoice with the joy of harvest. (*Verse* 3 (AV) reads 'Thou hast *not* increased the joy', which is not logical: the RV gives the correct sense by leaving out the negative). A son of the house of David would bring about this happier state of affairs. Looking backwards, it seemed to Isaiah and his contemporaries that the reign of David had been one of almost undisturbed peace, and that a return of that tranquillity would come with the looked-for prince of that lineage. His names were a revelation of his accomplishments—Wonderful Counsellor (wise in judgement and administration), Mighty God (powerful with the power of Yahweh behind him), Everlasting Father (caring for his children), Prince of Peace (subduing their enemies).

(255) *Isa.* 11¹⁻⁹. THE MESSIAH AND HIS KINGDOM

After the overthrow of the world power of Assyria, a new order
of life would be established. Possessed of the qualities of a perfect
ruler, the deliverer would proceed to set up an ideal government.
Verse 3 seems to suggest that, not only will he possess himself a
true personal religion; he will also be quick to sense its presence
in others. In his judgements of men, he will not depend merely
upon what he sees and hears, their external conduct; he will be
able to discern their moral condition. For the oppressed and
defenceless, he will have a special care. Righteousness and
faithfulness are to be the strength of his government, and he will
institute an order of peace that will affect even the brute creation.
It will make the lion lie down with the lamb.

(256) *Isa.* 32¹⁻⁸. THE MESSIANIC COMMONWEALTH

The prophet looks forward to a new age in which the upper
classes will be reformed and men of position and power will have
developed a new sense of social responsibility. They will regard
it as their first duty to give protection to the poor (*vv.* 1–2).
Public opinion will be enlightened and purified, and, with a
quickened moral perception, the people will no longer be misled
easily (*vv.* 3–4). False class distinctions will go, and men will
find their proper level according to character (*v.* 5). The fool
(vile person, or churl) and the liberal man are set in contrast;
people will no longer fail to distinguish between the two (*vv.* 6–8).

(257)* *Isa.* 2²⁻⁴. UNIVERSAL RELIGION IN THE MESSIANIC AGE

In the coming golden age, Mount Zion (Jerusalem) will take
its place and be pre-eminent amongst the mountains of the
world because it is the acknowledged seat of Yahweh-worship
(*v.* 2). People will come from all nations, eager to learn of the
true religion and ready to walk in the ways ordained by Yahweh.
The Jewish people are not amongst those who are destined to
create a world empire, for the reign of Yahweh is to be established
by His word and not by the sword (*v.* 3). His authority will be
accepted by the nations and bring an end to their disputes. Thus
there will be a universal reign of peace. (This passage occurs also
in Micah 4¹⁻⁴.)

E. *The Prophet Micah*

(258) Isaiah's contemporary, Micah, was a man of the village rather than the cities. Throughout his message, we are conscious of his concern for the dwellers in the countryside, the peasants oppressed by the wealthy landowners who were steadily getting into their own hands the property which once had belonged to ordinary families. Many of the truths proclaimed by Amos, Hosea, and Isaiah found a place in his teaching. We find the same denunciation of the sins of the nation and the same prediction of a coming judgement. Like Isaiah, Micah believed in a righteous remnant that would survive and prosper. As perhaps we should expect from him, he foresees the coming of the Deliverer, not from the city of Jerusalem, but from the small village of Bethlehem.

(259) *Micah* 6[1-8]. YAHWEH'S CONTROVERSY WITH HIS PEOPLE

The picture in the prophet's mind is that of a Court of Law to which the nation is summoned to answer the charges brought against it by its God. The works of nature are to act as judge. The people can do nothing but plead guilty. How can they conciliate an offended deity? He does not require ritual or sacrifice, not even the sacrifice of their firstborn. *Verse* 8, which has been described as the greatest verse of the Old Testament, expresses Yahweh's demands and seems to sum up the very essence of the message of the eighth-century prophets. 'What doth the Lord require of thee, but to do justly (Amos), and to love mercy (Hosea), and to walk humbly with thy God?' (Isaiah).

F. *Deuteronomy and the Reform of Religion*

We are now to consider a practical effort, on a nation-wide scale, to give effect to the teaching of the four great prophets whose work we have been studying.

(260) The reign of Manasseh of Judah lasted for some forty-five years (692–638 B.C.), and even the compilers of *Kings*, who were partial to the Judean monarchy, rank him as lower than Ahab of Israel. The worship of Yahweh was not definitely and openly suppressed, but every encouragement was given to foreign

cults. It is more than likely that Manasseh had to acknowledge the overlordship of Assyria and, in the desire to stand well with his masters, took up with enthusiasm the cult of Assyrian deities, the sun, moon, and stars. Divination was practised on a large scale and there seems to have been a recurrence of child sacrifice. The loyal followers of Yahweh, especially those who had been influenced by the teaching of Amos, Hosea, Isaiah, and Micah, must have been, to say the least, unpopular. Many were subjected to persecution, and some met their death as martyrs, including, so the tradition runs, Isaiah himself. It would suit Manasseh's policy to be rid of those whose religious views were likely to make them opponents of his subservience to Assyria. The loyal followers of the prophets wisely went underground for a time, and we can well believe that they spent this period collecting and writing down the words of their masters.

(261) An opportunity for improvement came with the accession of Josiah, who, though a mere lad of eight, was growing up with sensitive and wise understanding. He himself was a sincere worshipper of Yahweh and realized the necessity of ridding the land of foreign influences. Imported religions must go! To be strong the nation must have a common faith, and that faith must be a revived loyalty to Yahweh. The weakening power of Assyria, and the recovery of Judah's political independence, together with the underground work of the followers of the prophets, gave him his opportunity.

(262) 2 *Kings* 22–3³⁰. THE LAW BOOK AND THE REFORMATION

In the eighteenth year of his reign (621 B.C.) Josiah ordered a repair of the Temple, which was carried out under the Priest Hilkiah. Workmen discovered a roll which presumably had been hidden by some loyal follower of Yahweh during the reign of Manasseh. On the basis of the prophetic teaching, it set out a clear code of conduct for the life of the nation of Yahweh. After consultation with Shaphan the Scribe, the king was notified of the discovery, and he decided to make it the basis of a religious reformation. A prophetess, Huldah, warned him that Judah would not escape the judgement that it deserved, but that Josiah himself, as a reward for his efforts, would not have to see the coming doom. Representatives of the nation were gathered together at Jerusalem and the new regulations put into operation. How far this attempt met with success is a matter of doubt. In all probability it only partially achieved its objectives. When we come to the ministry of Jeremiah, we shall see his sense of disappointment that it had not gone deep enough (*see para.* 285).

(263) THE PRINCIPLES OF JOSIAH'S REFORMATION

(*a*) The temple at Jerusalem had been used for the 'mixed' worship which Manasseh had encouraged. Baal worship and Assyrian worship had taken place alongside that of Israel's true God. Therefore, the sacred building must be cleansed and purified.

(*b*) The Valley of Himmon, just outside the city, had been defiled by the offering of child sacrifice there. It was to be declared polluted for all time. In fact, it became a rubbish dump, known in the New Testament period as Ge-henna.

(*c*) The high places, the little local shrines which had been erected all over the country for the worship of Yahweh, had also been used for Baal worship and the immoral rites of Canaanite religion had been practised there. They were to be suppressed.

(*d*) All worship of Yahweh was to be centralized at Jerusalem where it could be properly supervised, and no sacrifice was to be offered except in the Temple, 'the place which Yahweh thy God shall choose'.

(*e*) Sacrifices were to be offered only by priests of the Tribe of Levi. The priests from the suppressed high places were brought to the Temple and given subordinate duties.

(*f*) Every loyal Jew was commanded to observe three annual feasts at Jerusalem—Passover, Pentecost and Tabernacles (or Booths).

(264) THE BOOK OF DEUTERONOMY

It is now generally believed that the book discovered in the Temple was our book of *Deuteronomy* (The Second Law), or at any rate a part of it (Deut. 12–19[13]). The book as we have it was probably compiled by a group of writers, and it purports to be a long speech delivered by Moses to Israel shortly before his death. Obviously, however, many of the ideas in it only developed in the centuries after Moses' death. The motive of the speech is to remind the people of the Covenant which bound them to Yahweh. The troubles that had befallen Israel were the result of its disloyalty to that bond, but, if only the nation would return to its obedience, all would be well. Indeed, Yahweh appeals for that return, using as His ground the great mercy He has shown to His people.

(265)   Before we turn to our selected readings, we may note certain characteristics of *Deuteronomy*.

(*a*) The final editors, in their idea of God, have reached the stage known as 'monotheism'. They are no longer content to leave other nations to worship their own national deities. Yahweh is unwilling to share His power and authority with the gods of other peoples, even of Assyria or Egypt. He alone is the true God of all mankind (Deut. 4^{35}, 6^4). Hence the book has an attitude of intolerance towards other religions and pours scorn upon the gods of wood and stone, which neither see, hear, eat, nor smell, but are merely the work of human hands.

(*b*) Yahweh must be worshipped with the proper ritual. Because ritual has become degraded in Manasseh's reign, it has to be reformed, and it was assumed in the book that the principles of reform had been laid down by Moses himself. Worship and sacrifice, as we have seen, were to be centred in the Temple. *Deuteronomy* regards sacrifice, not as the offering to Yahweh of something He is needing, but as a token of gratitude and joy. Details are given for the burnt offerings and the peace offerings, both occasions of merrymaking.

(*c*) Because Yahweh is a moral God, social righteousness is one of His first demands from His followers. So regulations must be laid down to guide the Israelite in the right treatment of his fellow Israelites, of strangers and slaves and criminals. The standard of *Deuteronomy*, both in regard to family life and the position of women, is very high, and throughout the legislation there breathes a fine humanitarian spirit towards strangers (those who were not Jews), and the poor (*see* Deut. 15^{19}, 20^{19}).

(*d*) For the first time, Hebrew religion found a basis in a book. The words of the prophets, which carried divine authority, were now written down. The way of Yahweh had been revealed, and future generations would be able to turn back and consult the records.

(266)   *Deut*. 6.   THE FUNDAMENTAL IDEAS OF DEUTERONOMY

The motives behind the laws were the fear of Yahweh and the importance of keeping them in order to receive benefits from Him (*vv.* 1–3). Israelites must give an undivided loyalty to Him, for He is the only God. They must keep His words in their hearts and teach them to their children (*vv.* 4–9). Beguiled by the material blessings of the Promised Land, they will be tempted to forget their duties and to attribute their gifts to other gods (*vv.* 10–15). To reduce this danger, when they enter Canaan, they must drive out the inhabitants (*vv.* 16–19). Future generations are to have explained to them that the Laws are the nation's response to Yahweh, in return for His deliverance of them from bondage, and are His way of preserving them as a nation (*vv.* 20–5).

(267)* *Deut.* 7¹·¹¹.   THE DISTINCTIVENESS OF ISRAEL

No friendliness must be shown to the people of the land (Canaanites), lest Israel be drawn into idolatry. The symbols of pagan religion must be destroyed. Israel has been chosen and is beloved by Yahweh, and must therefore keep His laws. This is *Deuteronomy's* doctrine of election.

(268)   *Deut.* 12.   THE LAW OF THE ONE ALTAR

After an introductory verse, we have a first statement of the Law of the One Altar. This reform stands in contrast to the customs of the Canaanites with their numerous high places (*vv.* 2–7). There follows a second statement of the same law, this time set in contrast to the practice of the wilderness wanderings, 'the things that we do here this day' (*vv.* 8–12). A third statement of the law is combined with a list of the offerings to be brought (*vv.* 13–19). Because of the confinement of sacrifice to one place only, it was necessary to sanction the non-ritual slaughter and eating of animals. Up to this time, the killing of domestic animals had been a religious matter, carried out in connexion with a nearby shrine. But now it will be impossible to go to Jerusalem on each occasion. Therefore, non-religious slaughter is to be permitted to those who do not live near the one altar, provided that the blood of the slain creature is poured upon the ground. Since the blood represented the principle of life, it was regarded as too sacred to be eaten. It belonged to God and had to be poured out as an offering to Him. This refusal to eat blood persists amongst Jews even to this day.

TEST QUESTIONS

(Send answers to TWO *questions to your tutor)*

1. Show how the teaching of Isaiah is bound up with the political events of his time.
2. What do you think Isaiah intended to convey to his own generation in the passages expressing Messianic hopes?
3. (*a*) Show the importance of the Book of Deuteronomy. (*b*) In what ways do you connect it with Josiah's Reformation?

Study Eight

Jeremiah and the Fall of Jerusalem

A. The Fall of the Southern Kingdom

(269) As the prophetess Huldah had predicted, Josiah's zeal for reformation was not sufficient to re-create the spirit of Judah and make it strong enough to ward off the disaster which threatened. It was becoming obvious during his reign that the power of Assyria was weakening, but another world empire was about to take its place and assert its mastery over Yahweh's people. Before we can study the great prophet Jeremiah, we must get as clear a picture as we can of this situation.

(270) The immediate danger to Judah came from the Scythians, hordes of wild and barbarous people from north of the Crimea, who began to move southwards and to ravage the territories under Assyrian rule. About the year 630 B.C., a body of them swept through Syria and reached as far as Ashkelon. It is said they were only prevented from attacking Egypt by the gift of a ransom. Their approach brought a serious threat to Judah and we can catch something of the terror they created in the earlier writings of Jeremiah (*see paras*. 282–3). They did not trouble Judah beyond this, but one of the effects of this invasion was to loosen the control of Assyria over the Palestinian states.

(271) Nearer home, Assyria had to reckon with the revolt of Babylon. Nabopolassar was able to establish himself as an independent king in 625 B.C. and began the dynasty of the Chaldeans (Babylonians). He set himself to destroy utterly the power of Assyria, a project in which he was helped by the Medes. Assyria found an ally in her ancient enemy, Egypt, which was probably anxious to prevent the creation of a still more powerful foe, a Babylonian Empire. But Assyria was still too weak. The decisive blow came when the Medes marched against Nineveh and sacked it in 612 B.C. Though remnants of the Assyrian armies still fought on, they had no real chance of recovery.

The vassal states awaited the fall of Assyria in the hope of regaining their freedom and independence, and, further south, under Pharaoh Necho, Egypt also was making the most of the opportunity. Its armies marched again and again against the Babylonians, either in the hope of weakening their growing power, or in order to capture for itself some of the provinces of Assyria. In 608 B.C., Pharaoh tried to take possession of Syria. Josiah of Judah went to meet him at Megiddo. There is a certain mystery about the incident (2 Kings 23^{29}); we cannot be sure why Josiah took a stand against the Egyptians. The most likely explanation is that he was resisting Pharaoh's attempt to bring Judah under Egyptian influence and to exact tribute. At any rate, it brought to an end the finest reign Judah had known in its history as a separate kingdom. Josiah was slain, possibly murdered, and his body sent back in a chariot to Jerusalem.

(272)   Judah then fell under the influence of Egypt. Necho deposed Josiah's successor, Jehoahaz, and replaced him with his own puppet, Jehoiakim (originally his name was Eliakim, but the Pharaoh changed it to this, which means 'Yahweh-has-promoted'). Egypt exacted from Judah a very heavy tribute and its citizens in consequence were loaded with a grievous weight of taxation. We can hardly blame Jehoiakim for trying to play off Babylon and Egypt against each other. Meanwhile, the Egyptian forces penetrated to the upper Euphrates, where they met the new and vigorous troops of the Babylonians under their brilliant young general, Nebuchadrezzar. At Carchemish (605 B.C.) he routed both the Egyptians and the remnants of Assyria, and made ineffective any further opposition from these sources. The sudden death of Nabopolassar provided an opportunity for Nebuchadrezzar to take possession of the throne of Babylon.

(273)   There fell to him the task of consolidating the new Babylonian empire. Its western tributaries were still in a state of unrest. In Judah, Jehoiakim resented the new overlordship and, in spite of the advice of Jeremiah the prophet, plotted and intrigued against it. In 598 B.C. the Babylonian king was sufficiently provoked to march against Jerusalem; but, by the time of his arrival, Jehoiakim was dead, though he lived long enough to realize how futile was his hope of Egyptian support. The wrath of Nebuchadrezzar fell upon the unfortunate son of the Judean king, a mere youth of eighteen, named Jehoiachin (or Coniah). Jerusalem was compelled to surrender and to accept the hard terms imposed upon it by its conqueror. According to the custom of the times, the king, the queen-mother, the nobility, many of the priests, in a word, all the potential leaders of the city, were transported to Babylon (597 B.C.).

(274) Only the bad figs were left behind, to quote the phrase used by Jeremiah. The Babylonians put on the throne the weak Zedekiah. Jeremiah repeatedly pointed out to him and his advisers that, in view of the demonstration of Babylonian might, the only possible course now open for Judah was one of complete submission to its conquerors. Nevertheless, Zedekiah allowed himself to be swayed by counsellors who thought otherwise, and proceeded to plot against the occupying power. The result was inevitable. Once again Jerusalem was besieged by the armies of Babylon. For a moment it looked as if Zedekiah's pathetic hopes might be realized, for the Egyptians did make an attempt to throw off the besiegers. But it came to nothing. The city was left to bear its own burden, isolated and helpless. Within, there were constant dissensions between those partial to Babylon, and those who still were attracted to Egypt.

(275) For nearly two years the city managed to hold out; but at last, when not a scrap of bread was left, it had no alternative but to surrender (586 B.C.). Zedekiah, with some of his supporters, made an attempt to break away, only to be caught by the Babylonian chariots in the plain of Jericho. The wretched king was forced by his captors to watch his sons slain before his eyes and then, having himself been blinded, was carried away a prisoner to Babylon. With him was taken a further convoy of Jerusalem's citizens, and this time only the poorest of the poor were left behind.

(276) The city itself was razed to the ground. Over the pathetic remnant that remained in the devastated country, the Babylonians placed a governor of Jewish blood, Gedaliah, though they took the precaution of moving his seat of government to Mizpah. Still, the survivors were not cured of their love of intrigue. The land was full of quarrels. Finally, a young pretender to the throne, Ishmael, supported by an armed gang of Ammonites, treacherously murdered Gedaliah in his house at Mizpah. A group of Jews who were loyal to the governor, and who feared the wrath of Nebuchadrezzar, fled for safety to Egypt, carrying with them the prophet Jeremiah. For the next fifty years, the history of Judah is a blank; all we know is that it remained a dependent part of the Babylonian Empire.

(277) 2 *Kings* 23²⁹–25²⁶. LAST EVENTS IN JUDAH

The account given here is a brief and condensed summary, but adequate for our purpose. A more detailed record is preserved in *Jeremiah*.

I

B. *The Prophet Jeremiah—the First Phase*

(278)   Jeremiah was born about 650 B.C. into a priestly family of Anathoth, in the territory of Benjamin, about three miles from Jerusalem. Amongst his ancestors may have been Abiathar the priest, who survived David's massacre at Nob (*see para.* 142), and Eli the priest of Shiloh (*see para.* 127), though he himself does not appear to have acted as a priest. Growing up in the reign of Manasseh, he witnessed the reformation of Josiah, taking an active part in the troublesome and confused years that brought the Southern Kingdom to its close. In character, he was a sensitive and lonely soul; always upon his conscience lay the weight of his own sins and the sins of his people. The message he had to deliver in the name of Yahweh was one which was bound to be anything but popular, and he knew it. At a time when the people of Judah were clinging desperately to the slenderest rays of hope they could find, he had to tell them that most of their trust was misplaced. Small wonder he was greatly disliked, even hated and persecuted, for he could not utter the pleasant words and insincere comfort in which people would have rejoiced. But however heavy the strain upon him, he never flinched from his duty, never ran away from his obligation, never lacked courage.

(279)   Many of the ideas in the message of Jeremiah had already been proclaimed by his predecessors, though there were distinctive and unique elements. Amongst the prophets of the Old Testament, he stands alone by reason of the revelation he has given us of his own self and his intimate relationship with God. Religion to him was a personal and spiritual experience. Made for human friendship and love, he discovered it was the will of God that he should not marry or share the delights and comfort of a home. Such things would have meant much to him and would have offered him a refuge from a bleak and hostile world. More and more the circumstances of his life and ministry isolated him and drove him to depend utterly upon God. In his writings, he lets us see into his very heart, and reveals the very essence of the faith that sustained him.

(280)   His ministry involved him in misunderstanding and loneliness, in much suffering and apparent failure. From the beginning he distrusted his own power. He felt he was 'but a boy', in experience and wisdom even more than in years. Yet

he was so made that he could not help loving the very men he had to condemn. As he shouldered his heavy and heartbreaking responsibilities, we are permitted to see what his religion meant to him—something very individual, spiritual, intimate, warm, loving. His great contribution to the world is not the immediate application of his vision of divine truth to the complexities of his day, but the deepened conception he has given us of the very nature of religion. It is no surprise that he has been regarded as the greatest character in the whole of the Old Testament. In the judgement of very many Christians who have come to know him, no one comes nearer to the spirit of Jesus Christ.

(281) *Jer.* 1¹⁻¹⁰.   THE CALL OF JEREMIAH

The call to prophesy came about the year 626 B.C., some five years before the Reformation under Josiah. It was brought home to Jeremiah that he had been pre-destined for his life's work by Yahweh, and that it was his special mission to be a prophet 'unto the nations'. Judah had now been brought into contact with the great world-empires, and in consequence his work was to be on a wider scale than that of the prophets before him. On Yahweh's behalf he was to act amongst men (*v.* 10, 'have set thee over'), plucking up and breaking down, destroying and overthrowing, building and planting. Thus his mission was to be both destructive and constructive. At first, Jeremiah was reluctant to accept this clearly-defined vocation, pleading his youthfulness and inexperience (*v.* 6, 'child' =young man). This sense of personal inadequacy was overcome by the promise of divine help, symbolized in the touching of his mouth.

(282) *Jer.* 1¹¹⁻¹².   THE VISION OF THE ALMOND TREE

The burden of Jeremiah's early preaching was that Yahweh was using the Scythian raiders from the north as His instruments to punish Judah for its faithlessness (*see para.* 270). In a vision, he saw a tree, lately bleak and bare, breaking into springtide blossom. There is a pun in the Hebrew, a characteristic device of the prophets, which cannot be brought out in our English translations. The Hebrew word for the almond tree means 'the waker'. The suggestion is that, whilst nothing seems to be happening, Yahweh is awake and will in due course give effect to His will.

(283) *Jer.* 1¹³⁻¹⁹.   THE VISION OF THE BOILING CAULDRON

Though the details of this vision are difficult to understand, the general meaning is clear. A pot of water on a fire looks still and unchanged until someone blows upon the fire under it; then the water bubbles and boils ('seething' = blown upon). There is no doubt that Jeremiah expected trouble to come from the north to stir up Judah. The remainder of the chapter describes the enemy reaching Jerusalem in order to execute Yahweh's judgements against the nation that had forsaken Him. The prophet must speak the word laid upon his conscience, but, once again, he is promised divine protection. The probability is that, when Jeremiah first uttered these words, he had in mind the threat from the Scythians (though they did not fulfil all the details of his prediction), but, later in his ministry, he revised them and made them apply to the Babylonians.

(284) *Jer.* 2¹⁻¹³. BROKEN CISTERNS

This is a passage from the prophet's early work, the central thought being that Judah is the faithless bride of Yahweh; a message reminiscent of *Hosea*. Yahweh remembers Israel's love for Him in the wilderness, like the love of a honeymoon when infidelity was just unthinkable. Israel then was 'holy' (*v.* 3), that is 'inviolable' or 'taboo', rather than morally upright. Why has she revolted? Other nations do not abandon their gods, even though these gods are worthless. Let Israel send to Kittim (Cyprus), and Kebar (an Arabian tribe), to both west and east, and see if there has been any conduct parallel to theirs. Israel's offence is two-fold—she has forsaken Yahweh, a spring of pure, cool, plentiful water that never dries up; and she has made for herself idols, which were like cisterns, hewn out of the rock to store water which would be flat and stagnant rather than fresh and sparkling, cisterns that were liable to crack and let the water out.

(285) JEREMIAH AND THE DEUTERONOMIC REFORMATION

The discovery of the roll in the Temple and the reforms carried through by Josiah, a true son of David, opened up to Judah the possibility of a new relationship to Yahweh (*see para.* 262). Much debate has taken place concerning the attitude of Jeremiah towards these reforms. The generally accepted view is that, at the beginning, they had his full support. He believed that the events of 621 B.C. were a divine call to the nation and that there was much in *Deuteronomy* of which he could approve. Jer. 11¹⁻⁸ suggests that he was enthusiastic about the inauguration of the new order and that he accepted a commission as one of the agents whose business was to proclaim the law to the people.

(286) This advocacy may, in part, account for his un-popularity, especially for the hatred and antagonism of his own kinsmen. If he championed the centralization of worship at Jerusalem, he was opposing the interests of his own family who were the custodians of a shrine at Anathoth. This, too, may be the explanation of his long silence during the later years of Josiah's reign. The king must be given his chance to lead his people back to Yahweh and, for the time being, the word of prophecy was not necessary.

(287) By the time of Josiah's death (608 B.C.), and the accession of Jehoiakim, Jeremiah decided that he must raise his voice against the situation created by the Deuteronomic move-ment. The reforms, he realized, had been largely ineffective in their aim of bringing the nation back to Yahweh. Perhaps during the lifetime of Josiah himself they had not achieved all the king had hoped for; certainly any good they had done was largely destroyed by his successor. What the principles of the reforms had done was to give the people a false sense of security (Jer. 8⁸). In any case, Jeremiah realized that they were too external. Any real return to Yahweh must take place at a deeper and more spiritual level.

C. *The Prophet Jeremiah—the Second Phase*

(288) The accession of Jehoiakim (607 B.C.) marks the beginning of the second half of Jeremiah's ministry, and the one which shows him as one of the greatest figures in Old Testament history. In the tragic drama of the decline and fall of Jerusalem, he never ceased to proclaim the word of Yahweh, however heavy the cost to himself. It was no pleasant or easy word that he had to utter. When, after Megiddo (*see para.* 271), Pharaoh Necho compelled Judah to accept Jehoiakim as its king and demanded so heavy a tribute that the whole land was crippled by its weight, the prophet must have been reminded of the bad old days of his boyhood, when Manasseh was on the throne. Josiah's reforma-tion seemed to have done nothing at all.

(289) As popular animosity towards him grew because of the disturbing nature of his prophecies, a young man, Baruch, who had been attracted to his personality, became his secretary, and stood by him when almost everyone else regarded him as a

traitor to his country and friends. To his pen we owe the record of Jeremiah's preaching and the intimate glimpses into his heart.

(290) *Jer.* 18$^{1-12}$. THE VISION OF THE POTTER AT HIS WHEEL

Having watched, probably hundreds of times, a potter at his work, Jeremiah one day came to discern a deep divine meaning in the commonplace performance. When a vessel was marred on his wheel, the potter did not fling it aside as waste, but moulded the clay into something else. The will of Yahweh was to deal with Israel in a similar way. Though the nation had proved a failure by its rebellion against His purpose, He was not finally frustrated; provided the people repented, He would remake it to His design (*vv.* 1–6). This seems to us an optimistic message, but *vv.* 7–12 apply it in a pessimistic way. Jeremiah reminds his hearers that Yahweh's intentions are thwarted by the unwillingness of the nation to repent. (It is sometimes thought that these verses were added by a later editor and consist of words of Jeremiah which were not originally attached to the story of the potter.)

(291) *Jer.* 7$^{1-15}$. THE TEMPLE SERMON

A belief had grown up in Judah that the Temple of Yahweh at Jerusalem was inviolable and that no enemy could ever destroy it. This sense of confidence probably began with Isaiah's faith that the city would remain intact in spite of the threats of foreign armies (*see para.* 250), a faith that seemed to have been confirmed by the remarkable retreat from its very gates of the Assyrian forces under Sennacherib. The Deuteronomic reformation, which centralized all worship in the Temple, certainly strengthened this idea. Jeremiah, however, was sent to the gate of the Temple to rebuke this false assurance on the part of Yahweh's worshippers, and to denounce those who were defiling the sanctuary with their sins. Social justice, moral conduct, and sincere worship were necessary; otherwise no temple could save the people from the just punishment of their sins. Certainly Yahweh was not prepared to let His Temple become a cave in which robbers could shelter, but would destroy it as He had destroyed the shrine at Shiloh (*see para.* 127), and banish Judah as He had banished the northern tribes (*see para.* 229).

The effect of the prophet's words is described in Jer. 26, a chapter which undoubtedly refers to this occasion. Priests and prophets (i.e. the official schools of prophets) were moved to a savage fury, and, in the presence of a great multitude, brought an accusation of blasphemy against their prisoner. 'This man is worthy of death.' Jeremiah defended himself by the argument that he had called the nation to repentance and reformation on the bidding of none other than Yahweh, and thus claimed the right of a prophet to pronounce doom upon a city, a privilege which everybody understood. The princes of Jerusalem were impressed by this plea, and Jeremiah was acquitted.

(292) *Jer.* 36.   THE WRITING OF THE BOOK

In a vivid and dramatic way, we are told how the oral pro-phecies of Jeremiah were first put into writing by his secretary, Baruch. For some reason or other, the prophet was unable to go to the Temple himself, possibly because he had been forbidden by the authorities. It does not seem likely that he was at this point a prisoner, but his public teaching may have been banned. Baruch read the roll to a crowd in the Temple courts, and later to an assembled council of princes, who, in their turn, proceeded to read the contents to King Jehoiakim. The message of the roll was not well received, for it predicted a successful Babylonian invasion. At this period, Judah did not seem to be in any immedi-ate danger. Nevertheless, the Battle of Carchemish had destroyed whatever solid hopes the nation may have entertained of Egypt's ability to give effective help if needed, and it was only a matter of time before the Babylonians began their advance towards Pales-tine. After the roll had been burned, neither Jeremiah nor Baruch was to be found; in some place of safety, the words were being rewritten.

(293) *Jer.* 29¹⁻¹⁴.   THE FIRST CAPTIVITY AND JEREMIAH'S LETTER

In the year 597 B.C. the threatened judgement fell upon Judah. Jehoiakim had accepted the authority of Nebuchad-rezzar, but after three years he thought he saw a chance of escape and refused to pay his tribute money. The Babylonians (Chaldeans) marched upon Jerusalem. As usual, the king of Judah relied upon Egypt to help him out of his difficulties, and, as usual, Egypt failed to give him the support he expected. During the siege of Jerusalem, Jehoiakim died and was succeeded by his son, Jehoiachin, who, after a brief reign of three months, was wise enough to surrender the city without further resistance. He and the leaders were transported to Babylon (*see para* 273).

Jeremiah, realizing that whatever there was of worth in Judah had been carried off, was sure that the future lay with the exiles and not with those who remained in Jerusalem. In a remarkable way, the events of 597 B.C. seemed to have created the Remnant of Israel which Isaiah had anticipated (*see para.* 242). Not that all the exiles were beyond reproach! Some of them, transferring to the vessels of the Temple the sanctity they had hitherto attached to the Temple buildings, were quite sure Yahweh would never allow these to fall into enemy hands (27^6), and in the spirit of superstition carried them with them to Babylon. They were confident that, although He might allow them to go on a journey, they could not be touched by Babylonian hands, and, in a very short time, they would be able to bring them home again. The prophet Hananiah even named two years as the limit of their absence (28^3).

Early in Zedekiah's reign, Jeremiah wrote a letter to the exiles to be carried by royal messengers. He advised them to settle down and make the best of their new life in Babylon, warning them that their captivity would last for seventy years. This, he said, was the will of Yahweh. Only then would they be restored to Jerusalem to fulfil the divine purpose. The gist of this message is in 29^{1-14}. (There is considerable doubt whether the rest of the chapter is part of the original letter.)

(294)   *Jer.* 37–8.   JEREMIAH DURING THE SIEGE OF JERUSALEM

Zedekiah, who was made king of Judah by the Babylonians in 597 B.C., did grudging homage to them for a few years, and then in 587 B.C. refused to pay his tribute, on the strength of promised help from Pharaoh Hophra. Once again Jerusalem was besieged by Nebuchadrezzar. This time, the Egyptians fulfilled their promise to the extent of sending an expedition to draw off the Babylonian forces. In the emergency, Zedekiah asked Jeremiah to intercede with Yahweh. The prophet added to his unpopularity by warning the king that, in spite of the temporary relief the Babylonians would return and ultimately capture the city (37^{1-10}).

During this interval in the siege, Jeremiah left the city to visit his estate at Anathoth, and was arrested on the charge of deserting to the enemy. This time, the princes did not take his side, and he was flogged and cast into imprisonment in a private house. Hoping for a more favourable forecast of the future, Zedekiah sent for him secretly, but did not receive the comfortable words he wanted to hear. However, in response to Jeremiah's protest of his innocence, he lessened the severity of his punishment and placed him in the guards' court (37¹¹⁻²¹).

Hearing that he was still predicting the fall of Jerusalem and advising individuals to surrender, some of the princes denounced the prophet to Zedekiah, accusing him of being a source of weakness to the defence. All the king dared do was to wash his hands of the affair. He allowed them to lower Jeremiah into the mud at the bottom of a pit originally intended for the storage of water. From this plight he was rescued by an Ethiopian, a man-servant whose duty was to take charge of a harem. He reported to Zedekiah what had happened and pleaded for the prophet's life (38¹⁻¹³).

Once again, the king enquired about the prospects before Jerusalem, first having promised to spare the prophet's life whatever his reply. Once again, Jeremiah had to say that nothing could save the city except surrender. More afraid of his own subjects than of the Babylonians, Zedekiah insisted that this interview should be kept a secret, and Jeremiah was returned to the comparatively comfortable imprisonment in the court of the guard, where he remained for the next eighteen months until the fall of the city brought him release (38¹⁴⁻²⁸).

(295) *Jer.* 39¹⁻¹⁴. THE FINAL FALL OF JERUSALEM

As the prophet had foreseen, the help from Egypt proved to be of no avail. The Babylonians returned to the siege and in the end the city was compelled to give up. In this reading two narratives have been woven together:

(*a*) 39¹⁻², ⁴⁻¹⁰. When a breach was made in the walls, Zedekiah took to flight. (Compare the accounts in 2 Kings 25¹⁻¹² and Jer. 52⁴⁻¹⁶.)

(*b*) The closing words of Chapter 38, with 39³, ¹¹⁻¹⁴. After the fall of Jerusalem, the Babylonian officers held a court (*v.* 3, 'sat in the gate of the city'). No doubt because they interpreted Jeremiah's policy during the siege as favourable to them, they set him free and directed the new governor Gedaliah to take him home.

(296) *Jer.* 43¹⁻⁷. THE FLIGHT INTO EGYPT AND THE FATE OF JEREMIAH

After the murder of Gedaliah, the governor appointed by the Babylonians (41¹⁻³), and his Babylonian bodyguard, it was almost certain that reprisals would be imposed upon the Jews who remained at Jerusalem. In their anxiety, the people turned to Jeremiah. He assured them that their fears were groundless, and particularly warned them not to attempt to flee to Egypt, but to remain in Judah. As the prophet had anticipated, their leaders refused to take his advice, and argued that his oracle was not a genuine one from Yahweh. They immediately set about the journey to Egypt and, by the use of force, compelled Jeremiah to accompany them. On their arrival at Tahpanhes, the prophet continued his work; though many of the refugees fell into the ways of the Egyptians and worshipped the Queen of Heaven. Jeremiah now had to tell them that they had finally broken the Covenant with Yahweh, and that He was no longer their God nor they His people. Tradition says that his unpopularity continued and grew to such an extent that in the end they turned upon him and murdered him.

(297) *Jer.* 31²⁷⁻³⁰. JEREMIAH'S DOCTRINE OF INDIVIDUALISM

Up to this point in its history, the prophets had declared to Israel that the troubles that befell it were due very largely to the sins that past generations had committed. Such a conception was bound up with the idea of corporate responsibility, an illustration of which we have had in the affair of Achan (*see para.* 113). The individual had no rights of his own, no values as an independent person; he only mattered in so far as he was a unit in a larger whole. Thus Achan's family had to suffer because one member of it had been guilty of a defiance of the will of Yahweh. All were held responsible for what one had done. Israel had to suffer because some of its members, in the past as well as in the present, had rebelled against the will of Yahweh. All were responsible for what some had done.

Jeremiah's first unique contribution to the spiritual heritage of mankind was his challenge to the way this doctrine of corporate responsibility was interpreted. There is truth in it, as we must all recognize. Mankind is bound together by the ties of community and we all must expect to bear some of the consequences of the stupidities and wickednesses of our fellows. None of us can live unto himself. But Jeremiah found his contemporaries consoling themselves with the thought that the disasters of their time were due entirely to the sins of past generations. They were the unfortunate innocents who had to bear the punishment for what had been done by their fathers, especially by Manasseh. They quoted the proverb, 'The fathers have eaten sour grapes and the children's teeth are set on edge'. That, they claimed, was the reason for their present miseries.

The prophet denied any such easy explanation. Every man, he affirmed, has to suffer the consequences of his own misdeeds. His hearers were themselves such grievous sinners that they did not need to look beyond themselves for an adequate explanation of their sufferings. They were merely getting what they themselves deserved, reaping the harvest of their own sowing, bearing the penalty of their own sin.

This doctrine of individual responsibility we shall find developed in the teaching of Ezekiel. We are not surprised that it was perceived by Jeremiah, for it is the attitude we should expect from one whose religion was so personal. In the past, religion had been thought of as a matter between the community as a whole and God. The effect of Jeremiah's struggles and sorrows, his efforts to bear the terrible burden that Yahweh had put upon him, was to isolate him from his fellows; and in that isolation, he came to see that religion was an individual matter, the intercourse of a man's own soul with his God. Out of that individual experience of religion, came his challenge to the current notions of corporate responsibility and his insistence that, if men defy Yahweh, each must bear the consequences of his rebellion.

(298) *Jer.* 31³¹⁻⁴. THE NEW COVENANT

The second great contribution of Jeremiah to the world was his insistence upon the necessity of a New Covenant. Along with his own personal experience, two things must have driven him to this position:

(*a*) The failure of Josiah's reformation. Whatever reforms this worthy king may have carried through, it would seem that little of value managed to survive his death. Perhaps the reform movement never went very deep. Its greatest weakness was that it was largely external. It tried to make men religious by passing laws, to make them good by imposing on them a code of conduct. It did not recognize that the human will needs to be changed from within, that man most of all wants a new heart, a new disposition.

(*b*) The imminent downfall of Jerusalem. To all intents and purposes, the surrender of the city meant the final defeat of the nation. What, then, had become of the Covenant that Yahweh had made with His chosen people under Moses, and which He had ratified again and again? Had Yahweh failed to keep His promises? Had His purpose been finally frustrated?

Jeremiah found a solution to these difficulties in the idea of a New Covenant, which differed from the Old in several ways. It did not, of course, involve a new Law. God's requirements from His people are unchanged. He still demands of them a proper standard of behaviour. What is new is the altered relationship between God and men. No longer must we think of it as a legal one: it must be conceived in terms of fellowship. The bond is to be so close, so personal that it will enable men to fulfil God's will in a way that was never possible before.

We must notice three distinguishing features of this New Covenant.

(i) It is *inward and spiritual*. The Old Covenant was external and based on the view that Yahweh would be satisfied if men observed the regulations He laid down for conduct and ritual. Henceforth religion was to be a question of spirit, of motive. 'I will put my law in their *inward* parts.' In fellowship with God, men would develop a purity of impulse and desire that would make them want to do His will, and an insight into that will that would enable them to deal with the various situations of life as they arose. The law of God would no longer be an external code which they were compelled to obey; it would be the inner principle of their lives, part of their very personality.

(ii) It is *individual*. The Old Covenant had been made with the nation as a whole and had been accepted by the nation acting as a whole; the New would be made with individuals, and each would accept it for himself. 'All shall know me.'

(iii) It is based upon the *divine forgiveness*. 'Their sin will I remember no more.' The new relationship was to be founded upon a reconciliation between God and man, in which the initiative was from God's side.

This new conception which Jeremiah sets out marks one of the highest peaks of Old Testament experience. We can see how it paved the way for Jesus and the personal religion of Christianity. In his day, Jeremiah realized that there could be no true reformation of men's lives, no revival of real religion, until there had come about an inward change in men's attitude to God, a change of heart. The Gospel insists on the necessity of a spiritual conversion, and the biggest factor in that conversion is our recognition of the grace and forgiveness of God towards undeserving sinners like ourselves. In Old Testament days, Jeremiah saw that truth from afar and caught a distant vision of its wonder.

TEST QUESTIONS

(*Send answers to* TWO *questions to your tutor*)

1. Sketch the historical situation behind the ministry of Jeremiah.
2. What contribution did Jeremiah make to the religion of his people?
3. Contrast the Covenant made at Sinai with the 'New Covenant' as taught by Jeremiah.

Study Nine

Israel in Exile

(299) Those carried into captivity were the better classes of the community at Jerusalem, most of whom had sufficient culture and sensitivity to appreciate the higher civilization of Babylon. From the material point of view, their new life was not hard; but from the spiritual aspect, it was the severest test that had yet come to any of their race. To those whose religion was not deeply rooted, it brought great loss, though they may not have been aware of what they were surrendering. They gave up the faith of their fathers with all its rich promises, and slipped into the ideas and ways of their captors, whose religion was both ethically and spiritually on a lower level. But for those whose faith was stronger, the worship of Yahweh became a richer and more precious thing because of the catastrophe.

(300) In their strange new surroundings, the more religiously minded Jews reflected upon beliefs they had always accepted and found in them deeper meanings than they had suspected. To old customs, such as circumcision and the observance of the Sabbath, which marked them out as a distinctive people, they clung more tenaciously than before. Set in the midst of the Babylonians, they grew into an ever-strengthening conviction that they were not as other people, and that, in their religion, they possessed something so exceeding precious that, whatever the cost, they must retain it in its purity. Even if it meant building a hedge about themselves which would shut out other people, they must not allow their faith to suffer any degree of loss (*see ANT, para.* 7(*b*)).

(301) In many ways, as it happened, their religious ideas grew and developed, especially in two significant respects:

(*a*) Now that the Temple no longer provided a living centre for Jewish faith and aspiration, an increasing importance came to be attached to the books of religion. A supreme value was placed upon the collections of ritualistic and ethical laws which provided a basis for the religious life of a devout Jew.

(*b*) A new note was heard more and more in the messages of the prophets. In the old days, their words from Yahweh were largely those of denunciation. Henceforth they increasingly came to speak of the hope and comfort He had to offer to His suffering people.

A. *The Prophet Ezekiel*

(302) The Book of *Ezekiel* divides into three main sections:

1. Ezek. 1–24—a series of prophecies concerning Judah and Jerusalem in the period 596–586 B.C.

2. Ezek. 25–32—a series of prophecies directed against foreign nations.

3. Ezek. 33–48—a series of visions and speeches concerning the restoration of Israel after the Exile.

(303) In recent years there has grown up a considerable uncertainty concerning the authorship of the book. Since the matter is still undecided by scholars, we state the two points of view:

(*a*) The traditional view regarded Ezekiel as a Jerusalem priest who was carried away to Babylon in the first captivity, 596 B.C. (*see para.* 293). There he heard the voice of Yahweh and experienced a number of visions in which he was permitted to see what was happening in Jerusalem until its final fall (*Ezekiel*, Part 1). In Babylon itself he had a particularly important task to fulfil in helping the exiles to preserve their nationality and their religion in a strange land. Above all he was able to encourage them with the hope that Yahweh would ultimately restore them to their own country (*Ezekiel*, Part 3).

The Book, as it has come down to us, supports this traditional view. Nevertheless scholars have been puzzled about the character of Part 1, and dissatisfied with the usual interpretation. Why did Ezekiel spend the early years of his exile in denouncing the Jews who were still in Jerusalem, instead of addressing himself to the task of helping his fellow captives? Still more important, how could he describe so vividly and realistically events that took place in Jerusalem, whilst he himself was nearly 1,000 miles away in Babylon? And how are we to account for his connexion with Jeremiah, in spite of the long distance between them?

(*b*) In the hope of overcoming these difficulties, various theories have recently been put forward. The simplest, and perhaps the most likely, is that Ezekiel was not exiled at the first captivity of

596 B.C., but remained in Jerusalem for the next ten difficult years and was a contemporary there of Jeremiah. We are not able to say what happened to him in 586 B.C., but we must suppose that the record of his prophecies in those years was carried by himself into the Exile. In Babylon, he revised these prophecies, giving them a Babylonian background and rewriting them as if they had been visions that came to him after his own exile (*Ezekiel*, Parts 1 and 2). To this he added Part 3, a series of visions of the restoration which did actually come to him in the period in Babylon.

Some scholars think that Part 3, and the revision of the whole book, were the work of a *disciple* of Ezekiel.

As the scholars have not yet made up their minds, we must leave them to settle the issue. In any case, the question of authorship makes no difference to the essential truths of God which come to us from this book. For convenience, we shall continue to use the name 'Ezekiel' to stand either for the prophet himself or for his disciple in Babylon (if it is necessary to believe in such a person).

(304) THE MESSAGE OF EZEKIEL

Ezekiel shared the views of many of the earlier prophets, and preached them. In particular, we find in his writings many echoes of the teaching of Jeremiah, which would be perfectly natural if they lived and worked together for a time in Jerusalem. There is the same doctrine of individual responsibility (*see para.* 297), the same emphasis on the need of a changed heart (*see para.* 298), and the same conviction of Israel's power to survive the captivity and the same faith in an ultimate restoration (*see paras.* 290, 293).

(305) The Exile raised difficult problems and, in his capacity as pastor of a Jewish community near Babylon, Ezekiel helped his countrymen to adjust themselves to the new situation. On the whole, the conditions of captivity were not too rigorous. The exiles were allowed to continue their distinctive social and religious customs, encouraged to take part in the commerce of the Babylonians, and permitted to administer their own system of justice. No restriction seems to have been placed upon freedom of speech. No doubt the conquerors hoped that they would soon settle down and merge in their new environment. Some of the Jews certainly were willing to accommodate themselves and make the best of things. It was the mission of prophets like

Ezekiel to prevent the Israelites losing their consciousness of being a distinctive race and to preserve their identity as the People of Yahweh.

(306) The first problem of the Exile was to assert that the presence and power of Yahweh were as real and effective in Babylon as in Jerusalem (*see* Psalms 137 and 139). Deeper still, the question of the divine sovereignty was raised. Why had disaster fallen upon Yahweh's people? Did it mean, as it must have looked to many, that He was weaker than the gods of Babylon? With his tremendous conception of the holiness of God, Ezekiel was confident that He would not allow His plan to be frustrated, either by the power of other nations or by the rebellions of His own people. Israel would be brought back to Jerusalem, if only in order that 'the nations shall know that I am the Lord' (36^{23}).

(307) In preparation for this return, Ezekiel visualized an order of life in which Yahweh really was accepted as Sovereign. This new state was to centre around His abode in the Temple. No less than nine chapters are concerned with its architecture and ritual. Since in His unutterable majesty, Yahweh was remote and unapproachable by ordinary mortals, a system of earthly priests and angelic beings was necessary to bridge the gulf. The function of the High Priest was to represent Yahweh on earth and to govern on His behalf. The priests were to be separated rigidly from the common people. They were to wear distinctive clothes; they were to be separated even more deeply by their spirit and way of life. The whole organization of the State was intended to proclaim the fact that Yahweh's people were a unique and exclusive race.

(308) Very much in Ezekiel's description, in Part 3, of the new city and its Temple may have little or no appeal for the modern reader. We must not forget, however, that all this planning for a restored community did more than preserve the identity of the Jews and keep up their spirits during the bitterness of the Exile. When they did ultimately return to Jerusalem, it provided the basis for their new corporate life; and later Judaism was based upon the principles and many of the actual regulations of Ezekiel.

(309)* *Ezek.* 2^1–3^{15}. THE CALL OF EZEKIEL

This account is usually taken to refer to Ezekiel's commission to prophesy in Jerusalem, and to pronounce the doom of Yahweh

K

upon the unfaithful city. The message he had to deliver was God's, but first he must assimilate it and make it his own. This truth was symbolized in the eating of the roll. Bitter at first, it became sweet as he digested it and made it part of himself. So grievous was the message of Ezekiel that he naturally shrank from it, yet there was joy in accepting his prophetic calling as a commission from Yahweh.

(310) *Ezek*. 18. EZEKIEL'S DOCTRINE OF INDIVIDUALISM

The message of Jeremiah on this subject (*see para*. 297) was taken up and re-emphasized by Ezekiel. With him too, it was a protest against the current fatalism which regarded the misfortunes of Jerusalem as an inevitable consequence of the sins of Manasseh. 'The fathers have eaten sour grapes, and the children's teeth are set on edge.'

Ezekiel made it clear that, in the sight of God, every man must stand upon his own feet; only the actual sinner himself would be condemned for his misdeeds. 'The soul that sinneth, *it* shall die' (*v*. 4). A bad man's son would not necessarily be involved in his father's doom. Whilst this message was a wholesome corrective to the wrong views of the times, we must not take it as a balanced and final judgement on the matter. Ezekiel carried his emphasis to extremes. Heredity is, after all, an important factor in life; and we are all more or less bound to the past and must to some degree suffer for the follies and sins of our ancestors. At the same time, each individual has a large measure of choice to determine what he makes of his life, and must accept responsibility for his decisions. When his sins come home to roost, he must blame no one but himself.

The concluding verses of the chapter (19–22) suggest that a man is not bound by his own past, any more than by the past of his fathers. It is always open to him to repent; there is always room for a change of heart and a change of life.

(311)* *Ezek*. 34. EZEKIEL AND THE GREAT SHEPHERD

With this reading, we turn to the Babylonian section of the prophet's ministry. He visualizes a new state of Israel. The nation has been brought to its present plight by bad leaders: a more satisfactory leadership will be required in the future. The evil shepherds, who have neglected and abused their flocks, will be replaced by Yahweh Himself, the great Shepherd of the sheep, who will bring them back from the Exile to their true pasturage.

The strong members of the flock will no longer be allowed to treat the weak with brutality. Whilst Yahweh will be the great Shepherd, there will also be an earthly Shepherd, a monarch with a shepherd's heart. He will rule in the spirit and power of David, the shepherd-king, and so will earn the title 'my servant David'. No longer will the kingdom of Israel be divided into north and south; it will be united under one Shepherd and enjoy prosperity and security.

(312) *Ezek.* 36[16-38]. THE CLEANSING OF ISRAEL

To the prophet's way of thinking, the fall of Israel in the eyes of the other nations of the world signified the weakness of its God, and therefore it was necessary for Yahweh to vindicate His reputation. It must not be assumed that He was unable to protect His people. The world must be given a true picture of the situation. The Israelites were not in exile because Yahweh was weak, but because He was strong. He was, in fact, showing His might by inflicting upon them punishment for their sins. But to clear away any misunderstanding, and to make a demonstration of His holiness and power, He had decreed that Israel should be restored to its own land (*vv.* 16-23). Before such restoration could take place, the people must be prepared in spirit by having their sins forgiven. This forgiveness is symbolized for Ezekiel by the cleansing of water (*v.* 25), and by the gift of a new heart or disposition (*v.* 26, etc.). Great fertility would then come to the land: Israel would turn from its sins with a double loathing, and the nations of the world would recognize the mighty power of Yahweh.

(313) *Ezek.* 37[1-14]. THE RESURRECTION OF ISRAEL

In his vision, Ezekiel saw a valley, possibly one which he was able to identify as outside the city of Jerusalem, and in it lay a multitude of dried and scattered bones, the remains maybe of those who had died defending the city against the Babylonians. These bones represented Israel, now lying as if dead in the land of Exile. There seemed no possibility of life in the dry bones, yet by the voice of Yahweh they were recalled to life, clothed with flesh, and given breath, until they were ready for Yahweh's purpose like an organized army. So it came to Ezekiel that it was not beyond the power of Yahweh to restore life and breath to His dead people. Israel would revive and the nation be restored to its own land.

(314) *Ezek.* 43¹⁻⁹. YAHWEH'S ENTRY INTO THE RESTORED
TEMPLE

One of the problems raised for the exiles in their captivity
concerned the presence of Yahweh. According to the ideas of the
time, so grievous had been the misdeeds of His people that He had
been compelled to leave His abode in Mount Zion. At first there
were many who did not realize that He was equally present in
Babylon, and who felt that it was no longer possible for them to
worship Him. 'How shall we sing the Lord's song in a strange
land?' (Ps. 137⁴). Under the guidance of teachers such as
Ezekiel, this localized idea of Yahweh was transcended. The
exiles realized the truth that monotheism implies omnipresence.
Since there was only one God, He must be everywhere and could
be worshipped in any place.

There was still a feeling, however, that Yahweh was without a
home (*see* 10¹⁸ and 11²²). In Babylon no attempt was made to
erect another temple for Him. The exiles gathered for worship in
synagogues, where instruction in the Jewish way of life was also
given—regulations for the observance of the Sabbath, circumcision, fasting and the distinction of clean and unclean foods.
Sacrifices were not allowed and these synagogues were not regarded as the home of Yahweh.

Part of Ezekiel's work was to make plans for the restoration of
the Jewish State at Jerusalem. The rebuilding of the Temple was
to take place before anything else. Our reading describes Yahweh's return from Babylon (*v.* 3—'I came' should be 'He came').
With great splendour, He enters by the Eastern Gate and
declares that He will now dwell in the midst of Israel for ever.
All traces of idolatry must first be removed. Even the graves of
the kings which were just over the boundary wall must go, lest
they defile the sacred abode.

(315)* *Ezek.* 47¹⁻¹². THE RIVER OF LIFE

The prophet sees Jerusalem bringing life to the whole world.
Water flows from the altar of the Temple eastwards, getting
deeper and stronger, until it finally reaches the Dead Sea. The
trees on the banks of this river are fair and fruitful, and are for
the healing of the sick nations, and for food for the hungry. The
Dead Sea becomes teeming with life like the Mediterranean, or
Great Sea. Only the salt marshes are unaffected so that the
supply of salt should not fail.

B. *Isaiah of Babylon*

(316) During the second half of their exile, the Jews in Babylon were ministered to by one of the greatest of all the Hebrew prophets. We know nothing about his personal life or circumstances: even his name has been lost. Probably between 550 and 538 B.C., he wrote down the main themes of his message, though his writings do not constitute a separate book in our Old Testament. They were added to the records of the teaching of Isaiah of Jerusalem (*see paras.* 234–57), to which was also added the surviving writing of another anonymous prophet who ministered to the Jews *after* their return from the Exile (known as Third Isaiah: *see paras.* 348–52). Scholars generally agree that *Isaiah* 40–55, with a few passages earlier and later in the book, are from the hand of this Babylonian prophet, whom we distinguish by calling him Second or Deutero-Isaiah of Babylon.

(317) He was born probably in the early years of the Exile and ministered to a generation that had grown up in Babylon. Many of them knew nothing about Jerusalem save the recollections of their fathers, and had come to regard Babylon as their homeland. We have reason to believe, however, that the conditions of exile, which at first had been easy and even pleasant, were becoming more oppressive. When Second Isaiah wrote, Babylon was still the supreme power of the ancient world, but its position was becoming more and more insecure. Cyrus, the King of Persia, had already conquered most of Asia Minor, and in time was bound to want to try conclusions with Babylon itself. Perhaps, as the threat of the crisis drew nearer, the exiles were compelled to give labour to their overlords.

(318) But the uncertainty also raised hopes. If the Babylonians were to be defeated, would the Jewish exiles get an opportunity of revenge upon their enemies? Would the way be opened up for a return to Jerusalem?

(319) THE MESSAGE OF THE UNKNOWN PROPHET

Against this background of history, Second Isaiah proclaimed his words of comfort and hope:

(*a*) He was a convinced monotheist who believed that there could only be one God. No longer was Yahweh merely the God of the Hebrew people: He was the God of all the earth, and the destinies of all the nations were in His hands. Other gods who were still worshipped had neither strength nor worth; they were but impotent shadows, mere nothings, doomed to disappear.

(b) Because there was no limit to Yahweh's might, He was able to restore His chosen people to their own land and to lead them forth to re-establish Jerusalem. As Second Isaiah saw it, this was partly a vindication of His power. He had to demonstrate His supremacy over the gods of the peoples who had compelled the Israelites to go into exile, and show that they were ineffective and worthless. But the intended deliverance was also the expression of Yahweh's never-dying love for Israel. Out of the compassion of His heart, He meant to compensate her for all her sufferings, deserved though they had been.

(c) As God of all the earth, Yahweh was able to make use, in the accomplishment of His purpose, of men who did not worship Him. Cyrus the Persian was a heathen. Nevertheless, since he was to issue a decree after his conquest of Babylon to permit the Jews to return to Jerusalem, he could be regarded as the servant of Yahweh. He could even be described as 'the Lord's Anointed' (45[1]).

(d) The restoration of Israel was to be a new challenge. A heavier responsibility would rest upon the nation, for the Jews were to be the evangelists of Yahweh to the whole world. Ezekiel had seen the vindication of Yahweh's power to be the destruction of His foes; to Second Isaiah, God's victory would be the conversion of all nations. Yahweh's enemies were not to be destroyed but to be given a chance to come to the light of His truth, and the restored Judah was to be the agent of that purpose. Unlike modern Christianity, Judaism was not to send out missionaries throughout the world to proclaim the truth, but rather to maintain the faith at Jerusalem in such purity and strength that people would come from afar, out of every nation, desiring to be initiated.

(e) Especially in the Servant Poems (see paras. 326–30), Second Isaiah saw that the sufferings of his people might be used by Yahweh for the salvation of the Gentiles.

(320) *Isa.* 40. YAHWEH'S CONSOLATION FOR THE EXILES

In this chapter, the exiles have not yet obtained their freedom, but we see their changing moods as they contemplate the great release, their hope and humility and reverence in the presence of the God who was to accomplish it.

(a) We begin with the prophet hearing a voice proclaiming comfort and pardon to Jerusalem (vv. 1–2).

(*b*) A herald cries out for a way to be prepared for Yahweh to return from Babylon (*vv.* 3–5), whilst another voice intervenes to reduce the exultations of the people to proper proportions by reminding them of the transience and decay of human life compared with the permanence of Yahweh (*vv.* 6–8).

(*c*) The glad confidence returns at the prospect of Yahweh leading His people back to Jerusalem and caring for them as a shepherd cares for his flock (*vv.* 9–11).

(*d*) Thought is directed to the power and majesty of Yahweh. The signs of His incomparable greatness are to be seen both in His works of creation and in His dealings with Israel. The might of men and of nations is as nothing before Him. They are as a drop of water that hangs from the bottom of a bucket and falls unnoticed to the ground. No image can be formed of Him. The very processes by which men make their idols should remind them of the absurdity of trying to represent Him. He sits aloof on the circle of the world, that is, on the firmament which over-arches the earth like a canopy, and the inhabitants of the earth are as locusts or grasshoppers. Has He not power to bring poten-tates to nothing? Scarcely are they planted, scarcely are they sown, when He bloweth upon them, and they dry up, and a whirlwind carries them off like stubble. The supreme token of the might of Yahweh is to be seen in the multitude of the stars on high. Who can make an image of such a God? (*vv.* 12–31).

(*e*) But, it may be objected, will One so high and exalted take any notice of the existence of individuals? On that score, there need be no fears. Israel is not too insignificant to be noticed, and Yahweh is of infinite power and discernment. He himself is never weary, but is able to give strength to those who are. Natural strength soon comes to its end and is exhausted, but the strength of those who wait upon God never fails.

(321)* *Isa.* 43¹⁻⁷. THE RESTORATION OF ISRAEL

These verses follow a description in the previous chapter of the dreadful sufferings and humiliation Israel had had to endure, calamities imposed upon the people by Yahweh for their sins. But Yahweh was about to deliver them. When water threatened to overwhelm them, or fires to consume, He would be at hand. Because Israel was precious in His sight, He intended to ransom it at the cost of powerful and wealthy nations. Cyrus, who was to be Yahweh's agent of deliverance, would be given territories on the Nile (Egypt, Ethiopia, Seba), as compensation for his act of emancipation. The Hebrew people, scattered abroad throughout the world, would be gathered together again at Jerusalem.

(322)* *Isa.* 44⁹⁻²⁰. THE FOLLY OF IDOL WORSHIP

Babylon was full of idols and it must have been a great temptation to the Jews to join in the practices of their neighbours. An exposure of idolatry was necessary to preserve the purity of Hebrew religion, and Second Isaiah subjected it to scornful satire. The idols worshipped by the Babylonians were useless, the work of frail men and possessing no power (*vv.* 9–11). With much detail he describes their manufacture and the human strength and ingenuity involved. Part is made of metal, part of wood. The very material the carpenter uses is selected at random in the forests and might just as easily be used to bake his bread or to warm himself (*vv.* 12–17). But idolatry blinds the minds of its worshippers and they have not the sense to realize plainly what they are doing (*vv.* 18–20).

(323) *Isa.* 44²⁴⁻45⁸. YAHWEH'S COMMISSION TO CYRUS

The restoration of Israel was part of the divine plan. Possibly, at the beginning of his ministry, Second Isaiah did not see how this was to be brought about, and may have looked for some supernatural intervention. The weakening of Babylon's power, and the rise of the Persian Cyrus, suggested that Yahweh might use the newcomer as His instrument.

In the first section of our reading (44²⁴⁻⁸), he visualizes Yahweh addressing His people and reminding them of His power. As Creator of the Universe, He can use what He has made for His purposes. In order that Jerusalem may be rebuilt, the Temple restored and the cities of Judah brought back to prosperity, He has determined to make use of Cyrus. He will support him in his task, and smooth out the difficulties he will have to face.

In the second section (45¹⁻⁸), Yahweh addresses Cyrus himself and makes him the promise of a successful career (*vv.* 1–3). It is in the interests of Israel that Cyrus has been called and in order that the godhead of Yahweh should be acknowledged throughout the world. All men will know that He is supreme.

(324) *Isa.* 55. YAHWEH'S INVITATION TO RETURN

The conquest of Babylon by Cyrus had apparently been

accomplished and the way was clear for the Jews to go back to Jerusalem, but some seem to have preferred to remain in the land of Exile where they had become profitably involved in its commerce. The chapter gives them a final challenge to leave their worldly business and begin the journey.

(a) *Verses* 1–5 speak of the blessings of the New Covenant which is offered to them. They will be given the true satisfaction of their hunger and thirst, whereas their present way of life was bound to end in disillusion. Yahweh was about to bring a great prosperity to Zion, and, by their obedience to His call, they could share in the good time which was coming.

(b) *Verses* 6–13 urge the people to accept Yahweh's offer, even though some of them have abandoned the religion of their fathers, for they can now repent and obtain pardon. Yahweh's thoughts and purposes are greater than those of men. Already His word has gone forth that a new world is to be established, and that word is as sure and certain as the fact that rain and snow do not return to heaven until they have accomplished their purpose of fertilizing the earth. Even as the exiles return to Jerusalem, they will perceive the signs of the new order of life in the transformation of nature along their route.

(325)* *Isa.* 35. THE BLOSSOMING WILDERNESS

Although this chapter has been included in our Old Testament amongst the writings of the First Isaiah (Isaiah of Jerusalem), its contents suggest that it is more likely to have come from the pen of the anonymous prophet of Babylon. Its background seems to be the period just before the Return and it speaks of the hopes and joys of those who are to be restored. The way back to Jerusalem across the desert will become like the most fruitful parts of Palestine. A great causeway will carry the ransomed over in safety. Not only will nature be transformed, but bodily infirmities will be removed (*vv.* 5–6). The mirage, which so often tantalized desert travellers, will in this case prove to be reality and not illusion.

C. *The Servant of Yahweh*

(326) Embedded in the writings of the unknown prophet of Babylon are a series of passages which draw the picture of an

ideal Servant of Yahweh. They are four in number: 42^{1-7}, 49^{1-6}, 50^{4-9}, and $52^{13}-53^{12}$. Whom had the prophet in mind in these descriptions? There have been two lines of interpretation:

(a) An individual, some representative of Yahweh amongst men, who in loneliness and through agony and death, accomplished the divine purpose. Various characters of Hebrew history have been suggested as fulfilling, at least to some degree, the portrait: for instance, Moses, Jeremiah, Isaiah of Babylon himself, or Zerubbabel the leader of the returned exiles in Jerusalem (see para. 336).

(b) A corporate personality, some group of people spoken of as an individual. Here again there is a variety of views. Some scholars think that Isaiah had in mind the *nation* of Israel whose sufferings, especially during the Exile, were to be redemptive, enriching the whole world and drawing all men to Yahweh. More prefer the idea that we have the portrait rather of the faithful *Remnant* of Israel through whom Yahweh's work was to be accomplished, a Remnant that was not only saved but that was to become a saving influence. Still others think that the passages refer to the *Ideal* Israel, the Israel of which Yahweh had dreamed but which had never come fully into being, the Israel that was not yet realized either in the nation as a whole or in the Remnant.

Whatever may have been in the mind of Isaiah, Christians have seen the perfect fulfilment of his prophetic vision in Jesus Christ.

(327) *Isa.* 42^{1-7}. THE FIRST POEM OF THE SERVANT

In this passage, Yahweh is the speaker. The first four verses describe the gentle and undemonstrative character of the Servant who is to accomplish the world-wide mission of calling the Gentiles to the true God. His function is to sustain and restore the weak and broken, and he will proclaim the religion of Yahweh with unending and unwearied persistence. *Verses* 5–7 speak of the ground of this prophecy, the might of Yahweh who is the Creator and Preserver of mankind.

(328)* *Isa.* 49^{1-6}. THE SECOND POEM OF THE SERVANT

Here the Servant himself is the speaker. The nations of the world are addressed. The announcement he has to make (v. 6) concerns them all. He compares himself to a weapon fashioned by Yahweh for His use. Yet, as the Servant reflects upon the story of his life, it seems to have been full of suffering and to have achieved nothing. However, he is quite ready to put his trust for the future in Yahweh who called him, and believes that by his sufferings he is to become a light to the Gentiles and the means of their salvation.

(329)* *Isa.* 50⁴⁻⁹.   THE THIRD POEM OF THE SERVANT

Once again, the Servant speaks of himself. He has the tongue of a disciple and has learned from Yahweh the art of persuasive and consoling speech. Indeed, daily he looks to Him for the message he has to deliver. To that message he has been loyal, but he has had to endure a series of persecutions in the course of his devotion. He has been beaten; he has been insulted by having his beard plucked and by being spat upon; but he has endured with patience. As if he were on trial in a court of law, he is conscious of God's support. Yahweh declares that he has been in the right; 'who shall condemn him?'

(330)   *Isa.* 52¹³–53¹².   THE FOURTH POEM OF THE SERVANT

After the opening verses 52¹³⁻¹⁵, in which Yahweh speaks, the tribute to the Servant comes from observers who had misunderstood him in his lifetime, and who had only come to grasp the meaning of his sufferings and sacrifice after his death of shame.

The poem falls into three parts:

(*a*) *The Introduction* (52¹³⁻¹⁵). The exaltation that is given to the Servant is in contrast to his previous humiliations. 'My servant shall deal wisely' is better translated, as in the RV margin, 'My servant shall prosper'. His sufferings have 'startled' (rather than 'sprinkled') many nations, but so great is the honour coming to him, that kings shall shut their mouths in awe because of him. In him they see a glory of which there had been no announcement and for which they were quite unprepared.

(*b*) *The Servant's Career* as it appeared to observers in the days of his sufferings (53¹⁻⁹). Probably the observers were the Gentile nations. This familiar passage has caused great difficulty to the translators, but the alternative suggestions in the RV margin will help our understanding. The unparalleled sufferings described, especially in *vv.* 1–4, seemed to mark out the Servant as the object of Yahweh's anger. But those who saw him were compelled to reverse their judgement, for they could see that, in a deep sense, he was suffering as their substitute. His sorrows were, indeed, the consequence of their sins, and yet at the same time they were the remedy that restored them to spiritual health. Finally, after enduring violence and injustice at the hands of men, his life was cut short and he was laid in a dishonoured grave. The prophet seems, as do some of the Psalmists, to regard the 'rich' as being equivalent to the 'wicked', though a slight change in the Hebrew word would make it 'evil doers'. (For *v.* 8 *see* the commentaries: it is almost impossible to translate, though we can get the general sense of it.)

(*c*) *The Reward of the Servant's Obedience* (53[10-12]). These also are difficult verses, which are partly recorded in the words of the observer, partly in the words of Yahweh. The Servant will be instrumental in establishing true religion and in removing the burden of guilt from men's consciences, and, as a reward for his sufferings, a brilliant future is set before him. He will have a multitude of spiritual children and a position like that of a world conqueror enjoying the spoils of warfare.

(331) From these poems it would seem that the unknown prophet felt that, in spite of the immediate prospect of a return to Jerusalem, Yahweh's ultimate purpose of redemption would still remain to be accomplished. But in the end, it would not fail; it would be fulfilled through suffering and rejection.

(332) We have seen (*see para.* 326) the various attempts to identify the Servant of Yahweh, and we have said that Isaiah's portrait was not fulfilled perfectly save in the life and death and resurrection of Jesus Christ. This does not mean that he looked down the centuries and actually predicted in detail the coming of Jesus. Indeed, some of the features in his portrait of the Servant do not agree precisely with the character and circumstances of Jesus as given to us in the New Testament. None of us, for instance, think of Jesus as without form or comeliness. What Isaiah realized was that God's redemptive purpose would have to be accomplished by the principle of vicarious suffering, either on the part of an individual or a group of people. From our vantage point, we can see that only Jesus was able to give to God and to the world such a love and devotion that, while it brought upon Him heavy and altogether undeserved suffering, it made the way of redemption possible for the sons of men, and used these sufferings as a means of redemption. He did become in truth the perfect Servant of God, the one who in the deepest way fulfilled the vision that came to Isaiah of Babylon. 'By his stripes we are healed.'

TEST QUESTIONS

(Send answers to TWO *questions to your tutor)*

1. What truths are stressed by Ezekiel?
2. In what ways did the Exile influence the development of Jewish religion?
3. What was the message of Isaiah of Babylon to the Exiles?
4. Describe, in your own words, Isaiah's 'Servant of Yahweh'. Whom do you think he had in mind? Give reasons for your answer.

Study Ten

The Restoration of Israel

(333) In 538 B.C. the great city of Babylon fell, after only the slightest resistance, to Cyrus the Persian. One of the first things the conqueror did was to issue a decree permitting the exiled Jews to return to their own land (*see ANT, para.* 2). In the case of captives of other nationalities whom he released at the same time, he granted them permission to take their gods with them; but, as the Jews possessed no images of Yahweh, they were allowed to carry with them the Temple vessels that Nebuchadrezzar had appropriated at the fall of Jerusalem.

(334) Perhaps it is not surprising that the return was neither as numerous nor as glorious as Isaiah had anticipated. The majority of the Jews in Babylon had never themselves set eyes upon Jerusalem. They had grown up to take the civilization of Babylon for granted and appreciated its many advantages. Why should they undertake a difficult journey of nearly 1,000 miles across the desert for reasons that seemed to them largely sentimental? Very many of them, certainly those of the greatest wealth and position, elected to remain where they were. Neither in their own minds, nor in the minds of those who were ready to undertake the pilgrimage, does this decision seem to have been interpreted as an act of disloyalty to Yahweh. He could now be served in Babylon as well as in Jerusalem. A hundred years later, when the Holy City was in dire trouble, it was from the descendants of those who had remained in Babylon that help came, and it was from their stock that men like Nehemiah and Ezra sprang.

(335) There was, then, no wholesale trek of Jews making their way back to Judah. During the next 150 years, we can trace three or four movements homewards, and it is likely that betweenwhiles small groups of pilgrims ventured upon the journey. The first party set out in 537 B.C. under the leadership of Shashbazzar. They met with great difficulties that they had not anticipated. The 'people of the land' did not welcome them. The descendants of those who had survived the falls of Samaria (721 B.C.) and Jerusalem (586 B.C.), together with the descendants of the colonists the Assyrians had brought in after the fall of Samaria,

had come to regard themselves as the legitimate inhabitants of Palestine. They had settled down together, there had been a fair amount of intermarriage, and they looked upon the returning Jews as intruders whom they did not want. They were not prepared to allow them more than a foothold in Jerusalem and the land immediately surrounding it. In point of fact, the pilgrims found the city still lying in ruins and the countryside around utterly wasted. Nevertheless they managed to restore the altar of Yahweh, the daily sacrifices were resumed, and the Feast of the Tabernacles was celebrated. The attempt to rebuild the Temple, however, made little progress. Repulsed in their offer of help, the Samaritans replied by obstructing the building operations. Although the foundations were laid, things remained at that stage for the next fifteen or sixteen years.

(336) In 520 B.C. the erection of the Temple was resumed in earnest. Possibly after the accession of Darius I to the Persian throne, a further group of Jews arrived from Babylon, bringing new strength and hope to the depressed city. By this time, Zerrubbabel, a grandson of Jehoiachin a member of the royal house of David, had been appointed governor of Judea, and alongside him in authority was Joshua, the High Priest, a member of the priestly family of Zadok. Stimulated by the energetic words of the prophets Haggai and Zechariah, these two set about building operations with zeal and enthusiasm. An attempt by the Tattenai, the local Persian governor of Syria, to stop the work, led to an appeal to Darius. The original decree of Cyrus was unearthed and the Tattenai ordered to help and not to hinder (*see* Ezra 5–6). The new Temple was finished in 516 B.C. Compared with the magnificence of Solomon's building, it seemed small and poverty-stricken; nevertheless it supplied an essential need in the life of the restored community.

(337)* *Ezra* 1. THE FIRST RETURN FROM BABYLON

The Books of *Ezra* and *Nehemiah* were compiled by the editor of 1 and 2 *Chronicles*. He evidently made use of the memoirs of Ezra and Nehemiah themselves, and quoted from official reports which passed to and from the Persian court in the original Aramaic language. But scholars warn us to treat his information with a certain degree of caution. Almost everybody now believes that Nehemiah preceded Ezra (*see ANT*, paras. 3–4).

The first chapter of *Ezra* gives the account of the return of 537 B.C.

A. *Haggai and Zechariah*

(338) THE PROPHET HAGGAI

Nothing is known of the personal history of the prophet. In 520 B.C. he broke into the life of the tiny, depressed community at Jerusalem with a fervent appeal for the completion of the Temple. So concerned were the Jews with their own comfort, so busy were they building their own houses, that they were neglecting the House of God. 'Is it,' he asked, 'a time for you yourselves to dwell in your cieled houses, while this house lieth waste?' (1⁴). (A cieled house was one lined with timber, instead of being left rough on both inside and outside.)

For years, there had been a series of bad harvests. Haggai interpreted them as a sign that Yahweh was displeased at this neglect. He reminded them that the material power of world empires such as Persia would disappear, but that the Temple would stand for all time as the centre of true worship, and in due course all nations would come to Jerusalem to worship Him. Zerubbabel, Joshua and the builders were so fired with the prophet's enthusiasm that the Temple erection was immediately undertaken.

(339)* *Hag.* 1. THE PROPHET'S SERMON

In *vv.* 1–11, we have the notes of a sermon preached in the autumn of 520 B.C. The people are bidden to consider their ways (that is, reflect upon their past experiences), and to look to the future. The building of the Temple would bring greater prosperity. In the past their hopes had been disappointed, for Yahweh had 'blown upon the land', or, as we might say, put an evil spell upon it and destroyed its produce. Attention to Yahweh's house would remove the tokens of His displeasure.

(340) THE PROPHET ZECHARIAH

The appeal of Haggai was supported by that of a second prophet, Zechariah. Unlike his colleague, Zechariah was a member of one of the priestly families. Our concern is only with the first eight chapters of the book, since scholars are agreed that the rest was not part of the original writing. We begin with an exhortation to repent, after which there follows a series of visions recorded in the first person. The historical details behind Zechariah's work are far from certain. Obviously he had tremendous faith in the work of Zerubbabel as governor of Jerusalem and Joshua as High Priest and it is possible that he urged Zerubbabel to proclaim himself king of Judah and reassert his country's independence. Many commentators interpret 6⁹⁻¹⁵ to mean that two crowns were to be prepared for Zerubbabel and Joshua, for Zechariah was insistent that the high priest also should be given his rightful authority. The secular and religious powers were both necessary and must work hand in hand.

(341)* *Zech.* 8¹⁻²³. THE RESTORED JERUSALEM

Evidently the Temple has been rebuilt and the prophet draws an idyllic picture of the Jerusalem that is to be. During the years of trouble, the city had been no place either for feeble old age or for young children. All will now be altered. 'There shall yet old men and old women dwell in the streets of Jerusalem, every man with his staff in his hand for very age. And the streets of the city shall be full of boys and girls playing in the streets thereof.' Once again Zechariah repeats the message of Haggai, that indifference to the rebuilding of the Temple had brought calamity. But, with the Temple restored, the future of Jerusalem will be full of happiness. The four fasts are to be kept cheerfully, as holidays. So great will be the blessing of Yahweh upon the city that the whole world will turn to Zion for peace and salvation. 'In those days it shall come to pass that ten men, out of all the languages of the nations, shall take hold of the skirt of him that is a Jew, saying We will go with you, for we have heard that God is with you.'

B. *Nehemiah and Ezra*

(342) After the rebuilding of the Temple and its dedication in 516 B.C., the Old Testament has little to tell us of the affairs of the restored nation. From other sources, we gather that for a generation or so everything went reasonably well. The returned Jews had little to fear from any external interference. Palestine was a province of the Persian Empire, and Persia was strong enough to preserve peace. Judah might not have its own king in name—if Zerubbabel had attempted any such claim, we can be pretty sure how Persia would have dealt with him—but so long as he was

L

governor it could at least be felt that the house of David had been recognized. The tribe of Levi, together with the sons of Zadok, provided priests for the Temple and maintained its ritual. Besides the revived community in Judea, we must notice that there were also Jewish settlements at Susa, the Persian capital, in Babylonia, in Egypt and in North Africa. At all these centres, the knowledge of Yahweh was being maintained and spread.

(343)   The situation began to change with the accession to the Persian throne of Artaxerxes I (465 B.C.). Greece was trying at this time to detach Egypt from the Persian Empire, and Artaxerxes could not afford to neglect his line of communications through Palestine. A report that Jerusalem was quietly rebuilding its walls was brought to him by the Samaritans, who chose to interpret it to him as the first step towards a declaration of political independence. Orders were immediately issued that the building should be stopped.

The next twenty years are obscure, though a little light on the situation comes from two prophets, Malachi and Third Isaiah.

(344)   MALACHI

The book is anonymous, for the title 'Malachi' simply means 'my messenger'.

(a) From its contents we gather that the Jews had become careless about the Temple services, and that there was a danger of the worship of Yahweh being reduced to the level of heathen worship, even of its being blended with pagan religions. Malachi, who was extremely interested in the Temple ritual and the priesthood, roundly condemned the indifference of priests and people. Sacrifices should be of perfect animals: nothing less than the best was worthy of Yahweh. Tithes must be paid promptly and in full; to withhold them was to rob God.

(b) The particular social evil that aroused Malachi was the prevalence of 'mixed' marriages. Jews were even divorcing their Jewish wives in order to marry foreigners. All such entanglements, affecting as they did the life of the family, were a threat to the purity of Yahweh worship.

(c) At the same time, there was a remarkable note of universality in the prophet's outlook. He seems to recognize that the Gentiles' worship of their gods was, in fact if not in name, worship offered to Yahweh. 'From the rising of the sun even to the going down of the same, my name is great among the Gentiles; and in every place incense is offered unto my name, and a pure offering:

for my name is great among the Gentiles, saith the Lord of Hosts' (1²²).

(345)* *Mal.* 2¹⁷–3⁶. THE REFINER AND PURIFIER

People were complaining of the divine justice. Prosperity seemed everywhere to be the lot of the wicked instead of the righteous. Tired of their grumbles, Yahweh announced that He would intervene and send a messenger to purify both priests and people. His mission would be one of cleansing rather than destruction; he would judge men as the refiner separated silver from its ore in the fierce heat of a crucible. He would usher in the ideal age. It is noteworthy that Malachi looks for the return of the fiery Elijah, rather than the coming of a new prophet. A fresh prophetic voice might conflict with the written Law which was now becoming the basis of Israel's religion. What was needed was not the proclamation of new ideas, but the revival of the ancient messages of the prophets which had been forgotten.

(346)* *Mal.* 3⁷⁻¹². TITHES AND THE DIVINE BLESSING

Fertility would be the reward of those who duly paid their tithes and offerings. The curse of locusts ('devourers') and the drought would be removed, and showers of blessing would make the land bring forth plentifully.

(347)* *Mal.* 3¹³–4³. THE TRIUMPH OF RIGHTEOUSNESS

There were those who argued that it did not pay to be religious. In answer, Malachi maintained that there would be a final vindication of the righteous. Yahweh had prepared a record of His people, and in the day of His action would specially protect them. The godless would be punished, but the righteousness of the God-fearers would shine out like the radiance of the sun.

(348) THE THIRD ISAIAH

Once again, the name and personal circumstances of this prophet are unknown to us. The notes of his message were added to *Isaiah*, probably because of a similarity of tone to the message of the unknown prophet of Babylon. There are, however, differences of background which, amongst other reasons, convince scholars that in Chapters 56–66 we are dealing with a third prophet. It is quite clear that the Jews are back in Jerusalem, and that Third Isaiah is dealing with the situation that existed there.

(349) The general picture is one of a depression in civic, economic, and religious affairs at Jerusalem. The Temple services were still being carried on, but the challenging words of Malachi do not appear to have done much good. The little Jewish community was being oppressed by its Persian overlords and molested by its more immediate neighbours, in particular by the Samaritans and the Edomites. The population was in a state of poverty and evidently trying to cheer itself up by indulging in hopes of a materialistic Utopia.

(350) As Third Isaiah saw it, the first practical step ought to be taken by the Jews themselves. The walls of the city should be rebuilt as a protection against their enemies. If they did that, Jerusalem could depend upon Yahweh to raise it from its low estate. Great glory and splendour would be in store. The prospect of a visit from Nehemiah seemed to put such a prophecy on a firm footing.

Alongside this picture of a magnificent future for Jerusalem, in which the rest of the nations are to be made to act as its servants, Isaiah strikes a note of broadminded universalism. The Temple at Jerusalem is to be a House of Prayer for all nations (56[7]). Even those who were barred by strict Jewish law from the Temple were to be included amongst those who might worship God.

Constantly in the writings of this prophet we get these two divergent voices. There is an arrogant nationalism which we find repellant; and there are passages which just as surely are anti-materialistic and proclaim the universalities of religion.

(351) *Isa.* 60. THE GLORIES OF THE NEW JERUSALEM

Though the rest of the world is still in darkness, the light of Yahweh shines upon Zion and the nations are attracted to it (*vv.* 1–3).

The exiled sons and daughters of Jerusalem are brought back into the city by their captors, bringing with them the wealth of distant countries as a tribute to Yahweh (*vv.* 4–9).

Thus Zion becomes supreme amongst the nations, who indeed are forced to act as its servants, being set to build up its walls. Even kings have to minister to its needs. Through the open gates of the city their treasures are brought in to beautify the sanctuary and Zion is nourished by the Gentiles (*vv.* 10–16).

(352) *Isa.* 61. THE ACCEPTABLE YEAR OF YAHWEH

The speaker is the herald of the coming salvation; a year of favour to those who love Yahweh, but also one of vengeance upon His enemies (*vv.* 1–3).

The people are told of the glorious future that awaits Israel. Its waste places will be rebuilt (*v.* 4).

Members of other nations will recognize Israel as the priest and servant of Yahweh, and will themselves be ready to serve as its labourers (*vv.* 5–6).

The People of Yahweh, who have suffered so many wrongs, will be given a new Covenant as a recompense and be blessed to make up for what they have undergone. They will be vindicated in the eyes of all the nations (*vv.* 7–9).

Finally the prophet himself breaks forth into joy at the prospect (*vv.* 10–11).

(353) NEHEMIAH

In 445 B.C. Artaxerxes I appointed his cupbearer, Nehemiah, to be the governor of Judea, thus putting him on an official equality with Sanballat the governor of Samaria (*see ANT, para.* 3). Nehemiah retained the post for twelve years before he returned to Susa, leaving his brother Hanani in charge. In 432 B.C. he paid a second visit (*see ANT, para.* 4). During his governorship, he set before himself five main objectives:

(*a*) He insisted upon the rebuilding of the walls of Jerusalem. For this he received permission from Artaxerxes, and the story of his struggles and achievements is told in the book that bears his name.

(*b*) He set about rectifying the social abuses of which he had heard in Susa. The poor Jews could not pay the taxes that Persia demanded without mortgaging their property and sometimes even selling their children into slavery. The richer members of the community exploited this situation to the full. Nehemiah pleaded with them to return the houses and lands which had come into their possession in this way, and to forgo part of what was legally due to them. He himself set the example by refusing the customary salary attached to his office (5[14]).

(*c*) He forbade Jews to enter into marriage with women who were not of pure Jewish blood. He believed this to be necessary in order to preserve the purity of the race at a time when it might easily have deteriorated. This was a harsh measure of reform, and cannot have been popular, but he carried it through in spite of the fact that the High Priest, Eliashib, had allowed his grandson to marry the daughter of Sanballat of Samaria (11[25]).

(d) He prohibited work upon the Sabbath. On that day the gates of the city were to be shut against foreign merchants and no transactions were to be undertaken (11^{19}).

(e) He ordered offerings to be paid, regularly and in full, to the Levites, and thus made them the wealthiest and most powerful class in the community (11$^{11-13}$).

(354) *Neh.* 1^1–2^8. PERMISSION TO RETURN

Shushan = Susa, the winter residence of the Persian kings. To the best of his knowledge, Nehemiah had not appeared sad at the news he had received from Jerusalem, but the king noticed his distress and enquired its reason.

(355) *Neh.* 2$^{9-20}$. ARRIVAL AT JERUSALEM

The governors beyond the river were probably those of Hamath and Damascus, through whose territory Nehemiah would have to pass. Sanballat, the governor of Samaria, and Tobiah 'the servant' (a title which may indicate that he had once been a slave) soon showed their disapproval. A secret survey of the city by night made Nehemiah realize how the broken walls exposed Jerusalem to its enemies; but his proposal to repair them was construed by Sanballat, Tobiah, and Geshem as an act of rebellion against Persia.

(356) *Neh.* 4. THE SAMARITAN OPPOSITION

Nehemiah's work was seriously obstructed by the Samaritans. Though they had much Hebrew blood in their veins and were worshippers of Yahweh, the returned Jews despised them for their lack of racial purity and treated them as foreigners. Under their governor, the Samaritans did everything they could to prevent Jerusalem from being re-established. Because of their threats, it was necessary for Nehemiah's men to work with both trowel and sword ready to hand.

(357) *Neh.* 6$^{1-9}$. FURTHER SAMARITAN FRUSTRATION

Sanballat and his friends thought that, if they invited Nehemiah to a conference, they would get him into their power; but he refused to meet them on the ground that he was too busy. At this, Sanballat went further and accused him of conspiring to make himself king and threatened to report him to Persia, a charge that Nehemiah met with a simple denial.

(358) *Neh.* 6[10-14]. A PLOT TO DISCREDIT NEHEMIAH

Sanballat induced Shemaiah, who posed as a prophet, to try to convince Nehemiah that the latter's life was in danger, and that he ought to seek safety by going with him into the inner sanctuary of the Temple, where only priests were allowed. Had Nehemiah acted upon Shemaiah's suggestion, he would have been guilty of a serious offence and would have been discredited in the eyes of the people.

(359) EZRA

After the governorship of Nehemiah, there follows another period during which we know nothing of what was happening in the little community in Judea. It used to be thought that Nehemiah and Ezra were contemporaries (they are mentioned together in Neh. 12[26]), but there are good reasons for believing that Ezra's return was not until 397 B.C. (*see. ANT, para.* 5). The Chronicler who compiled the books of *Ezra* and *Nehemiah* has led us astray. First, he got the two men in the wrong chronological order, for Nehemiah should precede Ezra; secondly he left us with the impression that Ezra's permission to return was given in the seventh year of Artaxerxes I (Ezr. 7[8]), whereas it must have been in the reign of Artaxerxes II.

(360) Ezra belonged to a group of priests who had remained in Babylon and had been busy writing down the laws concerning the Temple worship in the days before the Exile, and in elaborating them. The results of their labour he was anxious to communicate to the Jewish community in Palestine. With the royal permission, he organized a caravan to Jerusalem, bearing rich gifts for the Temple both from the Babylonian Jews and from the state treasuries. But Ezra's richest possession was the collection of laws which were designed to be the basis of a holy nation. Upon his arrival, he realized the time was ripe for another movement of reform, and that he had in his hands the means of the reformation. The nation's life must be reorganized on the principles of the collected Law. Ezra was so convinced of the necessity of making Israel a holy nation and guarding its people from every kind of religious and racial contamination, that in imposing his reforms he was prepared to be much more drastic than Nehemiah.

(361) A general assembly of the people was called together, at which Ezra expounded to them the Law (either the whole Pentateuch, or 'P', or the 'Law of Holiness' = Lev. 17–26; *see para.* 444). In gratitude for the love and protection of Yahweh,

the people accepted the book as containing His directions for a new community life. It was in the tradition of Ezekiel. Henceforth, religion to the Jews became more and more a matter of correct outward conduct in the proper observance of ritual, ceremonial holiness, and the keeping of the Sabbath. To fulfil the Law was the sure guarantee that some day God, for His honour's sake, would deliver His people and make them once again an independent nation.

(362)   Ezra's anxiety to separate his people from everything that might defile them brought about an attitude of intense racial pride and exclusiveness on the part of the Jews. They lost the sense of a world-wide mission to the Gentiles which Isaiah of Babylon had so persuasively proclaimed. Whatever the price, they must now be separate from all other peoples. One sign of this narrowness can be seen in the strong line taken by Ezra in regard to mixed marriages. He went much further than Nehemiah. Not only were such marriages forbidden, but where they had taken place he ordered that they be dissolved. Jews must put away all foreign wives and disown the children born of them (Ezr. 10³).

(363)   It is very easy for us to condemn this policy. On the other hand, with the subsequent history of the Jews in mind (*see* Study Twelve), we are compelled to ask whether, if some such attitude had not been imposed, the Jewish race would have survived as a separate body. The pressure to merge with other peoples must have been very strong, and it was only resisted by this spirit of exclusiveness. After all, the knowledge and worship of Yahweh had to be preserved until, in the fulness of time, it might be shared by all mankind. It may very well be that the harshness and narrowness of Nehemiah and Ezra were the only way in which this could be accomplished. Much as we prefer the breadth and universality of Second Isaiah, we have to recognize that the spiritual successors of Ezekiel had an essential part in the working out of the divine purpose, and in their own way helped to prepare the way for Jesus and His message to the world (*see ANT, para.* 7).

C.   *Voices of Protest*

(364)   The policy of Ezra did not go unchallenged. There were those in Judea to whom it did not commend itself, and the

problem was how to make an effective protest in an age when freedom of speech was not encouraged. At least two more catholic-minded Jews turned to the written word. From this period two short, anonymous books have survived, each in its own way registering its protest against the growing exclusiveness of post-exilic Judaism. The Books of *Ruth* and *Jonah* are welcome signs that the Jewish conviction that Yahweh had called His chosen people to undertake a mission to the wider world was not entirely lost.

(365) *Ruth* 1–4. A STORY OF TAINTED BLOOD

The unknown author set his story in the time of the Judges, and centred it around a custom which by his own day had become obsolete. In the earlier period, the old Law of Levirate marriage (Deut. 25⁵⁻¹⁰) laid it down that, if a man died without children, his widow should be taken by his next-of-kin, in order that the estate should not pass out of the family, and that the first son of this union should be reckoned as the dead man's, and should carry on his name. This Levirate marriage was not a true marriage, but merely a way of producing offspring to a dead man. However, our author does not seem to have understood the old custom properly, and has assumed that it involved a real marriage.

Driven by the stress of famine, Elimelech, his wife Naomi, and their family left their ancestral home in the district of Jerusalem and migrated to Moab, where the two sons contracted the kind of foreign marriages that Ezra condemned. After their deaths, one of the widows, Ruth, though a Moabitess, elected to return with her mother-in-law to Judah. (Ruth 1¹⁷ should read '*not even* death', instead of '*if aught but* death'.) In Judah, Ruth met a relative of her late husband and they fell in love. Boaz was not the nearest kinsman to the dead man; there was one who was closer and who should have fulfilled the legal obligation of re-purchasing the land that had been sold by Naomi's husband, and of marrying the childless Ruth. He, however, was persuaded to waive his claim. The writer of the story, as we have said, had mistaken what the ancient custom demanded. Also (4⁷) the practice of drawing off a shoe was not, in the beginning, a way of ratifying a bargain, but of insulting a man who refused to undertake the obligation of Levirate marriage.

These misunderstandings do not in any way detract from the point of the story. A great grandchild of the union between Boaz and Ruth was David, Israel's ideal king ($4^{21\text{-}2}$). Thus in the Royal House of Judah, and in its finest representative, there was a taint of Moabite blood, the very kind of impurity which had made Ezra demand the dissolution of 'mixed' marriages. In a quiet and delightful way, the author makes this protest against the narrow and inhuman policy which the leaders of his country were bent on pursuing.

(366) *Jonah* 1, 3, 4. THE RELUCTANT MISSIONARY

The author of this book wove his story around the name of an ancient prophet about whom little or nothing is known (2 Kings 14^{25}). He depicted Jonah as a sincere but bigoted Israelite who, to his deep dismay, was commissioned to preach to the heathen city of Nineveh. When the book was written, Nineveh had long since been destroyed, but it had left behind in the mind of every Jew a reputation for terrible cruelty and violence. No field for missionary work could have been less attractive or promising. In the story, it obviously stands for the heathen world at large.

Preferring to see its inhabitants destroyed rather than converted, Jonah tried to escape from his task by taking ship to Tarshish. In a terrible storm, he was compelled to confess to the superstitious sailors that it was probably his presence that was endangering their lives, and that he had better be thrown overboard. Conveniently swallowed by a big fish, he was brought to land and given a second chance of obeying the divine command. The unexpected conversion of the inhabitants of Nineveh made him furious, for he had been hoping for a grimmer result. Under the shelter of a gourd, he complained to God that he had been deceived. When the gourd withered, he was sorry for it; a strange contrast to his severity towards the inhabitants of the city.

Small as the book is, it has been acclaimed as the 'high water mark of Old Testament theology'. We note:

(*a*) It proclaims the impossibility of escape from Yahweh. He is everywhere, both in Nineveh and on the high seas.

(*b*) It recognizes in men like the heathen sailors a natural piety and humanity, a genuine kindliness of heart. They were willing to spare Jonah, though he was not willing to give Nineveh a chance.

(*c*) It stresses the generosity of the divine love. Unlike the prophet, Yahweh is concerned that even a heathen people should be saved rather than punished. He is ready to forgive all men if they will turn to Him in penitence.

(d) Yahweh's compassion extends even to dumb cattle as well as to humans.

(e) The essential missionary character of Judaism is throughout stressed and underlined. How can any of Yahweh's servants who realize the divine mercy be other than evangelists? How can Israel, the beloved of Yahweh, do any other than fulfil its mission and spread the light of true religion to those still in darkness?

In this way, the anonymous author of *Jonah* makes another protest against the narrowness and exclusiveness which were descending upon Israel after the Exile. Jonah stands for the Jewish people, called to their evangelical mission; a mission they were steadily refusing. Though they had been swallowed up in the Exile, though they had been brought back with their commission renewed, they were still reluctant. The Gentiles, they were saying in effect, could not possibly be saved. The author believed otherwise. He was convinced that the love of Yahweh was broader than the measures of man's mind, and sought to recall his fellow countrymen to their true task as servants of the one and only God of mankind.

TEST QUESTIONS

(Send answers to TWO questions to your tutor)

1. What part did Nehemiah take in the return from the Exile?
2. Show how the messages of (a) Haggai and (b) Malachi are related to the conditions in Judah in their day.
3. Tell the story of the Book of Ruth to show why it can be interpreted as a defence of marriages between Jews and Gentiles.
4. What is the importance for religious thought of the Book of Jonah?

Study Eleven

The 'Writings' of the Old Testament

A. The Creation Stories

(367) The Book of Genesis, in its first eleven chapters, contains a number of traditional stories about the creation of the world, its original inhabitants, the entry of sin into human life, the beginnings of agriculture and industry and the arts, the rise of different languages, a primeval flood, and so on. In their present form, these accounts were probably not compiled until a late date in Hebrew history, during or shortly after the Exile. They were, however, based upon earlier stories, some of which no doubt had been long in circulation. Our study is concerned with those in Gen. 1–4.

(368) The unknown authors did not set out to give us an account of the creation of our world in terms of modern science. That, of course, would not have been possible. They were ignorant of very much that is familiar to us. What they did was to make use of the views that were current in their own day. As scientific explanations of the creation, we are bound to regard their ideas as primitive and inadequate, and turn to the scientists of our time for a detailed and more accurate account of *how* the world came into being. The point always to remember is that the Old Testament writers set out primarily to proclaim profound *religious* truths and especially the truth that Yahweh was the Creator of all things. He, and He alone, had made the world, and all that is in it. We certainly accept that truth, for it is an essential part of our faith. Once having accepted it, the particular way in which the world was created is only of secondary importance. The writers go on to tell us stories which were meant to explain how the world is what it is, again using the ideas of their time. It is a spoiled world, for by his sinfulness man has marred God's original design. The first few chapters of *Genesis*, then, are full of religious teaching and their ancient stories bear witness to the greatness and glory of Yahweh, the Creator and Sovereign God of all mankind.

(369) *Gen.* 2⁴⁻²⁵. AN ANCIENT ACCOUNT OF THE CREATION

If you read through the first two chapters of *Genesis*, you will probably perceive a natural break after 2³. As a matter of fact, we have been given two distinct accounts of the Creation, and it is generally agreed that the one which comes second in our Bible is actually the earlier. Of the two it is more vivid and picturesque, and comes to us from the document 'J' (*see para.* 442); it is the kind of account that we should expect from a simple, nomadic people. At the beginning, we have a barren world, for there is no one to cultivate it. God, therefore, models a man in clay, breathes life into him, and puts him into a garden which is meant to provide him with both a home and work. Since man cannot be satisfied with this solitary existence, animals are created by God and brought into man's presence for him to name them. However, the problem of making man content and satisfied is still unsolved and God tries again. This time, by taking a rib out of man's body during a heavy sleep, He creates woman, and in this companionship man sees the possibility of happiness.

The whole account brings home the truth that God, and God alone, is the Maker of the physical world; that all things, including man, exist because He created them. The vegetable and animal orders have been put at the service of man, who stands at the highest point of the divine creative activity. Indeed, man is shown to belong to a higher order than the rest of creation: he is akin to God in a way that is not true of any other creature.

(370) *Gen.* 1–2³. A LATER ACCOUNT OF THE CREATION

This is a much more profound and dignified and orderly account, coming from the document 'P' (*see para.* 442). It reflects the attitude of the priests at the end of the Exile, and proclaims their faith in monotheism and their interest in religious institutions like the Sabbath. There are differences between this and the former account, which should be noted. We are told, in Gen. 1, of three acts in which, by the decree of God, something new was created for which no materials, or only some of the materials, were already existing—dead matter (*v.* 1), animal life (*v.* 21), human personality (*v.* 27). According to the priests, the animals were created before man, not as in Gen. 2¹⁸ᶠ; and man and woman were created at the same time. Yet 1²⁷ does not really differ from 2⁷. Both accounts drive home the same truths about man and his relationship to God.

(371) *Gen.* 3. THE BEGINNING OF SIN

As we read this story, in which the Biblical writers set out to tell us how sin got into the world, and its consequences, we are shown the condition of mankind in every age. 'Adam' in the Hebrew language simply means 'man'. The fall of man is not merely a single incident that happened long ago to the first ancestor of us all. It is an experience that comes to each one of us every time we, knowing the right, choose the wrong; and it is similar in character to the experience of Adam. Whatever may have been the limitations of the authors of *Genesis* in regard to scientific knowledge, they knew a great deal about the human heart and its motives, and were very wise in their psychological insight. This story reminds us that:

(*a*) Though man had a great deal of freedom given to him, it was not absolute; he could not do exactly as he liked; some things were forbidden him.

(*b*) The forbidden thing attracted him.

(*c*) He welcomed the idea of release from obedience to God and of becoming a law unto himself.

(*d*) He yielded to the attraction of the forbidden and disobeyed God of his own free will, though afterwards he tried to blame his wife.

(*e*) Through his disobedience, he came to know himself and experienced the sense of guilt that follows in the train of wrong choice.

(*f*) His sin brought with it a series of penalties. The Book of Genesis seems to suggest that the pain of childbirth, the subjection of woman, the curse upon man's labour, the drudgery of agriculture and the fact of death are all part of the consequence of man's choice of evil. Christian thought has travelled a long way from such ideas. It does not believe that these things are necessarily tainted with evil or are the consequences of evil, but it does recognize that human sin possesses the power to poison and corrupt every part of life.

(372)★ *Gen.* 4. MORE STORIES OF THE ORIGINS OF THINGS

(*a*) Crime (*vv.* 1–15). The story of Cain and Abel sets forth God's condemnation of murder and also seems to suggest the origin of the custom of blood revenge (*v.* 15). (Unfortunately we are not given the reason for the rejection of Cain's offering and must assume that this has been lost from the story as it was once told.)

(*b*) Urban civilization (*v.* 17).

(*c*) Nomadic, pastoral life (*v.* 20).

(*d*) Musical instruments (*v.* 21).

(*e*) Metal forging (*v.* 22). Lamech's song, in *vv.* 22–4, is thought to be the earliest poem of the Bible. It celebrates Lamech's sense of power because of his son's invention, and suggests how soon inventions came to be turned to destructive uses.

B. *The Book of Psalms*

(373) Our word 'psalm' is said to be derived from a Greek word which signifies the twanging of strings, suggesting that the psalms were meant to be set to music. It is generally agreed that the collection of Psalms that we have in the Old Testament was used as the Hymnbook of the Second Temple. As in all hymn-books, there is a great variety of subjects, and many different levels of spiritual experience and vision. All the moods of life are reflected—hope, fear, success, frustration, joy, sorrow, elation, despair—and every mood is brought into relation with God. Some Psalms are obviously more suitable for private devotion, but it is not difficult to imagine the majority of them being used for public worship at Jerusalem. Most of the singing was probably done by choirs or musical guilds, and not by whole congregations. The ordinary worshippers had to be content to join in the responses, and in some Psalms (e.g. 145) we can easily detect their parts. At the head of many Psalms there are names which suggest that the particular hymn belonged to a collection owned by a well-known choir (e.g. Asaph (Ps. 50), or Song of Korah (Ps. 42)). The term 'Selah' which has often puzzled readers is usually taken to be a musical instruction.

(374) THE AUTHORSHIP OF THE PSALMS

Any good hymnbook contains hymns written at various dates, some very old, some quite modern, and many of them revised by later editors and considerably altered from the original version. So it is with the Book of Psalms. They were composed at various dates, some far back in the time of the Monarchy, others just as certainly in the years immediately after the Exile, and yet others at a very late date in Hebrew history, possibly in the time of the Maccabees. To attempt to find out who wrote them is, in most cases, a waste of time. The superscription that stands at the head of many of them was added later, and we are far from certain that it was meant to tell us the name of the original author. 'A Psalm *of* David' could just as easily be translated 'A Psalm *for* David', and may be a kind of dedication rather than a statement of authorship. It is more important to consider the character of the Psalm itself, for its contents will often give us a clue to the period of history in which it was written. Whilst there are good reasons for thinking that some of the Psalms have come from King David, with or without later revision, we certainly cannot accept the idea that he was the author of them all. Still, a hymn can move and inspire us even though we don't know who wrote it, and the Psalms continue to be a source of deep spiritual help to Christians, in spite of the difficult problem of their authorship.

(375)   THE PLACE OF THE PSALMS IN OLD TESTAMENT RELIGION

After the return from the Exile and the re-establishment of the Jews in Jerusalem, the prophetic note seemed to fade into silence. The effect of the work of Nehemiah and Ezra was to put the emphasis upon the importance of correct ritual in worship and the scrupulous observance of the Law. Judaism, as we commonly understand it, came into being. Though this policy of strict adherence to the legal code may have been necessary in order to keep Israel from being contaminated by contacts with other nations, there was always the danger of its stifling a more spiritual type of religious experience. Religion might become no more than a matter of outward behaviour, which it did in many cases.

(376)   The Psalms are welcome evidence of the existence of a higher type of religious experience in what otherwise would have been a very cold and formal period of Hebrew history. They reflect the best spirit of Judaism, the response of pious men and women to God's demands, and their aspirations for an intimate and rich fellowship with Him. The Law is not regarded as the burden it came to be in later times. Men can find real joy in observing it. But, deep in the human heart, there was an instinct that wanted to give to God something more than a formal response. The soul hungered to come face to face with its Creator. That note of spiritual longing rises to its height in the Psalms.

(377)   We can well believe, too, that the high tone of the Temple hymns became more than an expression of what was in the hearts of the finest men and women of Jerusalem: they were creative of a similar spirituality in the lives of ordinary Jews whose

religion might otherwise have been little more than a matter of form. The fervent passion of the Psalmists for God, and their obvious joy in their fellowship with the unseen, awakened the deeper qualities in the lives of those who took part in the worship. Thus, the Temple Hymnbook provided a needed corrective to the stress placed upon ritual and ceremony, upon the importance of animal sacrifice and upon correctness of outward conduct. The Psalms kept alive the prophetic element in Hebrew religion.

(378) THE PSALMISTS' IDEA OF GOD

Coming as they do from many hands and from widely separated periods of history, we should expect the theological ideas of the Psalms to be on a variety of levels. It is difficult to generalize and to say 'This is the view of the Book of Psalms'. In the end, each Psalm must be studied by itself. Nevertheless, there is a more unanimous picture of God than might be thought likely:

(a) Throughout the Psalms, we are conscious of a robust monotheism. Idol worship is futile (Ps. 96).

(b) Though in some way God's presence is localized in the Temple, His dwelling place is above the firmament which divides the earth from the heavens. He is high and lifted up. Heaven is His throne and earth is His footstool.

(c) The Psalmists do not as a rule think of God as dwelling in the hearts of men. He is their Creator, a transcendent Being. Nevertheless He is not inaccessible and is man's Protector.

(d) Special emphasis is put upon His righteousness or justice. God has a standard for Himself from which He will not depart, and a standard from men which He expects them to keep (Ps. 97).

(e) Equally important is His lovingkindness. This is a word coined by Coverdale (A.D. 1555) to translate the Hebrew word 'chesed'. It signifies something more than kindness and mercy, and indicates the bond which exists between Yahweh and His people, a bond like a family tie. Because of this bond, He will not desert them, but will show them all His goodness.

(379) THE PSALMS IN CHRISTIAN WORSHIP

Though we find much inspiration and devotional value in the Psalms, and frequently use them in our church services, we need to remember that they are pre-Christian and often sub-Christian. The national pride of the Jews found its way into their hymnbook. Though the prophets had called them to see that Yahweh purposed to gather all nations under His sovereignty, the Hebrews

M

combined this universal vision with a deep and bitter hatred of other races. They hoped that Yahweh would annihilate those who resisted Israel in any way, and prayed for that punishment to fall upon their enemies (e.g. Ps. 137). Their anger was just as fierce towards those Jews who, during the Exile and afterwards, succumbed to pagan influences, for these were denounced as traitors to their faith and worthy of the most terrible retribution (e.g. Ps. 139$^{21-2}$). The Psalmists who breathed out such fearsome threats were at the same time too emphatic about their own faithfulness to Yahweh and frequently indulged in protestations of righteousness which are apt to sicken the modern reader.

(380)   We can, of course, explain these blemishes by reference to the historical circumstances in which they were written. In any case, the Psalter needs to be read, as everything else in the Old Testament, in the light that comes from Jesus Christ. Everything that is out of harmony with His spirit must be rejected. The greater part of the Christian Church, until comparatively recent times, has been content to take over the Hymnbook of the Second Temple in its entirety and without reservation. Its members, being human, have still possessed certain unredeemed elements in their make-up, and have therefore been relieved to find that, under the guise of sanctity, they could still curse their enemies, whosoever those enemies may have been. Nowadays, in nearly every branch of the Christian Church, there is a growing number of people who feel that some parts of the Psalter are quite unsuitable either for public worship or private devotion, and should be acknowledged frankly as sub-Christian.

(381)   THE CLASSIFICATION OF THE PSALMS

The Revised Version divides the Psalms into five books:

(i) Pss. 1–41
(ii) Pss. 42–72
(iii) Pss. 73–89
(iv) Pss. 90–116
(v) Pss. 117–50

This arrangement probably represents five different collections that were in use in the Temple worship, and some of the Psalms occur in more than one section (e.g. 14 is repeated in 53; 70 in 40$^{13-17}$).

(382)   Within these books smaller groups are found, e.g.:

Pss. 42–9 are described as 'of the Sons of Korah', doubtless one of the musical guilds.

Pss. 50, 73–83, are 'of Asaph', another guild (*see* Ezr. 2⁴¹).

Pss. 120–34 are described as 'Songs of Ascent', and were in all probability used by pilgrims making their way up to Jerusalem to celebrate the great Jewish feasts.

(383) Nowadays attempts have been made to group the Psalms according to the nature of their contents. No completely satisfactory scheme has been devised, for the range of subjects is so wide. The classification suggested here may prove useful for study purposes, but it is only one of many possibilities.

I. *Psalms set against a Historical Background*

(384) *Ps.* 46.   GOD THE STRONGHOLD OF THE NATION

The most likely setting for this Psalm would be the time when the army of Sennacherib seriously threatened Jerusalem in the reign of Hezekiah, and when the city was wonderfully delivered by what was regarded as divine intervention (*see para.* 250). In such case, the Psalm breathes the confidence of the prophet Isaiah that the Holy City will not be subdued.

(*a*) *Verses* 1–3. Though mountains and seas are tossed from their accustomed places, God is seen to be the refuge of His people.

(*b*) *Verses* 4–7. In troublous times, the city of Jerusalem is kept safe by the power and providence of God. To the psalmist, the river flowing from the Temple mountain was the symbol of the blessing which went forth from Zion and was to give healing and life to the world. Because of its mission, Jerusalem will stand sure, in amazing contrast to the raging of the seas. There has already been a great deliverance. The city has been saved by Yahweh and He will continue its beneficent ministry.

(*c*) *Verses* 8–11. From what He has already done we are bidden to look forward and see Yahweh, the God of all the earth, establishing an era of peace. (Compare M.H.B. 705, 'God is the refuge of the saints', to see what Isaac Watts made of the Psalm.)

(385) *Ps.* 103.   PRAISE FOR GOD'S DELIVERANCE

This Psalm commemorates the occasion of some national escape from danger and could very well belong to the period shortly after the Jews returned to Jerusalem from the Babylonian Exile. It looks backward to a long series of mighty acts on the part of Yahweh, beginning with the deliverance from the bondage of Egypt, in which Moses was the agent of the divine purpose and the leader who brought His people to an era of blessing and prosperity. The psalm has four parts:

(*a*) *Verses* 1–5. The writer summons himself to a great act of praise to Yahweh for His mercies, for personal benefits, for forgiveness, healing, daily blessings, food with its power of renewal.

(*b*) *Verses* 6–12. In Israel's national history, Yahweh has revealed His pity and His love. He has bestowed upon His people forgiveness after they had sinned, and restoration after they had experienced disaster.

(*c*) *Verses* 13–18. His motive is a boundless compassion for weak men. The Psalmist draws a contrast between God and man. He drives home the essential frailty and transience of human life compared with the permanence of Yahweh's mercy and righteousness.

(*d*) *Verses* 19–22. Because Yahweh is the Universal Sovereign, the whole earth is called upon to praise Him—all nature, all things, all men.

(386)* *Ps.* 72. THE IDEAL KING

Probably this was a coronation hymn, though there is nothing to indicate which monarch the Psalmist had in mind. It is dedicated to the memory of Solomon, and expresses the hope that the King will find a model in the character and reign of Solomon —the Psalmist has obviously forgotten his weaknesses! The King is to be just and beneficent and renowned. There is no suggestion that he is superhuman—the rather extravagant descriptions of his reign are such as might be ascribed to an eastern ruler by one of his subjects. His rule will extend far and wide. Tarshish was a Phoenician colony in Spain, Sheba was in South Arabia and Seba in Ethiopia.

Verse 15. 'May he live and may there be given to him of the gold of Sheba.'

Verses 18–19 are a doxology closing the Second Book of Psalms.

(387)* *Ps.* 126. REAPING WITH JOY

This is one of the Songs of Ascent (*see para.* 382). As it stands, there seems to be a curious contradiction between its two halves. In *vv.* 1–3 the restoration from the Exile has taken place; in *vv.* 4–6, the Psalm appears to be praying for it. The explanation is that two phrases 'turn the captivity' and 'turn the fortunes' are here, as elsewhere, confused. The opening of the Psalm recalls the joy the Jews felt when Yahweh 'turned the fortunes' and they were permitted by Cyrus to return from the captivity. But the actual re-settlement had proved full of difficulties and disappointments; so the Psalmist prays for another 'turning of their fortunes', a release from their distresses. He looks for a change that can be compared with the change that takes place when the torrents of fertilizing rain fall on the parched Palestinian soil. It is the contrast between a painful ploughing and the joy of harvest.

II. *Psalms which Portray God as the Creator and Sustainer of Nature*

(388) *Ps.* 8.   THE DIVINE REVELATION IN NATURE AND MAN

God has made a wonderful self-disclosure both in the world of nature and in man. Compared with the majesty of the natural order, man seems to be a very feeble and insignificant being, but in spite of this contrast he has true greatness. Has not God made him a little less than the divine ('a little lower than the angels'), and given him authority over all living things?

Verse 2 is difficult to translate. The sense seems to be: 'Let me sing of thy glory even though it be only with the mouth of a babe or suckling; Thou hast founded a stronghold, because of thine enemies, to still the foe and the avenger.' The Psalmist may be thinking of the powers of darkness being dispelled by Yahweh the God of Light.

Verse 4—The 'son of man' is merely another way of saying 'man'—it has no deeper theological significance.

(389) *Ps.* 19.   GOD IN NATURE AND IN HIS LAW

We seem to have here two independent Psalms linked together:
(*a*) The Revelation of God in Nature (*vv.* 1–6). This is generally thought to have been in origin an ancient hymn to the Canaanite sun-god, which has been taken by a worshipper of Yahweh and applied to Him. The world as we see it is always speaking the praises of Yahweh, though in a language that is inaudible to us. Day and Night, pictured as living beings, hand on from age to age the message of divine greatness. Their voice ('line') reaches the whole earth. The sun, for instance, goes on his way full of joy like a newly wedded bridegroom and warms all created things.

(*b*) The Revelation of God in His Law (*vv.* 7–13). This section is entirely different and sings the praises of the Law of

Yahweh. The study of the Law is invigorating and enlightening. By keeping it, the Psalmist hopes to be preserved from presumption and pride, the qualities that are to be seen in the 'bad' Jew who was disloyal to the faith of his fathers ('the great transgression').

(390)* *Ps.* 65.   A PSALM OF HARVEST THANKSGIVING

(a) *Verses* 1–4. It is fitting to praise God in the worship of the Temple, remembering the pardon He has bestowed upon us.

(b) *Verses* 5–8. In answer to man's praise and prayer, God will reveal His righteous power, terrible yet comforting. His sovereignty is revealed in the world of nature. We have here a strong suggestion that the Psalmist is reaching towards the conception of Yahweh-worship as universal. All people will be in awe at the tokens of God's power, and morning and evening, personified, will rejoice.

(c) *Verses* 9–13. In particular, the Psalmist proclaims the power of Yahweh as seen in the bounty of the natural order. It is He who visits the earth and waters it and makes it bring forth in abundance. The river of God is the ocean above the firmament, from whence the rain descends from time to time. Whenever God passes over the earth, fruitfulness follows in His steps.

III. *Psalms which speculate upon the Problems of Life and Religion.*

(391) *Ps.* 90.   THE ETERNITY OF GOD

(a) *Verses* 1–6. Man is frail and mortal; but he finds a refuge in the everlasting God. The transience, the nothingness, of human life stands over against the eternity of God. Generations follow generations in quick succession, like crops that are sown in the fields year after year; but God is for ever.

(b) *Verses* 7–10. The reason for the shortness of human life, as for the presence in it of so much suffering, is to be found, according to the thought of the times, in the fact of man's sinfulness.

(c) *Verses* 11–12. Man's lot, so puny and so painful, ought to teach him reverence and wisdom; for who can dare to risk facing the fury of Yahweh?

(d) *Verses* 13–17. The Psalmist finishes with a prayer for God's blessing on the future and a return of the divine favour.

In the hymn 'O God our help in ages past' (M.H.B. 878), we can see how Watts made use of this Psalm of ancient Israel, and made it serve the purpose of the Christian Church, the New Israel of God.

(392) *Ps.* 139. THE OMNIPRESENCE AND OMNISCIENCE OF GOD

Personal religion rises towards its height in this Old Testament hymn. The very intensity of the natural and individual sufferings of the Exile brought to many Jews a profound belief in God's care for the men and women He had made.

(*a*) *Verses* 1–12. The Psalmist speaks of Yahweh's intimate knowledge of him and His constant nearness. God is familiar with all his ways, his movements, his actions, his thoughts. He is in heaven and also in Sheol, the land of departed spirits. Were the Psalmist to be borne on the wings of the morning and carried to the western ocean, God would be there. Darkness and light are both alike to Him.

(*b*) *Verses* 13–16. The creating of man is a wonderful business. The days of his life were ordained by God before his birth, and visible to Him before his actual existence.

(*c*) *Verses* 17–18. The amazing thing is the providential care that surrounds man, and God's never ceasing goodwill towards him.

(*d*) *Verses* 19–24. Only one thing is necessary. If only God would destroy the wicked! The Psalmist is sure that God hates all evil and wants to get rid of it; indeed, he begs Him to see if there be any evil in his own heart that might bring affliction upon him, and asks that, if so, it may be removed. From the Christian point of view, these last verses fall short, and mar what otherwise would be amongst the very finest of the Psalms. There is no thought of attempting to convert the sinner, of winning him from his evil; he must be destroyed, and that is all there is to it!

(393)* *Ps.* 1. THE PICTURE OF A JEWISH SAINT

The Psalmist contrasts the righteous man who diligently studies the Law with the wicked who neglects it. The righteous will have nothing to do with the wicked and his ways, taking care to avoid his company; he delights in the fear of the Lord and in the Law, and will in consequence prosper in all his affairs. Not so the wicked: in the day of judgement he will not be able to stand.

The simplicity of this theory, of course, will not stand up to the facts of life. It takes no notice of the problem of the righteous man who may have to suffer. The problem of suffering comes up for discussion in the Book of Job (*see paras.* 404–12). There were those who explained Job's misfortunes along the lines of this Psalm; his sufferings branded him as wicked, for, had he been truly righteous, he would have prospered! In his own conscience, Job knew that what he was having to endure was out of all proportion to his sinfulness, and that the principle that prosperity was the result of faithfulness to Yahweh, and adversity the penalty of disobedience, would not hold.

(394)* *Ps.* 91.   THE DIVINE PROTECTION

Once again, we find the Psalmist holding the view that the righteous are rewarded with material prosperity, with long life and with protection against ills, whilst the prosperity of the wicked is a precarious thing and doomed to disappear. He assumes, as no Christian dare, that, because of his loyalty, God will intervene and save him from physical trouble.

Verses 1–2 should read: 'Blessed is he that dwelleth . . . that abideth . . . that saith of the Lord . . .'.

Verses 5–6. Yahweh would give protection against 'demons'— the spirits of the night; of sunstroke ('the arrow by day'); of sickness ('pestilence').

Verse 9. Read 'For as to thee, Yahweh is thy refuge . . .'.

IV.   *Psalms specially connected with Worship at the Temple*

(395)   *Ps.* 24.   GOD'S ENTRY INTO JERUSALEM

This is a processional Psalm, which may actually incorporate a very old fragment commemorating the bringing of the Ark to Jerusalem by David (*see* 2 Sam. 6). We see the procession winding its way up to the Holy City, singing of the greatness of Yahweh, the Creator of all things. The earth, in accordance with the thought of the time, is regarded as resting upon a boundless ocean (*vv.* 1–2). The pilgrims are challenged by the doorkeepers, 'Who shall ascend into the hill of the Lord?', and their reply describes what Yahweh requires of those who worship Him. The pilgrims proceed to summon the ancient doors (everlasting gates) to open and receive Yahweh as He makes His triumphal entry. A second series of doorkeepers issue another challenge. 'Who is this King of Glory?' and His worshippers make answer: 'The Lord of hosts, He is the King of Glory.'

(396)   *Ps.* 122.   THE BELOVED CITY

This is one of a small collection of pilgrim songs ('Ascents': *see para.* 382). They embody the thought and feelings of the nation as it returned from Exile, and were sung in after years by loyal

Jews on their annual pilgrimage to Jerusalem. The Holy City was the symbol of national unity, and the centre of Hebrew spiritual aspiration, and every true Jew, wherever he lived, counted himself as one of its citizens. In thought, if not in actual practice, members of all the tribes went up to it to give thanks to Yahweh. Recalling its ancient glories in the time of David, the poet prays for its future peace and prosperity.

(397) *Ps.* 84.   THE JOYS OF THE SANCTUARY

(*a*) *Verses* 1–4. The main theme is the happiness of those who inhabit God's house. As the pilgrims enter Jerusalem, the sight of the Temple makes them express their longing to be there, in God's house, where rest is to be found. We cannot suppose that an altar, with its fire and its crowd of worshippers, would be the best place for a bird to build its nest; nevertheless, we catch the poet's meaning. Just as the birds find their nests and homes, so the Jew who is worthy of the name looks for his rest and joy, and in his case finds it in nearness to the altars of his God.

(*b*) *Verses* 5–7. Within the Temple courts, the pilgrims sing of the happiness of those who seek God. The joys of the sanctuary reach out to those who have it in their hearts to make the three annual pilgrimages to Jerusalem, so that the thought of what awaits them brightens the whole journey, making even a parched valley seem rich in water. As they pass through it, it is as if the joy within them turns it into a spring and, instead of being wearied, the pilgrims are strengthened by the journey.

(*c*) *Verses* 8–9 are a prayer for God's blessing.

(*d*) *Verses* 10–12. The Psalmist returns to his main theme—the joy felt in the worship of Yahweh.

(398)★ *Ps.* 145.   THE UNIVERSAL REIGN OF GOD

This group of Psalms (145–50) seems to have been composed for use in the Temple services and forms a fitting climax to the Psalter. The one chosen for reading is an alphabetical one, each verse beginning with a successive letter of the Hebrew alphabet. The second half of each verse was probably sung as a response by the whole congregation. The theme is Yahweh's Kingdom, which will be based not so much on His power as on His loving-kindness (*see para.* 378 (*e*)). There is a fine breadth of vision. The Kingdom is for all men; the belief that God's care is only for one chosen nation has passed away; His love is now seen to be universal.

V. *Psalms of Personal Experience*

(399) *Ps.* 23. THE GOOD SHEPHERD

Largely because King David was a shepherd in his youth, this most precious of all the Psalms has been inseparably associated with his name. If, however, the phrase, 'the house of the Lord' in the last line refers to the Jerusalem Temple, he cannot have been its author, for the Temple was not erected until the reign of Solomon. Still, it is possible that the last two verses may have been added to what was actually one of David's Psalms.

(*a*) *Verses* 1–4. The picture is of God as our shepherd, supplying our needs and giving us His close personal care. In the varying experiences of life, He keeps us company. With His rod (the club carried by the shepherd) He wards off our foes, and with his climbing-staff He gives us strength for our needs (the real meaning of 'comfort').

(*b*) *Verses* 5–6. There is a change of metaphor. According to the custom of the East, a fugitive was safe from his enemies over-night once he was received into a tent, even the tent of a stranger. Until the light of morning, he was treated as a guest and, if necessary, would be defended by his host. So God, as well as being a Shepherd, is a Generous Host, and, taking refuge from our enemies, whether people or circumstances, we can be con-fident of His goodness, and not only for one night!

(400) *Ps.* 27. A JOYFUL CONFIDENCE IN GOD

The two distinct parts of this Psalm blend happily together.

(*a*) *Verses* 1–6. It is not the utterance of a recluse, but of one who is out amidst the storms, and who really loves God and finds in Him a refuge. The battleground is dark with violence. We hear echoes of strife and battle, of enemies waiting for him to make a slip, and false witnesses ready to trap him with their lies. But the victory has been already won, or is as good as gained. It all comes from God in whose presence the Psalmist would like to spend all his days. (The 'house of the Lord' could be used to denote 'life in fellowship with God'). He is confident that God will take care of him, sheltering him, as it were, in the vineyard hut (pavilion) used by the watchers as the grapes ripened, hiding him in the tent (tabernacle) in which the nomads of the desert kept their possessions, placing him upon the top of an unscalable crag (rock). Thus delivered, he will feast joyously with Yahweh in the common meal which, in the sacrifice of ancient Israel, was the symbol of communion with Yahweh (sacrifices of joy).

(b) *Verses* 7–14. The Psalmist is still in grievous trouble, bereft of friends, exposed to foes, and ready to faint and fall. Yet he has no doubt about God's willingness to help him, for he has always been one of His loyal followers, and his confidence is based upon his first-hand experience. Even if, in the last extremity, his parents were to forsake him, God would not leave him desolate. He asks, therefore, that he may be guided through the unknown country he has to travel to God, and declares his readiness to wait patiently for God to intervene on his behalf in His own good time.

(401) *Ps.* 51. THE PENITENT AND GOD

For many centuries, it was taken for granted that this was a Psalm of repentance on the part of David after the murder of Uriah and his sin with Bathsheba (*see para.* 155), though *v.* 4 makes this view unlikely, for David's sin was against man as well as God. It is more probable that this outpouring of a human soul in penitence came from a Jew who, during the Exile or the later domination of Judea by the Greeks, was guilty of the serious offence of adopting foreign ideas of worship.

(a) *Verses* 1–12. Here we have the Psalmist's confession and prayer for pardon and renewal. He realizes that his sin has separated him from God, and is bound to acknowledge that God would be perfectly justified in punishing him. The only plea he can offer is that he comes of sinful stock, inheriting tendencies to evil but not guilt. Only God can cleanse him.

'Hyssop' was the herb used in the purification of a leper or of one who had touched a corpse.

(b) *Verses* 13–17. In return for the joy of salvation, the Psalmist promises to proclaim God's mercy and to bring sinners back to Him. He does not altogether repudiate the value of the sacrificial system, but he recognizes that the essential thing is a contrite heart.

'Bloodguiltiness.' Commentators disagree as to what the Psalmist had in mind. He may have been praying to be kept from shedding of blood, i.e. murder, or the word could be used of death or disease which might come to himself, against which he asks for divine protection.

(c) *Verses* 18–19. The two final verses are a prayer for the restoration of Jerusalem, which will make possible again the sacrifices of the Temple and restore them to popularity. It is generally believed that they are an addition to the original Psalm, in order to correct the impression that sacrifices did not matter.

(402)★ *Ps.* 34. GOD'S PROVIDENTIAL CARE

It has been said that, in this Psalm, the first ten verses are a hymn, and the last twelve a sermon. On the basis of his own personal experience of God's goodness, the writer invites others to put Him to the test. There follows a series of maxims, in the fashion of *Proverbs*, holding out to the righteous the promise of length of days and deliverance from misfortune as rewards for their faithfulness.

(403)★ FURTHER READING IN THE PSALMS

When there is opportunity, the following Psalms should be studied for personal inspiration and enrichment:

  2 The Kingdom of the Lord's Anointed
 15 The Jewish Idea of the Good Life
 37 The Problem of the Prosperity of the Wicked
 40 A Thanksgiving for Deliverance
 42–3 The Sigh of an Exile
 73 The Problem of Suffering
 96 The Praise of Yahweh the Sovereign God
100 A Processional Hymn
104 The Glory of God the Creator
105 The Glory of God in History
107 The Glory of God in Personal Experience
121 Confidence in God's Care

C. *The Book of Job*

(404) Thoughtful men and women have never been able to escape the problem of suffering. Whilst it may have been necessary first to find a practical way of bearing their burden of pain, they have also had to wrestle with its challenge to their faith in God. The issue has been especially acute when they have felt that they were called upon to endure far more than they deserved. What has been the reason for such infliction? How can they reconcile the fact of their grievous fate with their thoughts about the divine character? If God is perfectly good, as they have always believed, why has He allowed so much pain

and misery to come into their lives? Can it be that He is power-less to prevent it? Surely an omnipotent God would be able to remove from them the weight of unmerited and undeserved suffering, and see to it that they were treated fairly! Equally, an all-loving God would want to release them! That is the dilemma. In view of all the undeserved suffering in human life, can we go on believing in the divine power and love? What are we to make of the divine justice?

(405) With such questions, the anonymous author of *Job* wrestles in his soul. He attempts to find a solution to the problem of suffering. The book has been variously described as a dramatic poem, a philosophical dialogue, and as the spiritual autobiography of a great soul fighting against despair. In fact, it is something of all three. We shall bear in mind that suffering can be not only individual but corporate, that communities as well as persons have to bear suffering which they feel they have not merited. The Book of Job deals with the problem on both levels. Job sitting on his dunghill is an individual asking the question: 'Why do righteous men such as I have to suffer so grievously?' He also represents Israel, small, poor, and pitiful, asking why it should be doomed to so painful a history.

(406) For his purpose, the author takes one of the three heroes named by Ezekiel (14^{14}), and makes him his central character. Just as Shakespeare frequently took an ancient story and adapted it to make one of his own plays, so this unknown writer made use of an old story concerning Job, a wealthy sheikh living in the age of the Patriarchs. In spite of the high quality of his character, the regularity with which he paid his religious dues, and the carefulness with which he fulfilled the righteousness of God's law, he was stricken by misfortune after misfortune. Scholars believe that the beginning and the ending of this ancient tale have been preserved for us, virtually unaltered, in the Prologue and the Epilogue of our book (Job 1–2, and 42$^{7-17}$). These, you will notice, are still written in prose.

(407) Within this framework, an author has set his own poem (3^1–42^6). This is the unique element of the book, the fresh attempt to solve the problem of suffering and to reconcile the sufferings of men and the nation with the justice and the love of God. Into this poem, some later hand has inserted yet another section, the speeches of Elihu (*see para.* 410).

In the course of the book, we are introduced to four possible solutions or attitudes to the problem of suffering.

(408) *Job* 1–2. SUFFERING AS A TEST OF RIGHTEOUSNESS

The scene, in the Prologue, is the Council of Heaven, where God's servants are gathered to report on their activities. Amongst them is 'the Satan' (i.e. 'the Adversary'). 'The Satan' is not here the Devil of later thought, but one of the 'sons of God', an angelic being whose special function is to test the righteousness of men, and see whether they live well or ill. He has become cynical and no longer believes in the possibility of disinterested goodness. God asks him to consider His servant Job, a man perfect and upright, who dwells with his family in health and prosperity, enjoying the rewards of a righteous life. The Satan questions whether the goodness of Job would stand up to the test of suffering. The only way is to subject Job to catastrophe. His property, therefore, is stolen or destroyed, his children are killed, and he himself is reduced to abject poverty. But, though he is ruined, he does not sin by making any foolish charge against God. He has stood the test.

In a further interview, the Satan asks permission to make a more penetrating test, and to be allowed to touch not only Job's possessions but his health. Afflicted with a foul disease, probably a repulsive form of leprosy, he becomes an outcast amongst men. Beneath this trial, even his wife fails him, for she bids him curse God and die. Yet he still remains steadfast in his faith and submits to his sufferings without rebellion. 'What? shall we receive good fortune at the hand of the Lord and shall we not receive evil?'

Thus the Prologue puts before us one of the current explanations of suffering. It was something decreed in the Council of Heaven as a test of human righteousness.

(409)* SUFFERING AS A PUNISHMENT FOR SIN

Three of Job's friends, Eliphaz, Bildad, and Zophar, also noble sheikhs, visit him in his distress, and their discussions with the sufferer form the main part of the book. The argument opens with a speech by Job, in which he curses the day of his birth. This is followed by three cycles of speeches, in which each of the friends presents his point of view on the problem of suffering and is answered by Job.

None of them has anything to say except to emphasize the most popular theory of the time, that trouble and calamity were punishments sent for sin. Job must have sinned greatly to have suffered so much, and, although he protests his innocence, he ought to search his heart to discover sins he has forgotten. Job's replies to his friends show little of that patience which is proverbially associated with his name. He asserts his guiltlessness with passion and persistence. He complains that he cannot put his case against an omnipotent God, for God always manages to put him in the wrong; therefore he longs for a 'daysman' or umpire to see that justice is done between them (9^{1-3}, 27^{30}). He claims to be as wise as his friends, yet it is quite clear to him that suffering is not always the result of sin. The wicked prosper, the righteous suffer (Chapters 12–14). Though to all appearances he has been condemned by God, he protests his own innocence and appeals to his friends for pity. He is quite sure that, after his death, his Vindicator (God) will establish that innocence and restore him to happy fellowship with Himself (19^{25-7}). He still hopes, however, to be given access to God here and now, to prove his guiltlessness and to learn the reason of God's dealings with him.

These chapters (3–31) are not easy to read with understanding, and we must turn to the commentaries for help. Special note should be taken of Chapters 29–31 in which Job, in reply to Eliphaz's accusation, gives a detailed statement of his innocence, and contrasts the virtue of his life with the miseries of his sufferings. These chapters have been claimed as the highest description of an ethical code in the Old Testament. The essential point, however, is that, on the basis of his own experience, Job repudiated the traditional theory that suffering was the penalty inflicted on men for their sins, and challenged God to provide him with a more satisfactory explanation.

(410)* SUFFERING AS A DIVINE DISCIPLINE

At Chapter 32, the young man, Elihu, enters the scene, to rebuke both Job and his friends for their attitudes. His speeches are long and bombastic, and most scholars think that this section (Chapters 32–7) was inserted into the book at a later date by a writer who felt there was another point of view that needed to be expressed. Elihu's contribution is the suggestion that suffering has a purpose; it is sent by God as a disciplinary agent, to chasten men and purge the righteous of spiritual pride. (*Note* especially 33^{14-30}.)

(411) *Job* 38^{1-11}; 42^{1-6}. SUFFERING AS AN INSOLUBLE MYSTERY

It is best to regard Chapter 38 as following on Job's challenge to God in Chapter 31. At last, God Himself appears and speaks direct to the sufferer. In some of the greatest poetry in the world, He calls attention to His own might and power, so that Job is overwhelmed by a sense of the divine majesty. He has to admit his own human limitations, his inability to see more than a little bit of the divine plan, his failure to understand in any clear way the wisdom and the power of the Almighty. All he can do is to acknowledge his humility and penitence. He has no right to question the way God governs His world; the matter is too great for his understanding.

Thus no intellectual explanation of his sufferings is given to Job. Like so much suffering in our world, it is an insoluble mystery. Yet Job himself has come to know God in a personal way, and that makes all the difference. He cannot accept the current solutions of his problem; he has no fresh theory to put in their place; but he has gained a new vision of God. He has been made certain of the goodness of God with a certainty that goes deeper than all his questionings. 'I had heard of thee by the hearing of the ear; but now mine eye seeth thee; wherefore I loathe my rash words, and repent in dust and ashes' (42$^{5\cdot6}$).

What *Job* tells us is that, whilst we may never be able to understand why men and nations have to suffer, especially beyond what they fully deserve, yet to have a personal and intimate vision of the true God is more important than to find an explanation. For that vision of God purges us of our self-righteousness—of which Job had more than his share—and enables us to carry our burdens without collapse. To be humble in the presence of our Creator is better than to understand His ways.

(412) *Job* 42$^{7\cdot17}$. THE EPILOGUE

Many have felt this conclusion of Job's story, with the restoration of all his prosperity, is out of place. For God does not give a guarantee, even to the greatest of His saints, that they will be recompensed on earth for what they have suffered, or that they will be blessed with material prosperity to make up for what they have had to endure. The simplest explanation of the difficulty is that this was the conclusion of the *original* ancient story of which our author made use, and that he did not trouble to alter it.

TEST QUESTIONS

(Send answers to TWO *questions to your tutor)*

1. What are the chief differences between the two Creation stories in Genesis 1-3?
2. Ought the Psalms to have a place in Christian worship? Give reasons for your answer.
3. How is the Problem of Suffering dealt with in the Book of Job?

Study Twelve

The Four Centuries before Christ

A. *Israel's History after the Return*

(413)   THE PERSIAN PERIOD (538–334 B.C.)

For nearly 100 years after Ezra, we know hardly anything of
the history of Judah. The nation was very small; its territory was
limited to a radius of about fifteen miles around Jerusalem. Yet
in this very difficult period it did manage to preserve its distinctive
life. Humanly speaking, this achievement was due almost entirely
to the determination of the priesthood and its policy of racial
segregation and exclusiveness, which we know as 'particularism'.
It would have been only too easy for the Jews to have become one
with their neighbours, especially with the Samaritans who were
so closely akin. We can measure the stubbornness of their resistance to anything that would lessen their thought of themselves
as an elect nation by the open breach between these two peoples.
The Jews would have nothing to do even with those who might
reasonably be regarded in both blood and religion as very largely
Jewish. Towards the end of this period, the Samaritans built a
temple in Mount Gerizim, a sign of the completeness of their
separation.

(414)   The priesthood, then, was in command of the nation.
To all intents and purposes the High Priest was the real King of
Judah. The descendants of Aaron, and the Zadokites who came
to be reckoned as Aaronites, were alone permitted to offer
sacrifices, and the members of the tribe of Levi undertook the
minor duties of the Temple. The Priestly Law, which Ezra had
brought back from Babylon, and which had formed the basis of
his reformation, became more and more elaborate and complicated. To teach it to the people, and to interpret its discipline,
a class of Scribes was established, most of whom were also priests.
The voice of prophecy was silent: the nation was priest-controlled.

(415)   The priests, however, were not able to close the doors
absolutely to every kind of foreign influence. There must have
been a continual coming and going of officials between Judah

and the capital of the Persian Empire, and in matters of religion it is likely that the Hebrews did learn something from their overlords. Though the Jewish religious leaders were now monotheists in thought, it is more than possible that the rank and file of the people found it difficult to rise fully, and at once, to this conception. Yahweh seemed so high and lifted up as to be remote from everyday experience, aloof in His holiness and majesty. Hence there arose the belief in an order of angelic beings, who acted as intermediaries between God and men, and made it possible for earth and heaven to have communication with each other. This development was probably helped by the fact that a similar process was taking place in Persia.

(416) At this period, Satan appears on the scene, first as an angelic being, 'The Satan' (*see para.* 408), later to become the Prince of Darkness. Slowly, also, there was growing a belief in the possibility of a future life for individuals. Probably it was Persian influence that stimulated the idea that those who departed this life would afterwards be divided according to their merits or demerits, inhabiting a glorious heaven or a revolting hell.

(417) THE GREEK PERIOD (334–320 B.C.)

Syria and Palestine fell to Alexander the Great as his armies made their way to Egypt. Judah was treated with considerable leniency, and the High Priest was allowed to continue in power as both the religious and political head of the state, and was given a Council of Elders to advise him. Greek influences in religion and culture began to make themselves felt in Judea (as we may now call it) and were resisted by the Jews at first in their desire to maintain their racial exclusiveness.

(418) THE GREEK-EGYPTIAN PERIOD (320–198 B.C.)

When Alexander died in 323, his generals fought for the various parts of his empire which disintegrated. At first Judea fell into the hands of the Egyptian, Ptolemy, and under him and his successors it was given a large measure of self-government. During this period, an increasing number of Jews migrated to Alexandria, where they became members of a community which now spoke Greek as a matter of course, and it was for these that the Jewish scriptures began to be translated (*see para.* 448).

(419) THE GREEK-SYRIAN PERIOD (198–142 B.C.)

The Greek-Syrian kings got possession of Palestine in 198 B.C., and Greek influences again threatened to submerge the distinctive qualities of Jewish life. There were now two definite parties, the Hellenists, which consisted of those who were willing to adopt Greek customs and ideas, and the Hasidim (or Pious) who, filled with religious and patriotic zeal, were determined to have nothing at all to do with any pagan way of life. After years of growing tension, the storm broke in the reign of Antiochus IV, a mentally unbalanced fanatic, whose surname 'God made manifest' (Epiphanes) gives us an insight into his character.

(420)   The Hellenizing movement did not progress sufficiently rapidly for the mad king. He looted the Temple, prohibited the celebration of the Sabbath and the rite of circumcision, tried to obliterate the distinction between clean and unclean foods, proscribed all sacred books, and forbade the offering of sacrifices to Yahweh. If the people wanted to offer sacrifices, let them make them to himself, and with pig's flesh! In the Temple itself he introduced Greek forms of worship and went so far as to erect an altar to the Greek god, Zeus, on top of the great altar of burnt-offering. ('The abomination of desolation . . . standing in the holy place', Mt. 24[15].) In a word, Antiochus tried to stamp out everything that was distinctively Jewish.

(421)   Many of the Hasidim resisted the decrees of Antiochus, even when he threatened to kill them if they did not sacrifice to Zeus. Not a few of them became martyrs. At last in 167 B.C., the Jews rose in revolt. They could stand no more. They found their leader in the aged priest, Mattathias, and his five sons. The third of these, Judas, called Maccabaeus, or the Hammerer, proved himself a genius in guerilla warfare. In less than two years, he drove the Syrian armies out of Judea. From the relative safety of the mountain passes, he harried them until they were forced to retreat. In 165 B.C., the Temple was re-dedicated and the sacrifices started again. After the death of Epiphanes in the next year, the Syrian government came to terms with Judas Maccabaeus and granted freedom of worship to the Jews. It was less than they wanted; they had set their hearts on achieving political freedom as well. For another twenty years the struggle continued until Simon Maccabaeus finally won independence for his country.

(422)   THE PERIOD OF INDEPENDENCE (142–63 B.C.)

For a spell of eighty years the ambition of the Maccabees was achieved and Judea managed to exist as an independent nation.

This happy interlude was brought to an end when rival claimants struggled for the royal power (after 69 B.C.) and the Roman armies under Pompey were called in to settle the dispute.

(423) THE ROMAN PERIOD (FROM 63 B.C.)

Judea fell under Roman domination and never regained its freedom.

A fuller treatment of these periods (*paras.* 422–3) will be found in Greville P. Lewis's *An Approach to the New Testament.*

B. *The Book of Daniel*

(424) In the Hebrew Bible, this book is not included amongst the 'Prophets' but with the 'Writings', a fact which ought to give us the necessary clue to its character. It was, indeed, written at the time of the Maccabaean revolt (*see para.* 421) and may be described as a pamphlet of the resistance movement. During the struggle it was essential to keep up the courage of the population until the victory was won, but, for fear of Antiochus Epiphanes, it was impossible for any writer or preacher to say openly what he wanted to say. The author of *Daniel*, therefore, used a method of conveying his message that would be unintelligible to his people's enemies but clear enough to themselves. In modern times, the book has been used to support many fantastic theories and predictions; but the only reasonable way to study it is to put ourselves into the position of those to whom it was first addressed and ask what it was meant to say to them.

(425) The book is divided into two parts, very unlike each other in character, but united by a single intention. In their different ways, they were intended to put iron into the faithful as they resisted the attempts by Epiphanes to suppress their ancient religion and to force them to adopt Greek customs.

I. *The Narratives of the Book of Daniel*

(426) In Chapters 1–6, we are told of a series of adventures that befell Daniel. There are references in Ezek. $14^{14, 20}$ and 28^3 to one of that name who possessed a reputation for piety and wisdom; otherwise the Old Testament has nothing to say about him. In the Book of Daniel, we are left to assume he was

a very young man, carried into the Babylonian Exile, who rose to a high place in the royal court. Presumably he continued to hold his position there after Babylon had fallen and the Persian conquest had taken place. If so, Daniel would be an extremely old man during the period of the Persian dynasty!

(427) We need not worry about such difficulties. We are dealing, not with the events of history accurately recorded, but with a series of romances told against an historical background. There are many details that do not agree with our knowledge of the history of that period, and are inconsistent with what is disclosed to us by Babylonian records. For instance, Belshazzar never actually ascended the throne, and no king by the name of Darius is known until after the time of Cyrus. But the value of these stories does not depend upon the correctness of such historical details; not even upon Daniel's being a real person. They were told for a specific purpose and in that they must have succeeded. Probably at first they were passed around by word of mouth, until some unknown author collected them and made them the first part of our book. But we can well believe they were excellent propaganda, and that many a weary Jew during the Maccabaean struggle received from them renewed confidence and energy for his resistance.

(428) *Dan.* 1. AT THE COURT OF NEBUCHADREZZAR

Along with three other noble youths, Daniel was taken prisoner by Nebuchadrezzar. (The spelling in this book, 'Nebuchadnezzar', is incorrect.) He was carried to Babylon where he was trained as an astrologer. (The word 'Chaldean' is sometimes used to denote a 'magician', sometimes it is an alternative for a 'Babylonian'). The question of food raised a serious issue for the captives. Babylonian food, 'the King's meat', might come from animals which the Jews were forbidden to eat by their laws, or it might not have been slaughtered in the ways described by Jewish regulations, or it might have been offered previously to the idols in the pagan temples of Babylon. If so, it would be regarded as bringing defilement. Daniel and his friends, therefore, were allowed to experiment with simple and harmless foods ('pulse' would denote all sorts of vegetable foods). After three years, they were proved superior in strength and appearance to the wise men of Babylon.

This story would put nerve into those Jews who were refusing the attempts of Antiochus Epiphanes to make them eat forbidden foods, especially those who were liable to be tortured for declining to eat the flesh of pigs.

(429)* *Dan.* 2. NEBUCHADREZZAR'S FORGOTTEN DREAM

Troubled by a dream in which he saw an image made of various materials, Nebuchadrezzar called for the royal magicians. To prove their powers, he demanded that they should not only interpret the dream, but recall it to his mind, for he had now forgotten it. When they were compelled to confess their inability to do this, he ordered them to be put to death. To save their lives, Daniel volunteered both to recall the dream and to interpret it. Its meaning, he said, was that after a succession of kingdoms, all of which would be in time overthrown, the everlasting Kingdom of God would be established. The statue represented the history of some 450 years (600–150 B.C.). The Golden Empire was that of Babylon; the silver that of the Medes; the brass that of Persia; and the iron that of the Greeks under Alexander. The two feet represented the two divisions of Alexander's empire which had battled to obtain possession of Palestine: the Syrian and the Egyptian divisions. All that, to the Maccabaean resisters, was past history. The important thing to them was that the fifth kingdom was to be the ideal kingdom of the near future, and it was to enable that kingdom to be set up that they were trying to break the power of Antiochus.

(430) *Dan.* 3. THE FIERY FURNACE

Daniel himself is not mentioned in this story. His three companions were thrown into a blazing furnace, because of their refusal to worship the image of gold set up by Nebuchadrezzar. They were miraculously preserved, and the king, anxious to see their fate, beheld them walking unharmed in the furnace. With them was a figure in human form, a heavenly being or an angel. After they were brought out, the king not only recognized Yahweh as the true God but forbade any criticism of Him. The faithfulness of these three heroes to their God provided an example to those whom Antiochus was tempting to betray their God, and their remarkable deliverance encouraged the hope of divine help in their resistance.

(431)* *Dan.* 4. NEBUCHADREZZAR'S SECOND DREAM

Daniel interpreted this dream as a sign that madness was coming upon the king and that he would be driven from human society. In a moment of great pride, he would become as a beast of the field. The moral of the story must have been plain to those who first heard it. If God so struck down Nebuchadrezzar at the height of his power, could He not bring a similar downfall to Antiochus Epiphanes? Indeed, was not Antiochus sometimes surnamed Epi-manes, the meaning of which was 'mad man'?

(432)* Dan. 5. BELSHAZZAR'S FEAST

This king gave a feast for his chief officers in which he used the sacred vessels captured from the Temple at Jerusalem. In the midst of the festivities, a hand was seen writing upon the wall. Daniel alone was able to interpret the message. It declared that Belshazzar had been weighed in the balances and found wanting; his kingdom would be divided and given to the Medes and the Persians. That night, the king was in fact killed, and Darius reigned in his stead.

Any contemporary reader would remember at once that Antiochus had desecrated the Temple at Jerusalem, and had forbidden sacrifices there. As the author anticipated, Antiochus was shortly to die (164 B.C.), though not in Palestine but in Persia (see 11^{45}).

(433) Dan. 6. IN THE DEN OF LIONS

The decree of Darius ordered any who worshipped Yahweh to be sent to the den of lions. A conspiracy of princes set out to get Daniel involved by reason of his habit of praying three times a day with his windows open towards Jerusalem—at the morning burnt-offering, the ninth hour (3 p.m.), and sunset. Though the sentence was carried out, the lions did him no harm and he was rescued safe and sound in the morning. His accusers themselves having been cast into the den where they were promptly destroyed, Darius issued a decree that the whole world was to honour the God of Daniel.

Once again, the sufferers under Antiochus were reminded that those who conformed to the practices of true religion, and were prepared to accept the consequences whatever they might be, were precious to God and would be looked after by Him.

II. The Visions of the Book of Daniel

(434)   The kind of writing we have in Chapters 7–12 is known as 'apocalyptic'. *Daniel* is the best example of it in the Old

Testament, though we have had a foretaste in *Ezekiel* and *Zechariah*. In the next two centuries, and in the beginning of the Christian era, it was a very popular form of literature. The word 'apocalyptic' suggests the revelation of what was hidden, the unveiling of the mysteries of God, but not openly. It makes use of visions and symbols. In *Daniel*, the author sets out to review recent history and to unfold its significance. He takes his stand, as it were, at some vantage point in the past, and looks forward and predicts events that had already taken place by the time he was writing, and also events that he believed to be about to take place in the immediate future. Thus, he speaks of the persecution of Antiochus as if it were something that had yet to take place, although, as a matter of fact, it was already in operation when he wrote.

(435) In apocalyptic writing, the actors in the human story are never referred to openly by name. Symbols are used. The Jews who read *Daniel* would know the people and the events to which the author made reference, but the Greeks would find the book unintelligible. For instance, in Chapters 8 and 11, we have a fairly accurate record, though in symbolic language, of the conquest of Palestine and the East by Alexander in 332 B.C., and the subsequent division of his conquests into four portions (8^{21-2}). There is also an account of the oppression under Antiochus Epiphanes and the setting up in the Temple of an altar of heathen worship. Indeed, there are many unmistakable references to Antiochus, to his war with the saints, the desecration of the Temple and the abolition of sacrifices. But names are not mentioned. When the author wrote, these events had, of course, already happened, but in his vision, he speaks as if they had still to come to pass. The important thing is that he traces the hand of God in the rise and fall of the kingdoms of men.

(436) From what had already happened, the writer turned in apocalyptic fashion to the future, and to what still actually lay ahead as he wrote. The persecution, he was sure, would become more intense. But the end would certainly come and the final judgement of God would be enacted. That would be the end of the world as he knew it. Upon the ruins of earth's powers, God would set up a Kingdom that would never be destroyed, a Kingdom symbolized by a human figure in contrast to the figures of beasts.

(437) In this way, the visions of *Daniel* sought to bring hope

to an oppressed and often despondent people. As we shall see, in the last chapter of the book, the author takes us further into theological truth than any Old Testament writer has been able to take us. Up to this point, there had been no clear belief in individual and personal immortality, but only a hope of the survival of the nation. To the author of *Daniel*, it seems that there must be a world beyond this, in which the good will be happy and the evil punished, and where many of the ordinary judgements of the world will be reversed. In particular, those who had suffered and given their lives in the Maccabaean Revolt would enjoy a resurrection to a life of happiness and joy beyond the grave.

(438) *Dan.* 7. THE VISION OF THE FOUR BEASTS

Here, in the form of a parable, we have a review of history and a prediction of the future. Four beasts rise out of the sea. (The sea represents the element of the world which is opposed to God.) These four beasts have been interpreted as signifying either the four divisions of Alexander's empire, or, more likely, the four great empires that had followed in succession—Babylonian, Median, Persian, and Greek. The concern of the vision is with the fourth beast. This has ten horns which represent the kings of the Greek empire. The little horn, which overthrows three of the ten, and persecutes the saints for three and a half years (a time, times and half a time), is Antiochus Epiphanes. But the little horn is doomed to destruction and its overthrow will be followed by the reign of the saints in an everlasting Kingdom. The saints, of course, are the oppressed Jews.

There is a change of scene. A throne is set up and the Ancient of Days, the divine Judge, takes his place upon it to execute judgement upon the kings and empires already referred to. It is not God Himself whom Daniel sees upon the throne, but His representative, a venerable old man. The kingdom of the future is given to 'one like unto a son of man' (*v.* 13) or to 'the saints of the most high' (*v.* 18). The two expressions are meant apparently to be equivalent, and have no reference to the Messiah. The ideal Kingdom, which does not arise like the beasts from the sea, but comes with the clouds of heaven into the presence of God, is symbolized by a 'son of man' because it is to be a human and a humane kingdom in contrast to the essential cruelty and brutality of the kingdoms it succeeds. ('With the clouds of heaven' means 'in triumph and glory'.) In conclusion, the vision gives us a further picture of Antiochus making war against the saints and attempting to change the times and the laws, by which is meant the Jewish feasts and the ordinances of the Jewish Law. His reign is doomed.

(439) *Dan.* 12. THE RESURRECTION OF THE DEAD

This Chapter is part of the final vision of Daniel which covers Chapter 11 as well. It is another summary of history from the beginning of the Persian era to the time of Antiochus Epiphanes. In Chapter 12, the great prince, Michael, the guardian angel of Israel, gives to Daniel a revelation of the deliverance that will come to Israel by the overthrow of Antiochus, and also a revelation of the resurrection of individuals. The life after death that is here spoken of is not universal—it is for many, and for individuals, but not for all. The martyrs of the Maccabaean period and the leaders of the people who have borne the strain of the struggle are promised compensations for all the trials they have endured. This is the earliest passage of the Old Testament in which there is definite teaching of a resurrection not only of the good, but also of the wicked (*v.* 2).

The book concludes (*vv.* 5–13) with a vision in which two angels answer enquiries about the duration of the troubles. They announce that the sufferings of the Jews will be over in three and a half years and then, at last, complete blessedness will be restored to Israel.

(440) THE RELIGIOUS VALUE OF THE BOOK OF DANIEL

In spite of the legendary and apocalyptic elements of this book, if we try to understand it we shall see its great religious worth.

(*a*) It is not intended to be a forecast of things that have happened in our time or are yet to take place. It was, indeed, a tract written for the Maccabaean age, and as such we must read it.

(*b*) Beneath its strange and often puzzling symbolism, we must recognize its high theology. Its emphasis is on the transcendence of God. By His infinite wisdom and power, He is far removed from the world of men, hence, angels, like Gabriel and Michael, are needed as the agents through whom He can communicate with men.

(*c*) The will of God must finally be taken into account by all men and by all nations. Those who oppose Him will be brought to nought and those who are faithful to Him will find that His power is able to preserve them.

(*d*) Not only is Yahweh the God of this world, but, beyond this, there lies a future life where also His will is supreme.

It is impossible to read the book without having a vivid awareness of the situation that called it forth. It was written at white heat amidst the fires of persecution, and by its passionate faith in God and the triumph of His Kingdom, it must have put new heart into many who otherwise would have been tempted to allow Antiochus to have his own way. As they were reminded that God was still in His heaven, that He was bound to reign triumphantly in the end, and that all attempts to exterminate the true religion were doomed to failure, how could they surrender? They were compelled to hold on to their faith and fight for it. In that way, it still has a message for our age.

C. *The Growth of the Old Testament*

(441) By the time of Nehemiah and Ezra, the idea that their religion had its basis in a *book* had taken a firm hold of the Jewish people, and the copying and preservation of manuscripts became an important matter. The Old Testament as we know it did not come into being as an authoritative religious book all at once, but slowly and by degrees.

(442) THE COMPILATION OF THE 'LAW'

When the Jews began to return from the Exile, there were in existence four holy books which contained the demands that Yahweh made upon His people as their part of the Covenant agreement. They also told stories from the history of the Israelite race to show, firstly, the ways in which Yahweh had kept His promises and had given Israel guidance and protection through many diverse and often painful experiences, and secondly how Israel had failed in spite of it all to fulfil its obligations. They were:

(*a*) *The 'J' Document.* This was a collection of stories about the origins of the Hebrew people which appeared in Judah some time between 850 B.C. and 800 B.C. It is thought to have been compiled under prophetic influence. It is graphic and human, written with poetic power and deep religious insight. It always uses the proper name for God (Yahweh or Jahweh. *See para.* 80).

(b) *The 'E' Document.* This collection of stories appeared in Northern Israel a little later than 'J'. Whilst still vivid and full of human interest, it is somewhat more spiritual and theological in character. It uses the ordinary name for God (Elohim), not the proper one, Yahweh.

(c) *The 'D' Document* (*see para.* 262). This was the law-book upon which Josiah based his reformation. In the main, it was a revision of old Jewish laws and customs in the light of the teachings of the great prophets of the eighth century. It was certainly revised and expanded, possibly many times. Our edition was probably brought up to date during the Exile, for it takes for granted that catastrophe (Deut. 28$^{63-5}$, 30$^{1-5}$).

(d) *The 'P' Document.* During the Exile, probably not long before the Return, a group of Jewish priests retold the story from their own special point of view; hence the title 'Priestly Document'. Their work was a compilation of old customs and stories rather than anything new. It contains some very old material. The priests revised ancient stories, purified them of undesirable elements and raised them to a higher religious level. They were not so much interested in social reform as in the establishment of a pure ritual for Israel. They were anxious about the worship of the Temple from which they were temporarily separated, and to which they hoped to return, and were concerned as to the laws which were to govern the life of God's chosen people.

(443) There is evidence that various attempts had been made to combine two or more of these documents. At some point, either soon after the first return from the captivity or in the period of Nehemiah and Ezra, or even after, all four documents were woven together by a body of priests who used 'P' as their framework. The result was the Pentateuch (i.e. the 'Five Books') known to the Jews as the Law or the Teaching ('Torah'). This was accepted as the first authoritative section of the Hebrew Bible, and no writings were ever regarded as quite so sacred or quite so binding. No Jew was ever absolved from his obligation to accept the Law.

We must not think of the Pentateuch in terms of a modern legal manual. First and foremost, it was a book of religion, though the word religion must be kept wide enough to include politics and sociology. The Jews did not make our distinction between the religious and the secular sides of life, or between the Church and the State. They saw all life as a unity and under the control of Yahweh. 'The earth is the Lord's and all that is in it.'

Thus the Law was the Word of God for every department of human activity.

(444)* THE HOLINESS CODE (H)

A study of *Leviticus* 17–26, reveals that these chapters consist of a code of laws different from the rest of the book. It is marked by a special insistence on ceremonial and moral holiness. 'Ye shall be holy: for I the Lord your God am holy' (Lev. 19²). There are many similarities in style and matter to the writing of Ezekiel and it is thought to have come from the prophetic circle to which he belonged. Its point of view is somewhere between that of Deuteronomy ('D') and that of the Priestly Code ('P') with which it became incorporated.

(445) It should be further noted:

(a) It is not certain whether the book referred to in Neh. 8–9 as read by Ezra was the 'P' Document, or the Holiness Code, or the completed Pentateuch. In any case, we imagine that he only read part of it.

(b) When, after the dissension caused by the racial policy of Nehemiah and Ezra, the Samaritans finally accepted separation from the Jews in matters of religion and built their own Temple on Mount Gerizim, they took with them the Pentateuch as the basis of their religion. With them, no additions were made to the Pentateuch; it, and it alone, became their Bible.

(c) The priests wrote another revision of Hebrew history which has been preserved for us in *1 and 2 Chronicles* and in *Ezra* and *Nehemiah*. It is not very reliable on matters of historical fact, but it does give us some of the personal memoirs of Nehemiah.

(446) THE COMPILATION OF THE 'PROPHETS'

After the succession of great Hebrew prophets came to an end, there grew up a natural desire to preserve the records of what they had taught. During the period 450–200 B.C., the second main division of the Old Testament came into being, consisting of eight books:

(a) Four books of history, *Joshua*, *Judges*, *Samuel*, and *Kings*, selected because they drove home the prophetic point of view. We do not know who compiled these histories in the form in which they have come down to us, but it is obvious that use was made of earlier records, such as the 'Chronicles of the Kings of Israel', and the 'Chronicles of the Kings of Judah'. In their present state they show clear signs of having been revised, especially by writers of the Deuteronomic school, and that the ancient stories were selected and edited to illustrate the teaching of the great prophets of the eighth century. If we bear in mind that these books were part of the 'Prophets', we shall look to them for religious lessons rather than for accurate reporting of historical events.

(b) Four books that recorded the words of the great prophets—*Isaiah, Jeremiah, Ezekiel,* and the *Twelve*—were added to the so-called 'histories'. We need to remember that the twelve minor prophets, *Hosea* to *Malachi*, were minor only in length, not in the quality of their work or the importance of their message. They earned the title because, being short, they were probably copied on to one single roll of parchment and treated as one single book.

In what circumstances this section of the Old Testament was added to the 'Law', we do not know, but, as far as we can judge, the question was settled by the year 200 B.C. Valuable as we perceive the 'Prophets' to be, in the estimation of the Jews they were never placed on the same level as the 'Law'.

(447) THE COMPILATION OF THE 'WRITINGS'

The third section of the Old Testament consists of a series of books very varied in character:

(a) Three books of poetry and wisdom—*Psalms, Job, Proverbs*.

(b) The five 'rolls' associated with Jewish festivals—*Song of Songs* (used on the 8th day of Passover), *Ruth* (Pentecost), *Lamentations* (9th day of Ab when the destruction of Jerusalem and the Temple was commemorated), *Ecclesiastes* (Tabernacles), and *Esther* (the Feast of Purim, a memorial to the Maccabaean revolt).

(c) *Daniel, Ezra, Nehemiah, Chronicles.*

In this collection, the Psalms were regarded as the most important and frequently gave their name to the whole section (*see* Lk. 24⁴⁴). The presence of some of the books was disputed until the end of the first century after Christ (e.g. *Esther, Ecclesiastes, Song of Songs*, and *Chronicles*), but the section was practically complete by 100 B.C. The two tests the rabbis applied in determining whether a writing should be admitted or not, were, Was it written between the time of Moses and that of Ezra? and, Was its teaching consistent with the Law?

(448) THE SEPTUAGINT (LXX)

After the fall of Jerusalem in 586 B.C., many Jews scattered throughout the known world, and some of them migrated to Egypt. One of the achievements of Alexander the Great was his creation of a new city in Egypt, which he called Alexandria after himself, and where he persuaded a number of Palestinian Jews to make their home. About 250 B.C. these Jews began to translate their scriptures into Greek, which was the universal language of the day. They would seem to have begun with the Pentateuch, and followed it by the rest of the Old Testament during the next two centuries. Legend says that the translation was carried out at the command of King Ptolemy II by seventy scribes (hence its name), who are said to have worked in cells, two by two. When they had finished it was discovered that they had all produced identical versions. Such a legend must be treated for what it is worth.

Two important differences between this Greek Bible and the Hebrew Old Testament should be noted:

(a) The Septuagint has changed the order of the books and it is more like that of our English Bibles. The histories come first, followed successively by the poetry, the wisdom literature, and the prophetic writings; thus: (i) *Genesis* to *2 Chronicles*, (ii) *Job* to *Song of Songs*, (iii) *Isaiah* to *Malachi*.

(b) The Septuagint contains a number of books not in the Hebrew Bible. These are not added as a separate section at the end, but intermingled with the others. They were obviously accepted as canonical at Alexandria, but not at Jerusalem.

(449) THE CANON

The Greek word signifies a rule or a measuring rod, and came to indicate the thing that was measured. We use it to denote the list of books that was selected as suitable for public reading amongst the Jews. Who made the selection we do not know, but there must have been a number of Councils that dealt with the matter. After their return from Exile, the Jews found themselves in possession of an increasing number of religious books, some highly esteemed by them, others thought to be of more questionable worth. It was a case of sorting out, and over a period of time, those that should be regarded as having religious authority. Those that were finally selected became the Canon of Scripture.

The Jews of Palestine did not finally fix the Canon of the Old Testament until the Council of Jammia (A.D. 90), since when they have regarded it as unchangeable. We have seen, in the previous paragraph, that the Greek-speaking Jews of Alexandria accepted a number of books that were not part of the Palestinian Canon. The Christian Church, which was largely Greek-speaking, took the LXX as its first Bible and therefore the wider list of religious books that were acceptable to Alexandria. The Roman and Greek Catholic Church still use this Greek Canon; but at the Reformation the Protestant reformers went back to the list of the Palestinian Jews, and that still determines the number of books we regard as being authoritatively part of the Old Testament.

(450)*   THE APOCRYPHA

The word 'Apocrypha' means 'hidden', and is used to indicate those books which were not included in the Hebrew Canon of the Old Testament, but were included in the Greek LXX. They are mixed in quality. Some were perhaps rejected in Palestine, because of the late date at which they were written (e.g. the *Wisdom of Solomon*, *c.* 70 B.C.); others were not regarded as suitable for the popular mind. *1* and *2 Maccabees* deal with history, but of a late date. *Ecclesiasticus* is full of wise religious and moral instruction. As we have seen above, the Roman and Greek churches regarded them as authoritative, but not the Protestant. In 1826, the British and Foreign Bible Society decided not to print them in their copies of the Scriptures. The Anglican Church, in its articles, recognizes them as profitable 'for the example of life and the instruction of manners', but not to be used for proving any point of doctrine. In recent years, Protestant scholars are giving more attention to the Apocrypha, because of the light it sheds on those centuries of change and preparation before the coming of Christ.

TEST QUESTIONS

In order that you may have adequate time for the revision of your previous studies, only one Test Question is included in this final Study.

In what circumstances was the Book of Daniel written? What were the chief lessons it was intended to teach?

Table of Dates

The purpose of this Table is to give a picture of the chief events in Israel's history in their proper time sequence. Some of the dates are still uncertain, and many are approximate.

Date B.C.	Important Kings	Outstanding Events	Chief Religious Characters
		THE PATRIARCHAL PERIOD	Abraham Isaac Jacob Joseph
1300			
		THE EXODUS	Moses
1200			
			Joshua The Judges
1100			
	Saul (c. 1025) David (c. 1000)	THE UNITED KINGDOM	Samuel Nathan
1000			
	Solomon (c. 970) Rehoboam Jeroboam I	THE DIVISION OF THE KINGDOM (c. 930)	
900			
	Ahab (c. 850)	Compilation of 'J' (c. 850)	Elijah Elisha
800			
	Jeroboam II (780–750) Ahaz (735) Hezekiah (720?)	Compilation of 'E' (c. 750) END OF NORTHERN KINGDOM (721) Sennacherib's Invasion (701)	Amos Hosea Isaiah Micah

Date B.C.	Important Kings	Outstanding Events	Chief Religious Characters
700			
	Manasseh (692)		
	Josiah (637)	Finding of the Law Book ('D') (621)	
		Fall of Nineveh (612)	
	Jehoiakim (607)	Megiddo (608); Carchemish (605)	Jeremiah
600			
	Zedekiah (596)	First Deportation (596)	
		FALL OF JERUSALEM (586)	Ezekiel
			2 Isaiah
		FIRST RETURN under Cyrus (538)	Zechariah
		Rebuilding of Temple (520)	Haggai
500			
		Compilation of 'P' (?)	
			3 Isaiah
			Malachi
		Rebuilding of Jerusalem	Nehemiah
400			
		Ezra's Reformation (398)	Ezra
		Composition of *Jonah, Ruth*	
		PERIOD OF GREEK DOMINATION	
		PERIOD OF EGYPTIAN DOMINATION (311) [(331)	
300			
		Writing of Septuagint begins	
200			
		PERIOD OF SYRIAN DOMINATION (198)	
		Persecution of Antiochus IV	Judas Maccabaeus (168)
		Composition of *Daniel*	
100			
		PERIOD OF ROMAN DOMINATION (63)	
		BIRTH OF JESUS CHRIST (6)	

THE KINGDOMS OF ISRAEL AND JUDAH

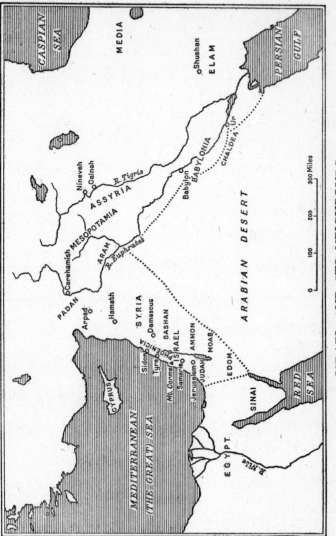

ISRAEL AND ITS NEIGHBOURS

INDEX

(The numbers refer to *paragraphs*)